Tearcard

VBA Data Types

DATA TYPE	STORAGE SIZE	RANGE
Byte	1 byte	0 to 255
Boolean	2 bytes	True or False
Integer	2 bytes	-32,768 to 32,767
Long (long integer)	4 bytes	-2,147,483,648 to 2,147,483,647
Single	4 bytes	-3.402823E38 to -1.401298E-45 for negative values; 1.401298E-45 to 3.402823E38 for positive values
Double	8 bytes	-1.79769313486232E308 to -4.94065645841247E-324 for negative values; 4.94065645841247E-324 to 1.79769313486232E308 for positive values
Currency	8 bytes	-922,337,203,685,477.5808 to 922,337,203,685,477.5807
Decimal	14 bytes	Numbers with 28 decimal places of accuracy
Date	8 bytes	January 1, 100 to December 31, 9999
Object	4 bytes	Any Object reference
String (variable length string)	10 bytes +	0 to approximately 2 billion
String (fixed-length)	Length of string	1 to approximately 65,400
Variant (number)	16 bytes	Any numeric value up to the range of a Double
Variant (text)	22 bytes + 1 byte/char.	Same range as for variable-length String

GW00361267

SAMS

Teach Yourself

Microsoft® Excel

2000 Programming

in 24 Hours

Useful Methods of the Application object

- **MailLogon and MailLogoff**   Used in conjunction with the MailSystem and MailSession properties, the MailLogon and MailLogoff methods allow you to log a user on and off of email.
- **Quit**   The Quit method is used to terminate Excel.
- **Run**   The Run method is used to execute Excel 4.0 macros.

Useful Workbook methods

- **Activate**   The Activate method is used to activate the workbook.
- **Close**   The Close method closes the workbook.
- **Save**   The Save method saves the workbook.
- **SaveAs**   The SaveAs method saves the workbook. The differences between this method and the Save method is that the SaveAs method has several useful optional arguments including *Filename*, *FileFormat*, *Password*, *WriteResPassword*, and *ReadOnlyRecommended*.
- **PrintOut**   The PrintOut method is used to print the entire workbook.
- **PrintPreview**   The PrintPreview method displays the workbook in Print Preview.

Frequently Used Worksheet Object Methods

- **Activate**   This method activates the sheet.
- **CheckSpelling**   As its name implies, the CheckSpelling method is used to check the spelling of the contents of the worksheet.
- **Delete**   If you need to delete a sheet, use the Delete method.

Useful Range Properties

- **Address**   The Address property returns the current location of the range.
- **Count**   The Count property is used to determine the number cells in a range.
- **Formula**   Returns the formula used to calculate the display value.
- **Offset**   The Offset property is useful for moving from one range to another.
- **Resize**   This allows you to resize the currently selected range.
- **Value**   Returns the value of the range.

Frequently Used Range Methods

- **Activate**   Activates a range.
- **Clear**   Clears the contents of a range.
- **Copy**   Copies the contents of the range on the clipboard.
- **Cut**   Places the contents of the range on the clipboard.
- **PasteSpecial**   Pastes the clipboard contents to the range.
- **Select**   Selects a range.

SAMS
Teach Yourself
Microsoft® Excel
2000 Programming
in 24 Hours

SAMS

A Division of Macmillan Computer Publishing
201 West 103rd St., Indianapolis, Indiana, 46290 USA

Sams Teach Yourself Microsoft® Excel 2000 Programming in 24 Hours

Copyright © 1999 by Sams Publishing

All rights reserved. No part of this book shall be reproduced, stored in a retrieval system, or transmitted by any means, electronic, mechanical, photocopying, recording, or otherwise, without written permission from the publisher. No patent liability is assumed with respect to the use of the information contained herein. Although every precaution has been taken in the preparation of this book, the publisher and author assume no responsibility for errors or omissions. Neither is any liability assumed for damages resulting from the use of the information contained herein.

International Standard Book Number: 0-672-31650-1

Library of Congress Catalog Card Number: 99-60558

Printed in the United States of America

First Printing: August 1999

01   00   99   4   3   2   1

Trademarks

All terms mentioned in this book that are known to be trademarks or service marks have been appropriately capitalized. Sams Publishing cannot attest to the accuracy of this information. Use of a term in this book should not be regarded as affecting the validity of any trademark or service mark.

Warning and Disclaimer

Every effort has been made to make this book as complete and as accurate as possible, but no warranty or fitness is implied. The information provided is on an "as is" basis. The authors and the publisher shall have neither liability or responsibility to any person or entity with respect to any loss or damages arising from the information contained in this book.

EXECUTIVE EDITOR
Brad Jones

ACQUISITIONS EDITOR
Sharon Cox

DEVELOPMENT EDITOR
Matt Purcell

MANAGING EDITOR
Jodi Jensen

PROJECT EDITOR
Dawn Pearson

COPY EDITOR
Mike Henry

INDEXER
Johnna Vanhoose

PROOFREADER
Jill Mazurczyk

TECHNICAL EDITOR
Lowell Mauer

TEAM COORDINATOR
Meggo Barthlow

SOFTWARE DEVELOPMENT SPECIALIST
Aaron Price

INTERIOR DESIGN
Gary Adair

COVER DESIGN
Aren Howell

COPY WRITER
Eric Bogert

LAYOUT TECHNICIANS
Brandon Allen
Tim Osborn
Staci Somers

Contents at a Glance

Table of Contents

About the Author

Sharon Podlin is a graduate of the University of Texas. She is president of PTSI, a consulting firm specializing in the development and presentation of computer training courses. Sharon also teaches courses at Coastal Georgia Community College. She has over 17 years in the industry and has worked for primarily Fortune 100 companies including J. C. Penney, Hyatt International Hotels, and United Airlines. She has worked with Microsoft Excel since the ancient days of the early 1980's.

Dedication

This book is dedicated to my husband, Mark, who supports me in everything I do, and my son, Hunter, who is the joy of my life.

—SJP

Tell Us What You Think!

As the reader of this book, *you* are our most important critic and commentator. We value your opinion and want to know what we're doing right, what we could do better, what areas you'd like to see us publish in, and any other words of wisdom you're willing to pass our way.

As an associate publisher for Sams Publishing, I welcome your comments. You can fax, email, or write me directly to let me know what you did or didn't like about this book—as well as what we can do to make our books stronger.

Please note that I cannot help you with technical problems related to the topic of this book, and that due to the high volume of mail I receive, I might not be able to reply to every message.

When you write, please be sure to include this book's title and author as well as your name and phone or fax number. I will carefully review your comments and share them with the author and editors who worked on the book.

Fax: 317-581-4770

Email: adv-prog@MCP.com

Mail: Brad Jones
          AssociatePublisher
          Sams Publishing
          201 West 103rd Street
          Indianapolis, IN 46290 USA

Introduction

You probably were drawn to this book because you need to learn to program with Microsoft Excel VBA in a quick and concise manner. With that in mind, before you get started, take a few moments to acquaint yourself with the design and layout of this book, which are described in the next few sections.

Who Should Read This Book

If you bought this book, you are either an Excel power user or a programmer who now needs to learn to automate Excel using VBA. This book is designed to teach programming to someone who knows Excel well, but doesn't know how to program (if you are a programmer, please keep reading). No assumptions have been made about your level of programming knowledge. On the other hand, if you do know how to program, you'll find some of the topics discussed familiar, such as variable declaration and control of flow constructs. As a programmer, you might not know how to use some of Excel's more advanced features, such as MS Query or pivot tables. These types of topics have added detailed to help you with your Automation requirements. This book does assume that you are familiar with the basic Excel skills needed to create and maintain Excel workbooks and worksheets.

This book starts with the basics. You are first taught how to record macros and why you can only do so much with recorded macros and, therefore, need to write VBA code.

The next step in your journey is an overview of key, basic VBA topics such as variables, controls, user input mechanisms, and so on. After you are familiar with the basics, more advanced topics are presented.

This 24-hour course uses Microsoft Excel 2000, the latest version of Excel. Excel 2000 requires Windows 95/98 or Windows NT 4.0 or higher.

What This Book Will Do for You

This book's overall goal is to teach you VBA in a practical and straightforward way. As you flip through the pages in this book, you'll notice that this is not a reference book. This is a training tool. It teaches you, topic by topic, the things you need to know to be able to automate Excel using Visual Basic for Applications. This book gives you the conceptual material quickly, and gives you every opportunity to work hands-on with Excel and VBA. It gets you up to speed with VBA in 24 hours, and provides you with the skills needed by most Excel VBA application developers.

This book gives you the background information that a new Excel application developer needs, but its focus is on the practical. It answers the "How do I...?" questions by providing you with step-by-step tasks.

Can This Book Really Teach VBA in 24 Hours?

Yes. You can master each chapter (referred to as an *hour* in this book) in approximately one hour. Some hours are longer and have more tasks in them. Other hours are shorter and have more background information in them. All hours provide you with key information, useful tips, and insightful notes.

What You Need

This book assumes that you have a Windows 95–compatible computer with Windows 95/98 or Windows NT 4.0 or higher installed on it. You also need Excel 2000 installed. If you meet these requirements, you are ready to go!

Files on the Web Site

You'll find some of the files needed to complete some of the lessons in this book on the Web site. You'll also find the completed workbooks for each hour on the Web site for your reference and use.

Conventions Used in This Book

This book uses different typefaces to differentiate between code and regular English, and also to help you identify important concepts.

Text that you type and text that should appear on your screen is presented in monospace type.

```
It will look like this to mimic the way text looks on your screen.
```

Placeholders for variables and expressions appear in a *monospace italic* font. You should replace the placeholder with the specific value it represents.

This arrow (➡) at the beginning of a line of code means that a single line of code is too long to fit on the printed page. Continue typing all characters after the ➡ as though they were part of the preceding line.

A Note presents interesting pieces of information related to the surrounding discussion.

 A Tip offers advice or teaches an easier way to do something.

 A Caution advises you about potential problems and helps you steer clear of disaster.

 New Term icons indicate clear definitions of new, essential terms. The new term appears in *italic*.

HOUR 1

What is Visual Basic for Applications?

Welcome to application development using Excel and Visual Basic for Applications! As an experienced user of Excel, you are comfortable with the native functionality of Excel. You are now ready to step up to the next level—automating Excel. Even if you've never programmed before, you'll be able to develop solutions using Visual Basic for Applications. Visual Basic for Applications is one of the easiest-to-learn, easiest-to-use—yet most-sophisticated—application automation languages (what used to be called *macro languages*) available today. In this hour, you'll start building the foundation of your knowledge by becoming familiar with the macro recorder.

The highlights of this hour include

- What Visual Basic for Applications is
- The benefits of application-based automation in the Excel environment
- Recording a simple macro
- Executing a macro
- Editing a macro
- The limitations of the Macro Recorder

What Is Visual Basic for Applications?

Until the early 90's, automating applications could be a challenging prospect. For each application you needed to automate, you had to learn another automation language. For example, you used Excel's macro language to automate Excel, WordBasic to automate Microsoft Word, and so on. Microsoft decided that rather than each application in its product line having a different automation language, the applications would share a common automation language—Visual Basic for Applications (VBA). Visual Basic for Applications is considered a subset of the very popular application development language, Visual Basic. VBA is actually an application-hosted version of Visual Basic. VBA differs from Visual Basic in several ways, including the following:

- Visual Basic is designed to create standalone applications. VBA is used to automate an existing application.

- Visual Basic is its own development environment. VBA has to be hosted by an application.

- To run an application developed in Visual Basic, a user does not need to have access to Visual Basic from his system because the developed application is executable. Because VBA applications are hosted, they require the user to have access to the parent application, such as Excel.

Even with their differences, the Visual Basic language and VBA are very similar in structure. As a matter of fact, if you already know Visual Basic you'll find yourself learning VBA very quickly. Conversely, after you learn VBA you have a great foundation for learning Visual Basic. Furthermore, after you learn to create solutions using VBA in Excel, you have most of the knowledge you need to create solutions using VBA in Word, Project, Access, Outlook, FoxPro, and PowerPoint.

A key feature of VBA is that the knowledge you learn about VBA in one Microsoft product or Visual Basic transfers to another.

To get more specific about what VBA is, it is the automation language you'll use to automate commonly used procedures and processes, create customized solutions, and, if you want, implement applications using Excel as a development platform.

Benefits of Application-Based Automation in the Excel Environment

1

You are probably wondering what you can do with VBA. Things that you might want to do using VBA include

- Automate repetitive tasks
- Customize Excel's interface with toolbars, menus, and forms
- Simplify usage of templates
- Add additional functionality to the Excel environment
- Create reports
- Perform sophisticated manipulation and analyses of data

You might not have thought of using an application as a development platform before. Most people think of languages such as Visual Basic or C++ when they think of application development. There are numerous reasons you might want to use Excel as a development platform. These reasons include

- Excel's application capabilities, including printing, file handling, formatting, and text editing
- Excel's extensive selection of built-in functions
- The familiar interface provided by Excel
- Connectivity to a variety of database formats

If you've ever programmed in a language before, you know that half of your work has to do with basic functionality, including file opening and saving, printing, and clipboard operations such as copying and pasting, and so on. This brings up one of the major benefits of using an application for solution deployment—basic functionality already exists in the host application. All you have to do is use it. You have access to everything that Excel can do, including file handling, text editing, and formatting.

Because you are developing a solution in Excel, you also have access to Excel's extensive library of functions. All the functions you are familiar with as an Excel user, including SUM, IRR, MAX, FV, PMT, and AVG, are available to you as an Excel developer.

From your solution's end users' point of view, they get the benefit of working with an application that they already know how to use. They are familiar with the menu system, toolbar, and worksheet areas of Excel. Because of this, they'll immediately feel comfortable with your automation solution.

Some of the other benefits of solution development using Excel are not immediately obvious. An example of this is Excel's database connectivity features. If you need to manipulate data in your solution from, for example, Microsoft SQL Server or Microsoft Access, you can easily do so because Excel can easily do so.

Recording a Simple Macro

Before jumping into writing VBA code, you should take a few minutes and experiment with recording a macro. Excel's macro recorder allows you to record a series of actions and it converts those actions to VBA code. Even when you become totally adept at writing VBA code, you'll use the macro recorder in your work. There are two reasons for using the macro recorder as a VBA developer. One reason is because the macro recorder saves you work. It is often used by developers to build the foundation of an application. The other reason is that the macro recorder can act as a teaching tool. If you are unsure of how to write a series of steps, record it and look at the code.

NEW TERM A *macro* is a series of commands saved with a name that Excel can execute.

The macro you are about to record is a very simple one that changes the font and color of selected cells. Although there are other ways to accomplish this type of task (for example, styles, AutoFormats, and so on), this series of steps provides a good demonstration of the macro recorder. Complete the following steps:

1. Open a new workbook. Make sure all other workbooks are closed—just in case they have macros or other VBA code in them—so that you can easily locate and work with the macro you are recording.

> You don't have to close other workbooks when recording a macro. You are doing it at this point to keep the environment simple and uncluttered.

2. In cell A1, enter your first name. In cell B1, enter your last name. In cell C1, enter the city you live in, and enter the country where you live in cell D1. This gives you some data to work with throughout this exercise.

3. Select cell A1.

4. Select Tools, Macro, Record New Macro. The Record Macro dialog box displays, as shown in Figure 1.1.

FIGURE 1.1

The Record Macro dialog box allows you to name the macro you are about to record.

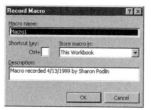

5. Enter `BigFont` for the macro name and press Enter to begin recording the macro. Notice that the word `Recording` displays in the status bar of the Excel application window. Typically, the Stop Recording toolbar displays as well.

A macro name can be up to 255 characters in length and must start with a letter. Other characters in the name can be letters, numbers, or underscore characters. Spaces are not allowed in a macro name. An underscore character is commonly used to represent a space.

To display the Stop Recording toolbar, right-click on a toolbar and select Stop Recording. The Stop Recording toolbar is available only when you are recording a macro.

6. Select Format, Cells. The Format Cells dialog box displays. Select the Font tab.

7. Set the font size to 16 and color to red. Click OK.

8. Click the Stop Recording toolbar button. The macro recording session ends.

If the Stop Recording toolbar doesn't display, select Tools, Macro, Stop Recording.

After you've recorded a macro, you can execute it.

Executing the Macro

When you execute a macro, it performs the same steps that you performed during the record operation. To execute the macro, use the following steps:

1. Select cell B1.
2. Select Tools, Macro, Macros. The Macro dialog box displays (see Figure 1.2).

> You can also access the Macro dialog box by pressing Alt+F8.

FIGURE 1.2

*The Macro dialog box
is used to select the
macro you wish to run
or edit.*

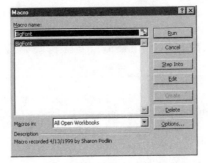

3. Select BigFont. Select Run. The font for cell B1 becomes 16 points in size and red.
4. Select cells C1 through D1. Run the BigFont macro again. Notice that both of these cells' fonts become 16 points and red, even though when the original macro was recorded only one cell was changed.

Viewing the Recorded Code

As you performed the steps you wanted to save to your macro, Excel converted your steps into VBA code. To view the generated code, complete the following steps:

1. Select Tools, Macro, Macros. The Macro dialog box displays.
2. Select BigFont and click Edit. The Microsoft Visual Basic Editor window opens, as shown in Figure 1.3.

The Microsoft Visual Basic Editor has several components to it. You'll learn more about the components of the Visual Basic Editor in Hour 4, "Understanding the Role of Variables and Constants." At this point, you want to focus on the code that is being displayed. The code displayed should be similar to Listing 1.1.

FIGURE 1.3

The Microsoft Visual Basic Editor is used to view and edit VBA code.

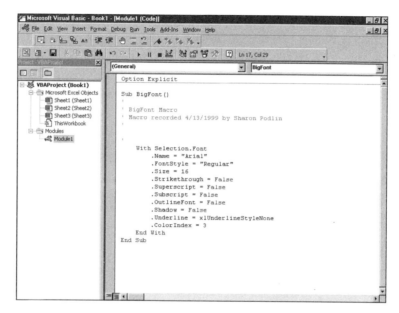

LISTING 1.1   The BigFont Procedure

```
Sub BigFont()
'
' BigFont Macro
' Macro recorded 4/11/1999 by Sharon Podlin
'


    With Selection.Font
        .Name = "Arial"
        .FontStyle = "Regular"
        .Size = 16
        .Strikethrough = False
        .Superscript = False
        .Subscript = False
        .OutlineFont = False
        .Shadow = False
        .Underline = xlUnderlineStyleNone
        .ColorIndex = 3
    End With
End Sub
```

The first line of code, `Sub BigFont()`, represents the starting point and name of the macro. The lines that follow and begin with a single quotation mark are comments that represent documentation about the macro; in this case, the name of the macro, when it was recorded, and by whom.

The actual working part of the macro begins at the word `With`. Note the word `Selection`. `Selection` is the word VBA uses to mean whatever is highlighted. This is why your macro works whether you select one cell or multiple cells. The other thing you probably notice is that a lot more has been recorded than the actions you performed. You only changed the font size and color, but all the font information has been recorded from the Format Cells dialog box's Font tab.

Editing Recorded Code

Editing code is done directly in the Visual Basic Editor. You can add lines, delete lines, and modify lines. The first thing you are going to do is delete the extra lines that were recorded, using the following steps:

1. Highlight the line that begins with `.Name`.

2. Delete the line. Don't worry if a blank line remains. VBA ignores blank lines.

3. Continue deleting lines until your procedure is similar to the following:

```
Sub BigFont()
'
' BigFont Macro
' Macro recorded 4/11/1999 by Sharon Podlin
'


    With Selection.Font
        .Size = 16
        .ColorIndex = 3
    End With
End Sub
```

4. Close the Visual Basic Editor window. You are returned to your workbook.

5. In cell E1, type `Test`.

6. With cell E1 selected, run the BigFont macro. Notice the macro works exactly as it did before you deleted the lines from the macro.

7. Select Tools, Macro, Macros.

8. Select BigFont and click Edit.

9. Right now, the font size is set to 16 points when you run this macro. Edit the macro so that the point size is 24. Your completed macro will look similar to the following:

```
Sub BigFont()
'
' BigFont Macro
' Macro recorded 4/11/1999 by Sharon Podlin
'


    With Selection.Font
        .Size = 24
        .ColorIndex = 3
    End With
End Sub
```

10. Close the Visual Basic Editor window.

11. Select cell A1. Run the BigFont macro. Now the point size for the cell's font is larger.

12. Save your workbook as Hour1.

You now see how easy it is to edit a recorded macro. There are a number of reasons why you might need to edit a macro. One reason is that you made a mistake while recording the macro. Another reason is that you changed your mind about what you wanted the macro to do. No matter what the reason, you can edit the macro using the Visual Basic Editor.

Limitations of the Macro Recorder

Many of the Excel processes you might want to automate can be accomplished by recording your actions. But the macro recorder does have limitations. Things that you can't do via the macro recorder include

- Prompting a user for information while the macro is running
- Performing different actions based on user input or cell values
- Displaying Excel's dialog boxes, such as the Save As dialog box
- Displaying and using custom user forms

These limitations are just some of the reasons why you'll want to create your own VBA code. For now, you'll work more with the macro recorder in the next hour.

Summary

This hour quickly got you using the macro recorder. You saw how to record, execute, and edit a macro. You even modified some VBA code. You are now ready to work with the macro environment in more detail.

The next hour focuses on more advanced macro topics. Understanding the how and why of macros is the first step to application development using VBA.

Q&A

Q Why do I need to know the macro recorder to program in VBA?

A Knowing the macro recorder has two major benefits. Your knowledge of the macro recorder will become the foundation of your VBA knowledge. Also you'll find that when you begin developing applications, you start by recording as much as you can and then modifying the recorded code.

Q If I've never programmed before, am I going to have a problem learning VBA?

A No! The main thing you need to know to start programming in VBA is Excel. You are going to use your knowledge of Excel in your solution development. The book will provide you with the rest of the knowledge you need.

Workshop

The quiz questions and exercise are provided for your further understanding. See Appendix A for the answers.

Quiz

1. Is VBA found only in Excel?
2. What language is VBA based on?
3. True or False: You can use Excel's built-in functions in your VBA applications.
4. When you edit your macro code, you work in the _____ (three words).
5. Name two limitations of the macro recorder.

Exercise

Create a new macro named Title that enters your name in cell A1 and today's date in cell B1. Also have the macro set the font size of A1 through B1 to 14 points. After you are through recording the macro, review the code that was generated.

HOUR 2

Working More with Recorded Macros

In Hour 1, "What is Visual Basic for Applications?" you focused on the basics of recording macros. This hour concentrates on advanced macro topics. Just as a reminder, the information you are learning here applies to VBA code creation. When you start writing VBA procedures, you'll use the techniques presented in this hour to decide where to store your code and how to use shortcut keys and buttons to execute your procedures.

The highlights of this hour include

- Assigning a shortcut key to your macro
- The role of location as it pertains to macros
- Creating a personal macro workbook
- Assigning a macro to a button or graphic

Assigning Shortcut Keys

NEW TERM   You might want to assign a shortcut key to your more commonly used macros. A *shortcut key* is a combination of keys that, when pressed, executes a command. You might be familiar with the shortcut key for the Copy command, Ctrl+C. Excel lets you assign a shortcut key to your macro. The shortcut will be a combination of the Ctrl key and a letter of your choice. After you assign a shortcut key to a macro, you can use the shortcut to execute the macro rather than going through the Tools menu.

The shortcut key you assign to your macro will override any default Excel shortcut keys while the workbook that contains the macro is open. This means if you assign the shortcut key of Ctrl+C to one of your macros, Ctrl+C will no longer execute the Copy command, which might cause you and your users both frustration and confusion. It's a good idea to print a listing of Excel's shortcut keys to have as a reference before assigning shortcut keys to your macros. Use the following steps to print a listing of Excel's shortcut keys:

1. Display the Contents tab of Excel's online help system.
2. Select the heading Shortcut Keys from the Using Shortcut Keys folder.
3. Right-click Shortcut Keys and select Print from the menu.
4. Select Print the Selected Heading and All Subtopics and click OK.

You can assign a shortcut key either when you create a macro or after you create the macro. To assign a shortcut key while creating a macro, enter the key you want to use in the Shortcut Key text box after typing in the name of the macro. After you record a macro, you can go back and assign a shortcut key. For example, to assign a shortcut key to the BigFont macro, use the following steps:

1. Open the Hour1 workbook, if it's not already open.

Depending on your macro security level, you may see a message box when you open this workbook. Select Enable Macros if this message box displays.

2. Select Tools, Macro, Macros. The Macro dialog displays.
3. Select BigFont and click Options. The Macro Options dialog box displays (see Figure 2.1).

2

FIGURE 2.1

The Macro Options dialog box is used to assign a keyboard shortcut to a macro.

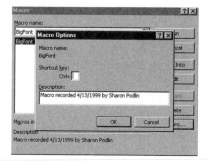

4. Enter the letter b for the shortcut key.

> The assignment for the shortcut key must be a letter.

5. Click OK. Close the Macro dialog box.

6. In cell A3, enter `Test`.

7. Select cell A3 and press Ctrl+B. The macro executes and the font size and color for this cell change.

If you are familiar with Excel's shortcut keys, you know that normally Ctrl+B would bold the contents of your selection. Because you assigned Ctrl+B as the shortcut key for your macro's execution, you have overridden the built-in functionality of Excel. That is the case as long as this workbook is open. Notice that Excel did not attempt to stop you from doing this. You didn't even get a warning message. Excel assumes that you know what you are doing!

Determining Where to Save Your Macros

When you created your first macro, you accepted the default location for the macro. In all, you have three possible locations where you can save you macro:

- This Workbook
- New Workbook
- Personal Macro Workbook

As the name implies, when This Workbook is the chosen location for the saved macro, the macro resides in the current workbook. This means the macro is available only when this workbook is open. You also have the option of saving your macro to a new workbook. If you select this option, the new workbook will be automatically created for you. The final option is to save your macro to the personal macro workbook.

Creating a Personal Macro Workbook

NEW TERM The *personal macro workbook* is a special hidden workbook reserved just for macros. The first time you elect to save a macro to the personal macro workbook, a new file is created called PERSONAL.XLS. After this file exists, it is automatically opened when you open Excel. Because the personal macro workbook is always open, any macro you save there is always available. That means if you are creating a macro that is generic enough to be used by multiple workbooks, you'll want to save it to the personal macro workbook.

On the Macintosh, the name of the personal macro workbook is PERSONAL MACRO WORKBOOK.

The personal macro workbook resides in the XLSTART folder.

Saving a Macro to the Personal Macro Workbook

Saving a macro to the personal macro workbook is basically the same as saving a macro to This Workbook. In this exercise, you are going to create a very simple macro that italicizes and underlines text. To save a macro to the personal macro workbook, complete the following steps:

1. Select Tools, Macro, Record New Macro. The Record Macro dialog box displays.

2. Enter FormatText for the macro name.

3. Select Personal Macro Workbook from the Store Macro in drop-down list box.

4. Click OK. You are now in record mode.

5. Click the Italic toolbar button. The hourglass pointer might display for a few moments—particularly the first time you save a macro to the personal macro workbook—because Excel needs to create the personal macro workbook file.

6. Click the Underline toolbar button.

7. Stop recording the macro.

Using a Macro from the Personal Macro Workbook

Now that you've saved a macro to the personal macro workbook, you can use it with any workbook. To demonstrate this, complete the following steps:

1. Close all open workbooks. This way you'll know that the macros you are using are saved in the personal macro workbook.

2. Open a new workbook.

3. In cell A1, enter your name.

4. Select cell A1.

5. Select Tools, Macro, Macros. The Macro dialog displays and you can see the FormatText macro listed as PERSONAL.XLS!FormatText (see Figure 2.2).

FIGURE 2.2

The macros saved to your personal macro workbook are available for you to use with all your workbooks.

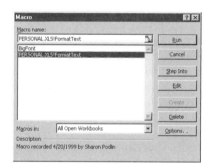

6. Select the FormatText macro and click Run. Your selected cell's text is now italic and underlined.

Editing a Macro in the Personal Macro Workbook

Editing a macro in your personal macro workbook is handled a little differently from editing a macro in other workbooks. The personal macro workbook is a hidden workbook and must be unhidden before you can edit its contents. To unhide the personal macro workbook and edit one of its macros, use the following steps:

1. Select Window, Unhide. The Unhide dialog box displays (see Figure 2.3).

FIGURE 2.3
The first step to editing a macro in the personal macro workbook is to unhide the workbook.

2. Select Personal and click OK. The personal macro workbook is unhidden and is now the active workbook. Look at the caption of the current workbook window. It says Personal.

3. Select Tools, Macro, Macros. The Macro dialog box displays.

4. Select FormatText and click Edit. If you tried to edit the macro without unhiding the personal macro workbook, you would get a message letting you know you must unhide the workbook first.

5. Make any changes you want to the macro, and close the Microsoft Visual Basic Editor window.

Deleting a Macro from the Personal Macro Workbook

To delete a macro from the personal macro workbook, the workbook must again be unhidden. Because you probably don't want the FormatText macro in your personal macro workbook permanently, you can delete it while the workbook is unhidden using these steps:

1. Select Tools, Macro, Macros. The Macro dialog box displays.

2. Select FormatText and click Delete.

3. A message displays asking if you want to delete the FormatText macro. Click Yes. The macro is deleted.

4. Save the workbook.

5. The last thing you need to do is hide the personal macro workbook. Select Window, Hide. The workbook is hidden.

Assigning a Macro to a Button

One of your main goals as an Excel developer is to provide an easy-to-use interface to your automated tasks. One of the most visual ways to accomplish this is to provide a command button right in the workbook the user will be using. Using the Forms toolbar , you'll add a button to a sheet in the workbook. After creating the button, you'll assign the macro to the button. Then your user can just click a button to execute your macro!

In this exercise, you'll create a button, assign a macro to the button, and then execute the macro using the button. Complete the following steps:

1. Open the Hour1 workbook.

2. Select View, Toolbars, Forms. The Forms toolbar displays as shown in Figure 2.4.

FIGURE 2.4

The Forms toolbar contains a variety of controls that you can use for the automation process.

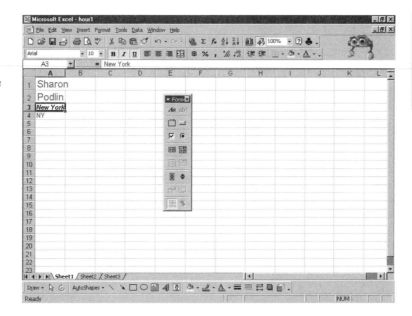

3. Click the Button button in the Forms toolbar. Your pointer becomes a crosshair (looks like a plus sign).

4. Point at the location where you would like the command button to be located and click and hold the left mouse button. Drag to draw a rectangle. This rectangle represents the size and shape of the command button. When you are happy with the size of the command button, release the mouse button. A command button is added to the sheet and the Assign Macro dialog box displays (see Figure 2.5). When you add a button to a sheet, you are automatically prompted to select the macro to assign to the button.

5. Select BigFont and click OK. The macro is assigned to the button.

6. Click before the letter B on the button. Press the Delete key until the text is removed.

7. Type Big Font and click OK.

8. Click outside the button to deselect it.

FIGURE 2.5

The Assign Macro dialog box is used to select the macro to be executed by this button.

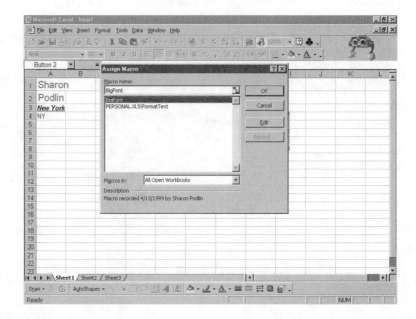

9. In cell A6, type today's date and press Enter.

10. Select cell A6 and click the Big Font button. The BigFont macro executes.

Buttons are a great way to add functionality to your worksheets. They are visible, familiar, and don't require the user to know the name of a macro to execute it.

Assign a Macro to a Graphic Image

You're not limited to using buttons to execute your macros. Any image you can place on a sheet can be used to execute a macro. This technique is useful when you want to create a very graphic and friendly interface. If, for example, you were creating an application that analyzed data for four different companies, you could use the companies' logos for buttons. To assign a macro to a graphic image, use the following steps:

1. Select cell G3.

2. Select Insert, Picture.

3. Select either Clip Art or From File.

4. Select an image to insert.

5. After the image is displayed on your worksheet, resize the image until it is approximately 2" by 2".

6. Right-click the graphic and select Assign Macro. The Assign Macro dialog box displays.

7. Select the BigFont macro and click OK.

8. Click outside the graphic to deselect it.

9. Enter 100 in cell A9.

10. Select cell A9 and click the graphic. The macro executes. The worksheet with the graphic "button" is shown in Figure 2.6.

2

FIGURE 2.6

Any piece of clip art or graphic file can be used to execute a macro.

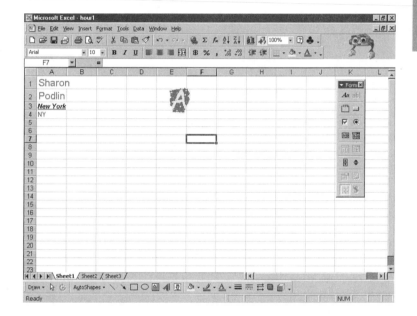

When you actually start writing VBA procedures, you can use this technique to assign them to graphics or buttons for execution.

Assigning a Macro to a Toolbar Button

If you don't want to add a button or graphic to your worksheet as a way to execute your macro, you have another alternative. You can assign the macro to a toolbar button. Excel lets you customize your toolbars by adding buttons to them. After you add a button to a toolbar, you can assign a macro to it. To assign a macro to a toolbar button, use the following steps:

1. Select Tools, Customize. The Customize dialog box displays.

> You can also right-click a toolbar and select Customize from the pop-up menu.

2. Select the Commands tab (see Figure 2.7).

FIGURE 2.7

The Customize dialog allows you to add buttons to existing toolbars and create new toolbars.

3. From the Categories list box, select Macros.
4. From the Commands list box, select Custom Button.
5. Drag and drop the custom button to a toolbar.
6. Right-click the newly added button.
7. Select Change Button Image. Select an image for your button.
8. Right-click the new button and select Assign Macro. The Assign Macro dialog box displays.
9. Select BigFont and click OK.
10. Click Close to close the Customize dialog.
11. In cell A11, enter 200.
12. Select cell A11 and click the new button. The BigFont macro executes.

Summary

Whereas the first hour focused on the basics of recording a macro, this hour had two focuses. First, you learned about the different locations in which you can store a macro. Then you covered the different ways you can execute a macro. Originally, you could execute a macro only by using the Tools, Macro, Macros menu. Now you know how to assign a shortcut key to a macro, as well as how to assign a macro to a button, a graphic, and a toolbar button. Don't forget, you can use these techniques when you write your own VBA procedures.

Q&A

Q How will learning macros help me be an Excel developer?

A One way is that learning macros reduces your development time. It is much faster to record actions than it is to write code from scratch. The other way is that by understanding the techniques for assigning macros to a variety of objects (buttons, graphics, and toolbar buttons), you are well on your way to knowing the basics needed for the interface design of your applications.

Q Can I assign my VBA code to buttons, graphics, and toolbar buttons?

A Yes, using the same techniques covered in this hour.

Workshop

The quiz questions and exercise are provided for your further understanding. See Appendix A for the answers.

Quiz

1. True or False: A shortcut key can be assigned only when you first record a macro.
2. Where are the three locations that you can save a macro?
3. Where is the personal macro workbook located?
4. True or False: The personal macro workbook is automatically opened when you start Excel.
5. True or False: Excel will not allow you to assign your macro to one of its already defined shortcut keys.
6. What are the basic steps for assigning a macro to a graphic?

Exercise

Assign the macro you created in Hour 1's exercise, Title, to a button, a graphic, and a toolbar button.

HOUR 3

Working with Controls

In the last hour, whether or not you were aware of it, you were starting to learn some of the components of user interface design. You learned about adding buttons, graphics, and toolbar buttons to your application's design. This hour expands on this with its concentration on controls.

The highlights of this hour include

- A brief introduction to Excel's development process
- A discussion of the different types of controls
- Adding controls to your worksheet
- Formatting controls to link them to worksheet cells
- Using UserForms in your application

A Brief Introduction to Excel's Development Process

As there is with building anything, there are numerous ways you can approach building an application. The approach presented here is one that I have used successfully for years. The first step to building your application is to learn as much as you can about the application. That means you need to find the answers to the following questions:

- Who is using the application?
- Where is the data coming from that is to be used by the application?
- What data is stored by the application?
- How is the data going to be used by the application?
- What type of output from the application is needed?

Who Is Using the Application?

Knowing the audience of your application gives you an idea of what type of look and feel your application needs to have. For example, if you are designing an application that is to be used by experienced Excel users, you might want to use worksheets as your primary data input mechanism. If, on the other hand, your users are not familiar with Excel, you will probably want to use forms for data input.

Where Is the Data Coming from That Is to Be Used by the Application?

Is the data already in an Excel workbook? Are you starting from scratch with all new data? Are you importing the data from another source? Your application's data current location is going to be one of the factors that controls the approach you'll use for your application's development.

What Data Is Stored by the Application?

Is the data going to be stored in the workbook where the application's code resides or in another workbook? Or is the data going to end up in another data file, for example, Microsoft Access, Microsoft SQL Server, and so on? If the data is going to reside in a workbook, you'll want to create the worksheet with the appropriate columns before you start writing code.

How Is the Data Going to Be Used by the Application?

In other words, does your application need to manipulate or analyze the data? Do you need to chart the data? Do you need to use the data in calculations? Do you need to set up pivot tables? Does the data need to be sorted? By asking yourself these types of questions, you find out what kind of worksheets need to be created as well as the formulas needed on the worksheets. You also determine what types of actions you can record using the macro recorder.

What Type of Output from the Application Is Needed?

This question leads you to designing and creating another set of worksheets. You'll probably need to create a worksheet for each report you want to output.

Answering these questions actually leads you to your application's design. Knowing this information up front makes your job as a developer easier.

The Different Types of Controls

NEW TERM   You can add controls to a worksheet or to a UserForm. *UserForms* are actually windows or dialog boxes that you create to be part of your application's user interface. The types of controls you can add to a worksheet are more limited than those you can add to a UserForm. The first controls discussed are those that you can use on a worksheet. These controls can also be used on UserForms.

Start by closing all open workbooks and opening a new workbook. Right-click on a toolbar and select Forms from the menu. The Forms toolbar displays (see Figure 3.1). This toolbar has 16 controls on it, but only 9 of them are enabled. These 9 controls can be placed on a worksheet.

FIGURE 3.1

The Forms toolbar has a variety of controls that you can place on a worksheet.

NEW TERM   The first control on the Forms toolbar is the label control. *Labels* are static areas of text that are used to label other interface elements and to provide information. Because labels are static, users cannot alter their content. Figure 3.2 shows an example of a label.

In Figure 3.2, the arrow pointing from the label control in the Forms toolbar points toward the label object on the worksheet.

The next available control for a worksheet is the group box control. The group box control is used to group other controls. The group box control provides a visual frame, letting users know that the grouped controls relate to the same thing. To see an example of a group box, select File, Print. The Print What group box contains a series of option buttons that are used to select the portion of the workbook to print.

FIGURE 3.2

A label allows you to place static text on your worksheet without placing it in a cell.

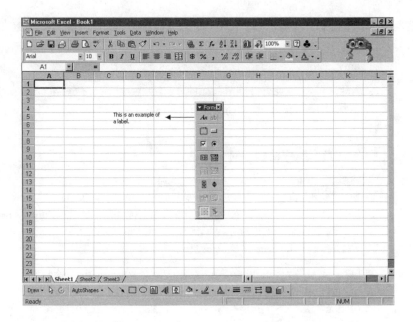

Next to the group box control on the Forms toolbar is the button control you are already familiar with from Hour 2, "Working More with Recorded Macros." Buttons are nice controls to use in your application because users are accustomed to them. Users see OK, Cancel, Yes, and No buttons throughout Windows.

The next two controls, the check box and the option button, have a similar goal: to allow the user to make choices from selections. This is where the similarity ends. A check box, shown in Figure 3.3, is a toggle control—meaning that repeated clicking on the control turns it on and off. If you have multiple check boxes in a group, a user can select one, several, or all of the check boxes. Think of check boxes as and/or selections (select check box 1, and/or check box 2, and/or check box 3, and so on).

If you have a group of option buttons (see Figure 3.4), on the other hand, you can only select one option in the group. Think of option buttons as either/or selections (select either option button 1, or option button 2, or option button 3, and so on).

Typically, you organize check boxes and option buttons using a group box.

FIGURE 3.3

Check boxes make it easy for a user to select from multiple choices.

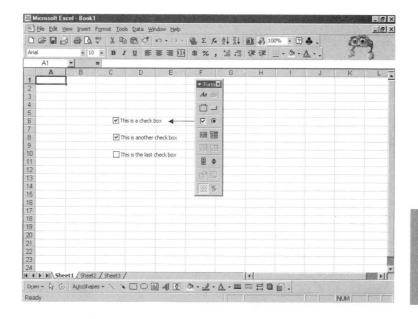

FIGURE 3.4

Option buttons let your users know that they can select only one of the available options.

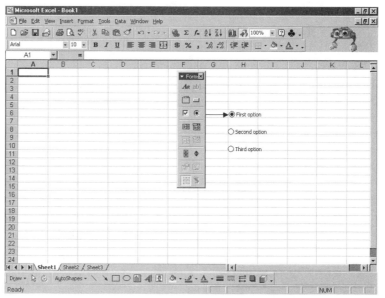

The list box and combo box controls are used to display multiple selections. If, for example, you wanted the user to select from a list of regions, you could present the regions in a list box. A list box (shown in Figure 3.5) only allows a user to make a selection, whereas a combo box (see Figure 3.6) allows a user to select from a listed item or enter in another value. A combo box gets its name from the fact it is a combination of a list box and a text box.

> A list or combo box has the same functionality as option buttons in that they all allow for selection from available options. The rule of thumb many developers use is that if you need more than three option buttons, use a list box instead. You don't want to do what I once saw a client do and create 50 option buttons, one for each state in America! This situation definitely called for a list box.

FIGURE 3.5

List boxes allow a user to select from multiple choices. If the available choices are too numerous to be shown in the list box, the user can use the scrollbar to see addition choices.

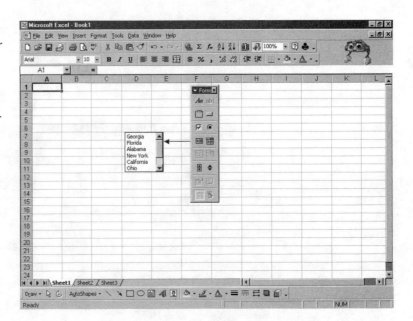

The last two controls that you can place on a worksheet are the scrollbar control and the spinner control. The scrollbar control (see Figure 3.7) is not something that you use to add scrolling ability to a long form. It is a selection mechanism. If you have used a graphic program, you might have used a scrollbar control to make an image lighter or darker or to select from different values of the same color.

FIGURE 3.6

*The combo control is
another way to give
your user the ability to
select from a list of
options.*

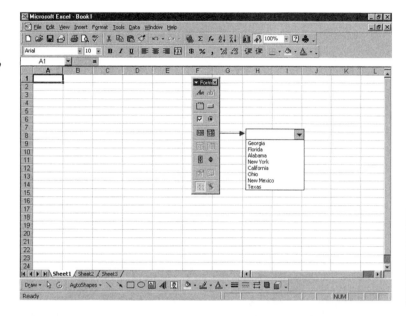

FIGURE 3.7

*Scrollbars can be
either horizontal or
vertical, depending on
how you draw them.*

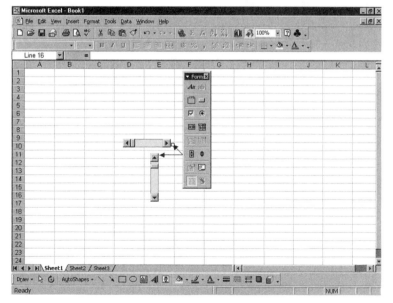

The spinner control (shown in Figure 3.8) is also a value selection mechanism. If you
have changed the date or time on your Windows system, you have probably used a
spinner control.

FIGURE 3.8

A spinner is a compact control that allows a user to click the arrow buttons to select values.

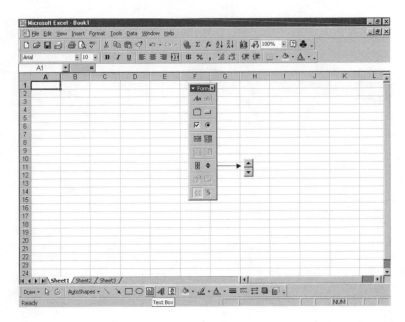

Adding Controls to Your Worksheet

I often tell students that if they can draw a rectangle in that famous Windows accessory, Paintbrush, they have the skills they need for interface design in the Excel environment. It really is that easy. To place any of the available controls on a worksheet or form, you use the following steps:

1. Select the desired control from the toolbar.

2. Position your pointer where you want the upper-left corner of the control to be.

3. Click and drag until you get a rectangle of the size you want the control to be.

4. Release the mouse button. The control is added.

Designing your interface seems like the process of drawing a bunch of rectangles. To illustrate this, complete the following steps:

1. Open a new workbook.

2. Display the Forms toolbar.

3. Select the Label button.

4. Position your pointer, which should look like a plus (+) sign, over cell E1.

5. Left-click and drag until you have a rectangle approximately the size of four cells. Release your mouse.

6. Click before the L in Label1. Press Delete until the text in the label is removed.

7. Type This is an example of a label control.

8. Click outside the label to deselect it. The finished product should look similar to Figure 3.9.

FIGURE 3.9

Adding labels to your worksheet allows you to place text that is not bound by a cell on the sheet.

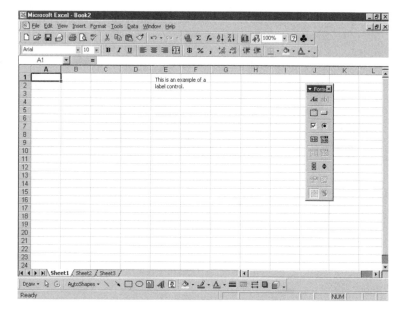

3

9. Select the Check Box button from the Forms toolbar.

10. Position your pointer, which should look like a plus (+) sign, over cell E5.

11. Left-click and drag until you have a rectangle approximately the size of four cells. Release your mouse.

12. Using these same basic steps, add a scrollbar and spinner control to your worksheet until yours is similar to the one found in Figure 3.10.

After you add the controls, you can resize or move them to suit your needs. The first thing you need to do to change the size and location of a control is select the control. Left-clicking a control will not select it for editing. To do that, you need to right-click the control. This places the control in an edit mode and displays a menu. Because you don't need to use the menu, left-click the selected control's border. A gray border surrounds the selected control. To move the control, position your pointer over the control's gray border until the pointer looks like a four-headed arrow. Click and drag the control to its new location. Notice that the selected control's border also has eight small boxes on it. These boxes are resizing handles. To resize your control, move the pointer over one of the resizing handles until it looks like a two-headed arrow. Click and drag the handle until the control is the desired size.

FIGURE 3.10

The worksheet with the added controls.

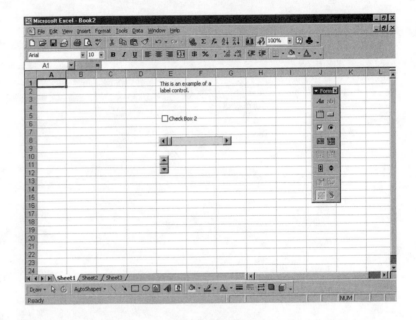

If you want to work with, move, or resize (and so on) multiple controls, select the first control. Press and hold the Ctrl and Shift keys. Click another control. Both controls are selected. Continue holding down the Ctrl and Shift key and clicking controls until all of the controls you want to work with are selected.

Formatting Controls

You might have been wondering how you are going to use these controls you've placed on your worksheet. You could assign a macro to them, but there are other ways of using them. You can use them to enter values into a worksheet. This is done by formatting the control. Formatting a control allows you to control its look and behavior. The following steps illustrate how to format controls:

1. Select the check box control that you placed on your worksheet.

2. Right-click the control and select Format Control. The Format Control dialog displays.

3. Select the Control tab (see Figure 3.11).

FIGURE 3.11

The Control tab of the Format Control dialog allows you to link the value of the control to a cell.

4. In the Cell Link box, type A1 and click OK.

5. Click outside the check box to deselect it.

6. Click the check box to place a check in it. The word TRUE is placed into cell A1. This means that the check box has been checked.

7. Click the check box again to remove the check from it. The work FALSE is placed into cell A1.

> You could use Excel's IF function to test the value of cell A1 and perform different actions or calculations based on whether the cell's value is TRUE or FALSE. For example, if you want to add 20% to a value if the check box is checked, you could use a formula similar to the following:
> =IF(A1=TRUE,A4*1.2,A4).

8. Select the scrollbar control you created earlier.

9. Right-click the control and select Format Control. The Format Control dialog displays.

10. Select the Control tab (see Figure 3.12).

11. In the Cell Link box, type A3 and click OK.

12. Click outside the scrollbar control to deselect it.

13. Click the right-arrow button of the scrollbar control. The value of cell A3 is increased by one. Continue clicking the right-arrow button of the scrollbar control to increase the value of cell A3.

14. Save the workbook as Controls and close it.

3

FIGURE **3.12**
*The Control tab
appears different
based on the type of
control selected.*

You can see that by using controls, formatting, and formulas, you can perform some simple automation (or at least it will appear so to your user).

Naming Controls

When you create a control, Excel assigns it an unimaginative name like Check Box 1 or Scroll Bar 7. When you get ready to write code that uses these controls, you might find it hard to keep track of which control is which using the Excel defined names. You should assign your own descriptive names to controls. Most developers use a naming convention when naming their controls. The naming convention typically used incorporates a prefix for the first three characters of the name that describes the control type. For example, if you were creating a check box that had to do with priority shipping, you might name the check box chkPriorityShipping. In this case, chk is the prefix used for check boxes. Table 3.1 lists commonly used naming prefixes for controls.

Table 3.1 Recommended Control Naming Prefixes

Control Type	Prefix
Check Box	chk
Combo	cbo
Command Button	cmd or btn

This is a control that for some reason Microsoft has given two names. In the Forms toolbar, it is called a button. In the Toolbox, it is called a command button. In Visual Basic, it is called a command button. Probably the most frequently used prefix for this control is cmd.

Control Type	Prefix
Group Box	grp or fra

 For some reason, Microsoft has used two names for this control. In the Forms toolbar, it is called a group box. In the Toolbox, it is called a frame. In Visual Basic, it is called a frame. Probably the most frequently used prefix for this control is fra.

Image	img
Label	lbl
List Box	lst
MultiPage	mul
Option Button	opt
RefEdit	ref
Scrollbar	hsb or vsb, depending whether it is horizontal or vertical
Spinner	spn
TabStrip	tab
Text Box	txt
Toggle Button	tog

Naming a control is done basically the same way that you name a cell or range. Select the control and use the Name box located on the formula bar to enter the control's name. Use the following steps to name your controls:

1. Right-click the label to select it.
2. Click the Name box on the formula bar (you'll probably see that the name is currently Label 1).
3. Enter lblExample for the control's name and press Enter. The control is renamed.

Working with UserForms

If you want to really add a professional look to your application and make input easier for your user, you'll want to use UserForms. UserForms act as the dialog boxes and windows for your application. Adding controls to a UserForm is done the same way as adding controls to a worksheet. The first step you need to take, however, is to add a

UserForm to your application. This is done using the Visual Basic Editor. Use the following steps to add a UserForm:

1. Create a new workbook.

2. Select Tools, Macro, Visual Basic Editor. The Visual Basic Editor opens.

 3. Select the Insert UserForm toolbar button or select Insert, UserForm. The newly added UserForm displays, as shown in Figure 3.13.

FIGURE 3.13

UserForms allow you to design windows and dialog boxes for your application.

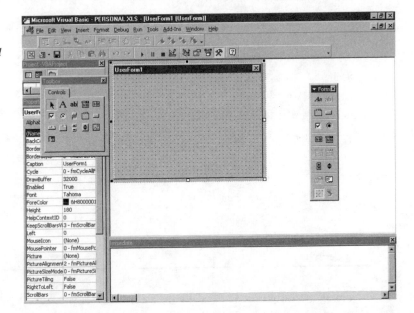

The newly added UserForm has a title bar with the caption of UserForm1. The grid that displays in the form is a design tool that helps you with control placement. The grid does not appear when the form is displayed by your application.

When a UserForm is open, the Toolbox automatically displays (see Figure 3.14). In the Toolbox, you'll see many of the controls you are already familiar with including the label control, the check box control, the option button control, and the button control. There are a few additional controls as well.

FIGURE 3.14

The Toolbox contains the controls that you'll place on your UserForm.

A *toggle button* control is a button that remains pressed in when clicked, and then releases when it is clicked again. Several toolbar buttons are actually toggle buttons. For example, when you click the Bold toolbar button from the Formatting toolbar, the button remains pressed (it appears indented) to indicate that bold is on. Clicking the Bold toolbar button again turns bold off and the button appears raised.

A *TabStrip* is a control that contains one or more tabs. A TabStrip control is used to organize and group related information. For example, you might want to use a TabStrip to display the sales information for each of your regions. Each region then would have its own tab. By default, a TabStrip includes two pages, called Tab1 and Tab2. More tabs can be added to the control.

A MultiPage control looks similar to a tab control. It is a control that contains one or more pages. Unlike the TabStrip control that has the same look and feel on each tab, the MultiPage control's pages are forms that contain their own controls and have a unique layout. A good example of a MultiPage control can be seen by selecting Tools, Options. The Options dialog contains a MultiPage control.

The Image control allows you to place a graphic on your UserForm. The following graphic file types can be displayed using the Image control:

- .bmp
- .cur
- .gif
- .ico
- .jpg
- .wmf

The last control you'll find in the Toolbox is the RefEdit control. A RefEdit control looks similar to a text box, but differs in that the RefEdit control has a button that allows you to collapse the UserForm so that you can select a range. Figure 3.15 shows a form that has a RefEdit control on it. Figure 3.16 shows the same RefEdit control after its button has been clicked and the UserForm has been collapsed. You might have worked with this type of control while using the Paste Function dialog.

3

FIGURE 3.15

The RefEdit control adds the range select functionality found in a variety of Excel dialog boxes.

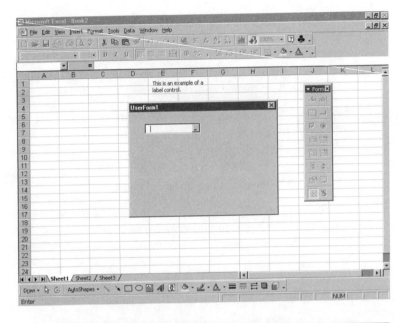

FIGURE 3.16

Use the RefEdit control to select a range of cells.

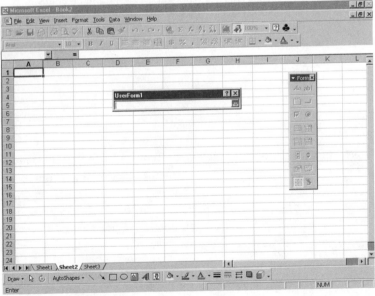

Adding these controls to your form is just like adding controls to a worksheet. Just as you could on a worksheet, you can move and resize controls. The UserForm itself can be resized using the form's resizing handles.

After you are happy with the design of your UserForm, you can preview it by selecting Run, Run Sub/UserForm. The form displays in the foreground of the current workbook, as shown in Figure 3.17. Close the form using the form's Close button (found in the upper-right corner of the form), and you are returned to the Visual Basic Editor. In the following hours, you'll learn how to automate a UserForm.

Another way to run the form is to press the F5 key.

FIGURE 3.17

Running a UserForm gives you a preview of how the form will look in your application.

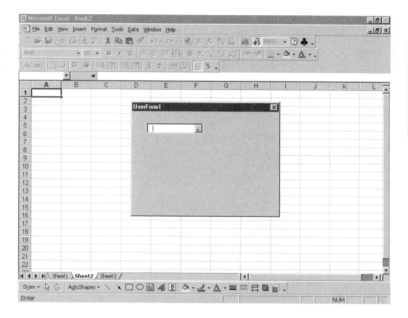

Summary

After this hour, you should have a good, basic working knowledge of designing the interface for your application. You now know how to add controls to a worksheet. You also know how to add a UserForm to your application and place controls on that form.

The remainder of your time spent learning Excel application development will shift from the interface to the code of your automation solution. So get ready to program!

Q&A

Q **How do I decide where to place my controls? Should I use worksheets or UserForms?**

A It really depends on your preference and your application's audience. If your audience members are very familiar with Excel, they might prefer interacting with worksheets. In that case, you would want to place controls directly on a worksheet. If your users are at a beginning level when it comes to Excel use, or if you want more of a standalone feel to your application, you'll want to use UserForms.

Q **When should I use a TabStrip instead of a MultiPage control?**

A By asking yourself the question, "Do I need each tab/page to have the same layout?", you'll know which control to use. If you answer yes to this question, you need a TabStrip. If you answer no, you need a MultiPage control.

Workshop

The quiz questions and exercise are provided for your further understanding. See Appendix A for the answers.

Quiz

1. Name two controls that allow a user to select from one possible option among multiple options.

2. True or False: A UserForm can be added only when the Visual Basic Editor is active.

3. How do you link a control to a cell?

4. True or False: The grid that displays on the UserForm when you are looking at it in the Visual Basic Editor also displays when you run the form.

5. _____ are controls that display static text.

Exercise

This exercise gives you the opportunity to work more with controls. Open a new workbook. Add the necessary controls to the worksheet so that it looks like the one shown in Figure 3.18. Name the option buttons optMale and optFemale. Name the check box chk401K.

FIGURE 3.18

The exercise's completed worksheet.

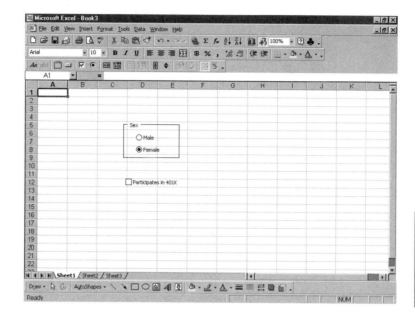

3

Hour 4

Understanding the Role of Variables and Constants

This is the first hour that you are going to focus on the hardcore business of writing VBA code. Five important concepts are introduced in the hour: modules, procedures, variables, constants, and scope.

The highlights of this hour include

- An overview of modules
- A discussion of procedures, including how to create a procedure
- How to use variables
- How to use constants
- How scope comes into play

Your Code's Home: Modules

VBA code must reside somewhere and that somewhere is a module. There are two basic types of modules: class modules and standard modules. Each procedure in a module is either a function procedure or a sub procedure. Later this hour, the difference between a function and sub procedure is discussed.

NEW TERM A *module* is officially defined as a collection of VBA declarations and procedures that are stored together as a unit.

NEW TERM VBA allows you to build your own objects. A *class module* contains the definition of an object.

The majority of your work takes place in a standard module (otherwise referred to simply as a *module*). When you record a macro, a module is automatically created for you if one doesn't already exist. You can also add additional modules if you want to do so. Excel and VBA don't care which module your procedure or procedures are located in as long as the procedure or procedures are located in an open workbook.

Overview of Procedures

NEW TERM This hour has introduced a term without defining it. That term is procedure. A *procedure* is defined as a unit of VBA code. The series of statements found in a procedure acts to perform a task or to calculate a value. Each procedure in a workbook will have a unique name to identify it.

There are two kinds of procedures: sub procedures and function procedures. Sub procedures perform one or more operations and do not return a value. You've seen an example of a sub procedure when you recorded a macro and looked at the code. Macros can record only sub procedures. They can't record functions. An example of a sub procedure is shown in Listing 4.1.

LISTING 4.1 Sub Procedure Example

```
1: Sub cmdSmallFont_Click()
2:     With Selection.Font
3:         .Name = "Arial"
4:         .FontStyle = "Regular"
5:         .Size = 16
6:     End With
7: End Sub
```

The procedure listed is actually an event procedure. You can tell by its name that this is an event procedure. The procedure's name is comprised of a name of an object, cmdSmallFont, and an event, Click, which is separated from the object name with an underscore. If you are wondering, cmdSmallFont in this case is the name of a command button. That tells you this is the event procedure that runs when you click the command button named cmdSmallFont.

Function procedures, more typically referred simply as *functions*, return a value. This value is often the result of a calculation or the result of a test, such as True or False. As I have already said, you can use VBA to create your own custom functions. If you've read Microsoft's marketing materials about VBA and Excel, you might have seen a statement that claims you can extend Excel with VBA. What Microsoft is trying to tell you is that you can create your own functions. As a matter of fact, you can use the functions you create in the cells of your worksheets. Listing 4.2 contains a simple function that calculates shipping as 10% of the price.

LISTING 4.2   Simple User-Defined Function Example

```
1: Public Function Shipping(Price)
2:     Shipping = Price * 0.1
3: End Function
```

4

Notice that this function uses an argument (Price). Both sub and function procedures can accept arguments. Whatever the value of Price, it is used to determine the amount of shipping. Price can be a number or a cell reference. This calculated shipping cost is returned from the function. This function can be used in a cell, as shown in Figure 4.1.

Creating a Procedure

Creating your first procedure requires two basic steps. First, you'll add a module to your workbook. Then you'll add a procedure to the module. You really need to add a module only once to each application you create. You can have multiple modules, but it's not necessary. Some developers like to have multiple modules so that they can organize their procedures by purpose, form, and so on. The procedure you are creating in this exercise is just going to display a message box. Although you haven't been introduced to the MsgBox statement yet, you are going to use it here because it provides a visual example. To create the procedure, use the following steps:

1. Open a new workbook.
2. Select Tools, Macro, Visual Basic Editor. The Visual Basic Editor window opens.
3. On the left side of the Visual Basic Editor, you should see the Project Explorer window (see Figure 4.2). Right-click on ThisWorkbook in the Project Explorer window. Select Insert, Module. A module is added to your application.

FIGURE 4.1

The user-defined function Shipping *is used to calculate the shipping cost based on the price.*

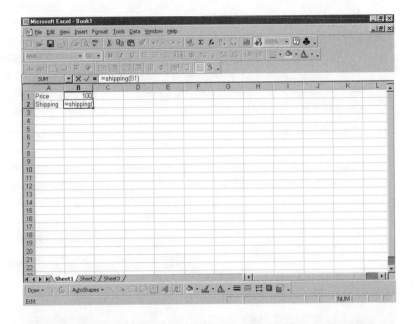

FIGURE 4.2

The Project Explorer window keeps track of the elements that make up your application.

Project Explorer window

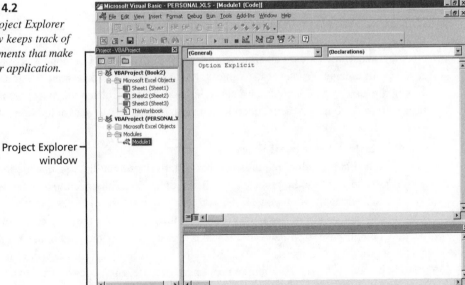

If you don't see the Project Explorer window, press Ctrl+R.

You might see an Option Explicit statement at the top of your module. The Option Explicit is used to force you to explicitly declare all variables using the Dim, Private, Public, ReDim, or Static statements. If you try to use an undeclared variable name, an error occurs at compile time. This statement is added to new modules when Require Variable Declaration is checked on the Modules table of the Tools, Options dialog box.

4. Select Insert, Procedure. The Add Procedure dialog displays (see Figure 4.3).

FIGURE 4.3

The Add Procedure dialog assists you in creating new sub procedures and functions.

5. Enter FirstVBAProc for the name of the procedure. In the Type frame, make sure that Sub is selected. Click OK. A new procedure is added to the module, as shown in Figure 4.4.

FIGURE 4.4

The newly added procedure begins with a Public Sub *statement and terminates with an* End Sub *statement.*

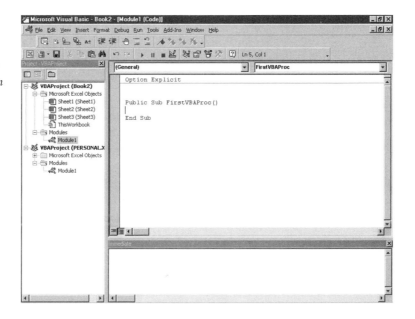

4

6. The insertion point should be on the blank line that is provided in the procedures. Press Tab and enter the following:

```
MsgBox "This is my 1st VBA procedure."
```

When you typed MsgBox, a box popped up giving you information about that command. This is called Auto QuickInfo.

> The indention provided by pressing the Tab key is not a requirement of VBA. Indention is used to make your code easier to read and follow.

7. Press Enter. The completed procedure is shown in Figure 4.5.

FIGURE 4.5
Your first procedure only has three lines of VBA code.

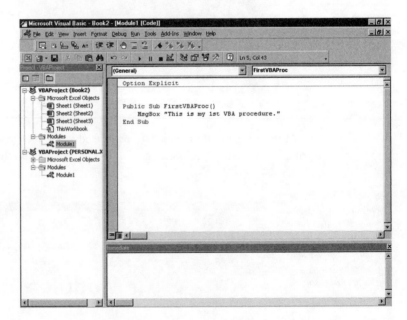

VBA has rules about naming sub procedures and functions. These rules are

- The first character must be a letter.
- Names can contain letters, numbers, and underscores.
- Names can't contain spaces, periods, exclamation marks (!), or the characters @, &, $, #.
- The maximum number of characters in the name is 255.

Running a Macro

After you create your procedure, you can immediately run it. There are several ways that you can run a procedure. You can use the Run menu, or the Run Sub/UserForm toolbar button, or press F5. Use the following steps to run your procedure:

 1. Click the Run Sub/UserForm toolbar button. The procedure executes and a message box displays (see Figure 4.6).

FIGURE 4.6

The one line of code you typed into your procedure resulted in this message box!

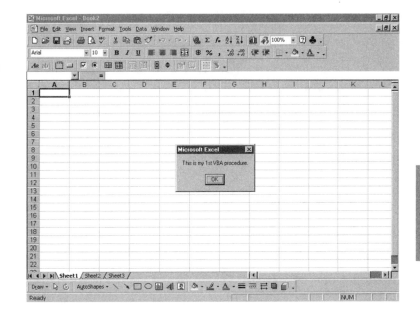

2. Click OK.

Saving Changes to Your Module

To save your new procedure, you need to save the workbook where the procedure resides. You can save the workbook from the Visual Basic Editor. Use the following steps to save the workbook:

1. Select File, Save Book. Because this workbook has not been saved before, you need to name it.

2. Enter First for the name of the file and press Enter. The workbook, module, and procedure are saved.

What Are Variables?

NEW TERM
Variables are temporary holding places for values. Variables contain data that might be different each time the application runs or change while the application is running. To demonstrate the need for variables, create a simple procedure using the following steps:

1. Create a new procedure named WhatsYourName.

2. Enter the following code for the procedure:

   ```
   InputBox "Enter your name: "
   ```

   Don't worry about the syntax of the InputBox statement yet. You'll get more information on this statement in Hour 6, "Conditional Logic."

3. Press F5 to run the procedure. An input box displays, asking you to enter your name.

4. Type your name and click OK. The procedure ends.

Where did your name go? How are you going to find out what a user entered into the input box? You need a variable to hold the result of the entry by a user.

Variable Data Types

NEW TERM
The first step to using variables is learning about data types. A variable's *data type* controls what type of data is allowed to be stored in the variable. Table 4.1 lists the data types supported by VBA. This table also contains information about how much storage a variable requires based on the data type it has been assigned.

TABLE 4.1 VBA Data Types

Data Type	Storage Size	Range
Byte	1 byte	0 to 255
Boolean	2 bytes	True or False
Integer	2 bytes	-32,768 to 32,767
Long (long integer)	4 bytes	-2,147,483,648 to 2,147,483,647
Single	4 bytes	-3.402823E38 to -1.401298E-45 for negative values; 1.401298E-45 to 3.402823E38 for positive values
Double	8 bytes	-1.79769313486232E308 to -4.94065645841247E-324 for negative values; 4.94065645841247E-324 to 1.79769313486232E308 for positive values

Data Type	Storage Size	Range
Currency	8 bytes	-922,337,203,685,477.5808 to 922,337,203,685,477.5807
Decimal	14 bytes	+/-79,228,162,514,264,337,593,543,950,335 with no decimal point; +/-7.9228162514264337593543950335 with 28 places to the right of the decimal
Date	8 bytes	January 1, 100 to December 31, 9999
Object	4 bytes	Any Object reference
String (variable length string)	10 bytes + 1 byte/char	0 to approximately 2 billion
String (fixed-length)	Length of string	1 to approximately 65,400
Variant (number)	16 bytes	Any numeric value up to the range of a Double
Variant (text)	22 bytes + 1 byte/char	Same range as for variable-length String

One of your goals as a VBA programmer is to select a data type that is as small as possible for the data you are storing. This is why the Storage Size column is provided in Table 4.1. For example, if you are storing a small number such as the maximum number of students in a classroom, you only need a variable with a data type of Byte. Why waste computer memory using a data type like Single in this situation?

Creating Variables Using the `Dim` Statement

Now that you are familiar with the data types available for variables, you are ready to create variables. You use the `Dim` statement to create variables. Creating variables is called *declaring variables*.

NEW TERM   The basic syntax for the `Dim` statement is as follows:

```
Dim varname As datatype
```

The *varname* in this syntax represents the name of the variable you are creating. The rules for naming a variable are the same as those for naming a procedure. The *datatype* portion of this statement refers to the data types listed in Table 4.1.

Variable names must start with a letter and can contain letters, numbers, and certain special characters. You cannot use a space, period (.), exclamation mark (!), or the characters @, &, $, # in the name. Names cannot be longer than 255 characters in length.

The next exercise is going to demonstrate how variables are used in VBA programming. You are going to create a procedure that prompts a user for his or her name and then displays that name in a message box. Complete the following steps:

1. Create a new sub procedure named KnowYourName.

2. Enter the following code for this procedure:

```
Dim sName As String

sName = InputBox("Enter your name: ")
MsgBox "Hi " & sName
```

The completed procedure should match the following:

```
Public Sub KnowYourName()
    Dim sName As String

    sName = InputBox("Enter your name: ")
    MsgBox "Hi " & sName
End Sub
```

The indention and blank lines found in this procedure are not required. Indention and line spacing are highly recommended because they make your code easier to read.

3. Place your pointer anywhere in the procedure and press F5 to run the procedure. An input box displays (see Figure 4.7).

4. Type your name and press Enter. The message box displays with your name as part of its text (see Figure 4.8).

FIGURE 4.7

*The input box stores
the entry from the user
in the* sName *variable.*

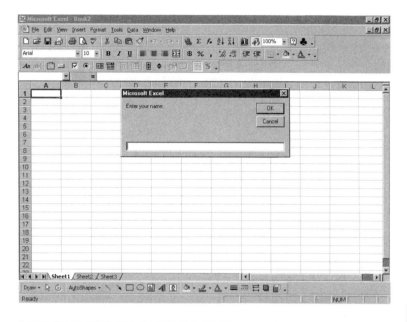

FIGURE 4.8

*The message box dis-
plays the value of the*
sName *variable as part
of its text.*

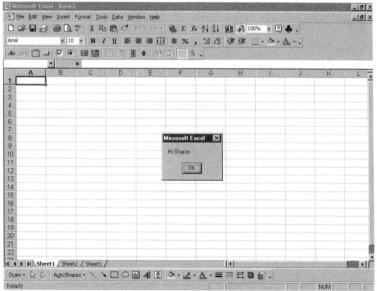

4

5. Click OK. You are returned to the procedure.

You don't have to supply the variable's data type in the Dim statement. If you don't supply a data type, the variable is assigned the Variant data type because the Variant data type is VBA's default data type. Your first reaction to this news might be, "Cool! I'll just let VBA do all the work and not worry about the data types." Wrong! You do need to assign data types. The first reason why you should assign data types is because of the memory usage involved with Variant variables. Looking at Table 4.1, you'll see that even when it's empty, a variable with the data type of Variant takes in between 16 and 22 bytes of storage. The second reason you should assign data types is that Variants can affect your application's performance. VBA has to figure out what kind of data is being stored in the variable instead of relying on you to tell it. The following exercise is something I frequently use to illustrate to students why they don't want to use all Variant data types:

1. Create a new procedure named VariableExample.

2. Enter the following code for the procedure:
   ```
   Dim StartTime
   Dim EndTime
   Dim i
   Dim j

   StartTime = Now()
   For i = 1 To 5000000
       j = i + 1
   Next i

   EndTime = Now()
   MsgBox "Start Time: " & StartTime & vbNewLine & "End Time: " & EndTime
   ```

   Because you didn't supply a data type for the variables in the Dim statement, they are automatically assigned the Variant data type.

3. Press F5 to run the procedure. It should take a few seconds to run. You need it to run at least 4 seconds. Because you might have a faster machine, this procedure might run too quickly for this example. If it doesn't run at least 4 seconds, increase the number 5000000 to 10000000. Note how long the procedure took to run.

4. Click OK to clear the message box.

5. Modify the procedure's code to match the following:
   ```
   Dim StartTime As Date
   Dim EndTime As Date
   Dim i As Long
   Dim j As Long
   ```

```
StartTime = Now()
For i = 1 To 5000000
    j = i + 1
Next i

EndTime = Now()

MsgBox "Start Time: " & StartTime & vbNewLine & "End Time: " & EndTime
```

6. Press F5 to run the procedure again. It should take about half the time to run that it did the first time.

7. Click OK to clear the message box.

Variable Naming Conventions

In Hour 3, "Working with Controls," you were introduced to a naming convention for your controls. Many developers use a naming convention for variables, too. Table 4.2 lists recommended naming prefixes for use with variables.

TABLE 4.2 Naming Prefixes for Variables

Data Type	Short Prefix	Long Prefix
Array	a	ary
Boolean	f	bin
Byte	b	bit
Currency	c	cur
Date/Time	dt	dtm or dat
Double	d	dbl
Integer	i	int
Long	l	lng
Object	o	obj
Single		sng
String	s	str
Variant	v	var

Listing 4.3 illustrates a variety of variable declarations. Notice the declaration for a string variable. If you know the maximum number of characters in a string, you can include it in the variable declaration.

> In this listing, you see lines that begin with a single quotation mark (').
> These lines are comments. Comments are used to document your code and
> are ignored by Excel when the procedure is run.

LISTING 4.3   Variable Declarations

```
1: 'The following line creates a variant
2: Dim StudentID
3: Dim iNumberOfStudents as Integer
4: Dim dTestDate as Date
5: 'The following line creates a variable length string
6: Dim sLastName as String
7: 'The next line creates a 2 char. fixed length string
8: Dim sState as String * 2
```

Note the way variables are named in this listing. They are named using mixed case. The prefix that describes the variable is done in lowercase. The rest of the variable uses uppercase and lowercase letters. This is a commonly used naming convention for variables.

Working with Arrays

NEW TERM   If you have worked with other programming languages, you are probably familiar with arrays. An *array* is a group of variables having the same data type and sharing a common name. The elements of the array are identified by an index number. The syntax for defining an array is

```
Dim array_name(n) As type
```

where *n* is the items in the array.

For example, if you wanted to create an array that could hold 10 student names, you would use the following statement:

```
Dim sStudents(9) as string
```

Note that the number within the parentheses is 9, not 10. This is because the first index number is, by default, 0. Arrays are useful for working with similar information. Let's say that you needed to process 15 test scores. You could create 15 separate variables, meaning that you would need 15 separate Dim statements. Or you could create an array to hold the test scores using the following statement:

```
Dim iTestScores(14) As Integer
```

Most of the time you will work with single-dimension arrays like the one in the previous example. However, multidimensional arrays are supported in VBA. For example, a 2-dimensional array could be thought of as similar in structure to a spreadsheet or table. To create a four-by-four array, you would use the following statement:

```
Dim iTable(3, 3) As Integer
```

NEW TERM Another option when declaring an array is to not give it a size. This gives you the flexibility of defining the size of the array after the program begins to run. For example, your application lets a user create a table. You prompt the user for how many rows and how many columns he wants in the table. By creating a dynamic array, you can do this and even allow the user to add and delete rows and columns after the table (which is really an array) is created. If an array is declared without a size, it is a *dynamic array*. The syntax for a dynamic array is

```
Dim dyn_array() As type
```

After declaring the array, size it at runtime using ReDim:

```
ReDim dyn_array(array_size)
```

The *array_size* argument represents the new dimensions of the array. To retain the values of the array, be sure to include the reserved word Preserve after the ReDim statement as shown in the following syntax:

```
ReDim Preserve dyn_array(array_size)
```

Assigning Values to Variables

After you have the variable declared, you can assign a value to it. Listing 4.4 shows a series of assignment statements for variables. Note the use of an index number when assigning a value to an array item.

LISTING 4.4 Assign Values to Variables

```
1: Dim iNumber As Integer
2: Dim iTestScore() As Integer
3: Dim i As Integer
4:
5: iNumber = InputBox("Enter the number of students: ")
6: ReDim Preserve iTestScore(iNumber)
7:
8: For i = 1 To iNumber
9:     iTestScore(i) = InputBox("Enter test score " & i)
10: Next
```

Using Constants

You now know that variables act as placeholders for non-static information. When you need a placeholder for static information, create it as a constant. Constants are used for two reasons. One reason is to hold a value referenced numerous times that does not change during the run of the program, but that might change in the future. A good example of this is a tax rate. Another reason to use a constant is to make a program more readable. TAXRATE is easier to read than .08167.

To declare a constant and set its value, you use the Const statement. After a constant has been declared, it cannot be assigned a new value. If you wanted to declare, for example, a constant to store the value of a sales tax, you would use the following statement:

```
Const SALESTAX As Long = .06231
```

Because you already know the value of a constant, you can specify the data type in a Const statement. Constants can be declared as one of the following data types: Boolean, Byte, Integer, Long, Currency, Single, Double, Date, String, or Variant. An often-used naming convention for constants is to use all caps for their name. This makes it easy to tell the difference between variables and constants in your code.

Scope

NEW TERM Up to this point you've learned how to define variables or constants, but not where to define them. Variables and constants can be defined in two locations. They can be defined within a procedure, and they can be defined at the top of a module in a section called the General Declarations area. The location of a variable's declaration determines its scope. When you create a variable within a procedure, only that procedure knows about it. No other procedures can use that variable and its value. It is referred to as a *procedural-level* or *local variable* because it is local to its defining procedure.

NEW TERM What if you wanted to set a variable or constant to a value and then use that variable or constant in another procedure in the module? You would need the variable or constant to have a different level of scope. If you defined the variable or constant in the module's General Declarations area, all procedures defined in the module could use that variable and its value. This is called a *module-level variable*.

> The concept of scope also applies to procedures.

NEW TERM There is another level of scope called public. *Public-level variables* can be used in any procedure in your application, whether or not that procedure is in the same module as where the variable or constant was defined. This makes public-level variables very flexible, but also means that they are loaded into memory the whole time you are running your application, and therefore are taking up system resources. To create a public-level variable, you use the `Public` statement. To create a public variable, use the following syntax:

```
Public variablename As datatype
```

To create a public constant, use the following syntax:

```
Public Const CONSTANTNAME datatype = value
```

Public variables and constants need to be defined in the General Declarations area located at the top of a module.

Summary

This hour focused on variables and constants. You learned how to create variables as placeholders for nonstatic data. As part of the variable discussion, you were introduced to the importance of choosing appropriate data types. You also learned to create placeholders for static data called constants. The last part of this hour introduced the role of location as it pertains to the scope of a variable.

At this beginning of this hour, you learned to create a procedure. In the next hour, you'll learn how to call procedures from other procedures and how to create and use functions.

Q&A

Q **Where do I need to define a variable if I want to use its value in more than one location?**

A You need to define it in the General Declarations area of a module. How you define the variable depends on the location of your procedures. If all your procedures are in one module, you can use the `Dim` statement. If they are located in multiple modules, use the `Public` statement.

Q **Are modules separate from my workbook?**

A No, they are actually a part of your Excel workbook. When you save your workbook, changes made to your module are saved as well.

Q Why shouldn't I declare all my variables as Variants?

A Because of the nature of Variants, they take more up more memory and affect your application's performance.

Workshop

The quiz questions and exercise are provided for your further understanding. See Appendix A for the answers.

Quiz

1. What are the three levels of scope?
2. You need a variable that will store numbers greater than 0 and less than 100. What data type should you use?
3. What is the maximum number of characters in a procedure, variable, or constant name?
4. True or False: A procedure name can begin with a number.
5. Where are public variables declared?
6. True or False: Constants can only be defined within a procedure.
7. Which function key do you press to execute a procedure?

Exercise

Create a new procedure called VarAndConst. Create a variable named sTest of data type String. Create a constant named iNumber of data type Integer, and set it equal to 2. Set sTest equal to "This is a test." Add the following lines of code to your procedures to display the values of sTest and iNumber:

```
MsgBox "sTest's value is: " & sTest
MsgBox "iNumber's value is: " & iNumber
```

Run the procedure.

HOUR 5

User Input

In previous hours, some of the procedures that have been used to illustrate various topics have used the MsgBox and InputBox statements. This hour, you are going to learn about these statements and how to use them in your VBA code. Hour 1, "What is Visual Basic for Applications?" discussed some of the limitations of recorded macros. One of those limitations was the ability to prompt users for information. In this hour, you'll learn to prompt your user for information and retrieve the result of the prompt.

The highlights of this hour include

- Using the MsgBox function
- Exploring the InputBox function
- Using the InputBox method and understanding how it differs from the InputBox function
- A discussion of named arguments
- How to use string concatenation

MsgBox Function

Take a look at Figure 5.1. This figure shows you what happens when you try to exit a workbook without saving it.

FIGURE 5.1

This is one of many application-generated message boxes.

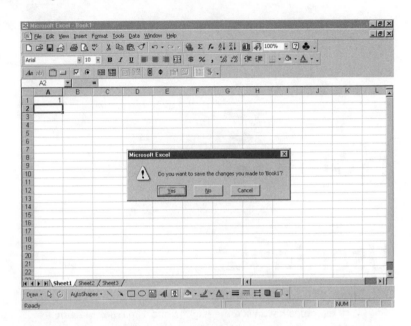

You might have thought that message boxes took long hours of programming. Wrong! That message box can be created with the following line of VBA code:

```
MsgBox "Do you wish to save the changes to '" & _
ThisWorkbook.Name & "'", vbYesNoCancel + vbExclamation
```

ThisWorkbook.Name is used in this code to retrieve the name of the current workbook.

The MsgBox function is used to display a message in a dialog box. Once displayed, the message box waits for the user to click a button. Based on the button clicked, an integer value is returned. The syntax for the MsgBox function is as follows:

```
MsgBox(prompt[, buttons] [, title] [, helpfile, context])
```

The *prompt* is the only required argument for this function. Its value is a string that is displayed as the message in the dialog box. Notice the use of parentheses in the given syntax. MsgBox is a function, meaning that it returns a value. In the example given earlier, there were no parentheses. When you drop the parentheses from a function's argument, you are telling VBA that you don't want the return value from the function. If you did want the return value, you would use code similar to the following:

```
Dim iResponse As Integer
IResponse = MsgBox("Do you wish to save the changes to '" & _
ThisWorkbook.Name & "'", vbYesNoCancel + vbExclamation)
```

Notice that the MsgBox statement is now broken into two lines. The line continuance character in VBA is a space followed by an underscore.

If you don't supply a value for the *buttons* argument, VBA assumes by default that you want only an OK button on the dialog box created. The optional *buttons* argument is a very useful argument. It allows you to control

- How many buttons the message box will have
- What types of buttons are placed on the message box
- The icon to display on the message box
- Which button is the default button
- The modality of the message box

Table 5.1 lists the available settings for this argument. In this table, you'll find that the arguments are grouped. The first group of values sets the number and type of buttons displayed in the dialog box. The second group selects the icon style. The third group sets which button is the default. The fourth group sets the modality of the message box. When adding values to create a final value for the *buttons* argument, use only one number from each group.

TABLE 5.1 Available Settings for the MsgBox's buttons Argument

Group	Constant	Value	Description
Group 1	vbOKOnly	0	Displays OK button only (default).
	vbOKCancel	1	Displays OK and Cancel buttons.
	vbAbortRetry Ignore	2	Displays Abort, Retry, and Ignore buttons.

continues

Table 5.1   Continued

Group	Constant	Value	Description
	vbYesNoCancel	3	Displays Yes, No, and Cancel buttons.
	vbYesNo	4	Displays Yes and No buttons.
	vbRetryCancel	5	Displays Retry and Cancel buttons.
Group 2	vbCritical	16	Displays Critical Message icon.
	vbQuestion	32	Displays Warning Query icon.
	vbExclamation	48	Displays Warning Message icon.
	vbInformation	64	Displays Information Message icon.
Group 3	vbDefaultButton1	0	First button is default.
	vbDefaultButton2	256	Second button is default.
	vbDefaultButton3	512	Third button is default.
	vbDefaultButton4	768	Fourth button is default.
Group 4	vbApplication Modal	0	Application modal; the user must respond to the message box before continuing work in the current application.
	vbSystemModal	4096	System modal; all applications are suspended until the user responds to the message box.
Additional Options	vbMsgBoxHelp Button	16384	Adds a Help button to the message box.
	vbMsgBoxSet Foreground	65536	Sets the message box as the foreground window.
	vbMsgBoxRight	524288	Displays message box right-aligned.
	vbMsgBoxRtl Reading	1048576	Specifies that text should be displayed as right-to-left reading on Hebrew and Arabic systems.

> To see a list of MsgBox and other intrinsic Visual Basic constants, use the Object Browser. Look for classes that begin with VB. Also look at the Constants class. You'll also find Excel's intrinsic constants.

The optional *title* argument can be set to a string expression displayed in the title bar of the dialog box. If you don't provide a value for the *title* argument, Microsoft Excel is placed in the title bar.

helpfile and *context* are optional arguments that are used when you create your own help file for your application.

MsgBox is a function and that means it can return a value. Table 5.2 lists the values that can be returned from the MsgBox function. The value returned is based on the button selected by the user.

TABLE 5.2 Return Values of the MsgBox Function

Constant	Value	Description
vbOK	1	OK
vbCancel	2	Cancel
vbAbort	3	Abort
vbRetry	4	Retry
vbIgnore	5	Ignore
vbYes	6	Yes
vbNo	7	No

Looking at the values returned by the MsgBox function, what type of variable do you think you would need to create to hold the result? The best data type to use when declaring the variable that will hold the result of a MsgBox function is Integer. In the following exercise, you are going to create a message box with multiple buttons on it, and then display which button was selected using another message box:

1. Go to the Visual Basic Editor.
2. Right-click ThisWorkbook in the Project Explorer window.
3. Select Insert, Module.
4. Select Insert, Procedure.
5. Enter MBExercise for the Name and press Enter.
6. Enter the following code for the MBExercise procedure:
   ```
   Dim iResult As Integer

   iResult = MsgBox("Select a button", vbYesNoCancel)
   MsgBox iResult
   ```
7. Position the insertion point within the procedure and press F5 to run the procedure. A message box displays, as shown in Figure 5.2.

5

FIGURE 5.2

*The message box con-
tains three buttons as
specified by the
buttons argument.*

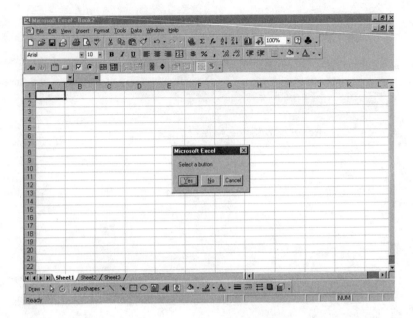

8. Click the Yes button. Another message box displays with a 6 in it. Referring to Table 5.2, you know that 6 is the result of clicking the Yes button. Click OK to dismiss the message box.

9. Press F5 to run the procedure again. This time, click the No button in response to the message box. The second message box displays a 7. Click OK to dismiss the message box.

10. Press F5 one more time. Click Cancel in response to the message box. The second message box displays a 2. Click OK to dismiss the message box.

You now know how to use a variable to display the value returned by a message box. In Hour 6, "Conditional Logic," you'll learn how to use the value in your VBA code.

InputBox Function

The MsgBox function is nice when you need a simple Yes/No, OK/Cancel type of answer. If you need other types of input, like numbers and text, you need to use the InputBox function. The InputBox function displays a dialog box and provides text for the user to enter data. The syntax for the InputBox is as follows:

```
InputBox(prompt[, title] [, default] [, xpos] [, ypos] [, helpfile, context])
```

The only argument that is required for the `InputBox` function is the *prompt* argument. Just like the *prompt* argument of the `MsgBox` function, its value is a string that displays as the message in the dialog box.

The optional *title* argument is a string expression displayed in the title bar of the dialog box. Like its cousin the `MsgBox`, if you don't provide a value for the *title* argument, `Microsoft Excel` is placed in the title bar.

To save your user time, you might want to set a value for the optional *default* argument. This argument can be set to a string expression that is displayed in the text box as the default response if no other input is entered. If this argument is omitted, the text box is displayed empty. If you were asking a user to enter a postal code and most of your clients lived in the same postal code, you might want to provide that postal code as a default.

xpos and *ypos* are optional arguments that control the position of the input box on the screen.

helpfile and *context* are optional arguments that are used when you create your own help file for your application.

The value returned from the `InputBox` function is the value entered into its text box. Complete the following steps to get some experience working with the `InputBox` function:

1. Insert a new sub procedure in the current module named `IBExercise`.
2. Enter the following code for the new procedure:
   ```
   Dim iResult As Integer

   iResult = InputBox("Please enter your favorite number:")
   MsgBox iResult
   ActiveCell.Value = iResult
   ```

   This code prompts you for a number and then displays the number in a message box. It also places the number in the active cell of your worksheet.
3. Position your insertion point within the procedure. Press F5 to run the procedure. The input box shown in Figure 5.3 displays.
4. Type a number and press Enter. A message box displays with the number you typed in it.
5. Click OK to dismiss the message box.
6. Go to your workbook. You should see the number also in the active cell of your workbook.

5

FIGURE 5.3

*The input box is ready
for you to enter a
number.*

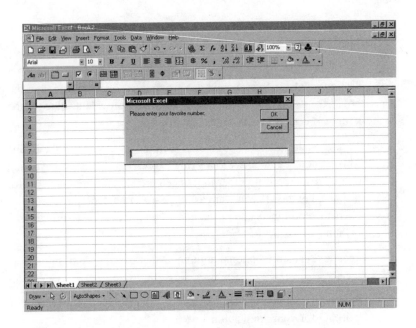

FIGURE 5.3

*The input box is ready
for you to enter a
number.*

If you look at the online Help documentation, it tells you that the InputBox function
returns a string. This isn't exactly the case. In newer versions of Visual Basic, including
the one implemented in VBA, the value acts like a Variant in that it takes on the characteristics of the data entered. That's why your procedure worked, even though the iResult
variable was assigned the Integer data type. Another thing that you need to know about
the InputBox function is what is returned if the user clicks the Cancel button. If the user
clicks Cancel, the InputBox function returns a zero-length string (" "). One last thing:
Users seem to always want to know how to control the size of input boxes. The bottom
line is that you can't. This is a case of "What you see is what you get!"

InputBox Method

Excel supports an additional way to get input from a user called the InputBox method. It
looks identical to its cousin the InputBox function, but it has a couple of slight, but useful, differences. The first thing you need to do is take a look at the syntax for the
InputBox method:

```
Application.InputBox(Prompt, [Title], [Default], [Left], [Top], [HelpFile],
[HelpContextId], [Type])
```

The syntax is similar to that of the InputBox function. Notice that the statement begins
with Application. Excel owns this method and therefore is the application.

Most of the arguments look familiar. A slight difference can be found with Left and Top. These are equivalent to *xpos* and *ypos*.

The argument you want to focus on is the last argument in the InputBox method, Type. The optional Type argument allows you to specify the data type of the return value. Table 5.3 lists the values that you can use for the Type argument.

TABLE 5.3   Values for the Type Argument

Value	Expected Return Value
0	A formula
1	A number
2	Text (string)
4	A logical value, such as True or False
8	A cell reference
16	An error value
64	An array of values

Looking at this table, you might wonder why there are gaps in the numbering, such as from 4 to 8 and from 16 to 64. This is because you can sum the allowable values. For example, if you want to accept both numbers and text, set the Type argument to 1 + 2. If you do not provide a value for the Type argument, the InputBox method returns text. To demonstrate the benefit of the InputBox method, complete the following steps:

1. Run the IBExercise procedure.
2. Enter the letter a in response to the input box, and press Enter. Take a look at what happens. Because you entered text instead of a number, your procedure failed (see Figure 5.4).
3. Click End to dismiss the message box.
4. Create a new procedure named IBMethod. This new procedure will use the InputBox method.
5. Enter the following code for the IBMethod procedure:

```
Dim iResult As Integer

iResult = Application.InputBox _
    ("Please enter your favorite number:", , , , , , , 1)
MsgBox iResult
ActiveCell.Value = iResult
```

5

FIGURE 5.4

This message box lets you know there is an error with your procedure. You don't want your users to see this kind of message box!

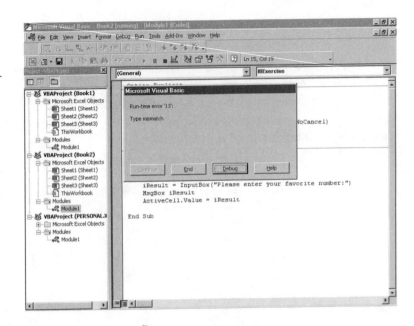

The commas used in the `Application.InputBox` statement act as placeholders for the arguments that you are not entering a value for. The *Type* argument is the last argument in the InputBox's syntax. It is set to 1, meaning that only numbers are acceptable. Notice that the only difference between the lines in this procedure and the lines of code in IBExercise is the use of the `Application.InputBox` statement.

6. Position the insertion point within the IBMethod procedure and press F5 to run the procedure. An input box displays.

7. Type a letter A and press Enter. Instead of the procedure failing, a message is displayed to explain the problem (see Figure 5.5).

FIGURE 5.5

The user is notified that his entry is not valid.

8. Press Enter to dismiss the message box.

9. Type a 7 and press Enter. A message box with a 7 in it displays. Click OK to dismiss the message box.

You now can see that one of the advantages of the InputBox method is built-in error handling. Another difference between the InputBox function and the InputBox method is the result that is returned if the user selects the Cancel button. If the user selects the Cancel button when the InputBox function has been used, a zero-length string is returned. The InputBox method returns False when the Cancel button is selected.

Named Arguments

In the previous exercise, you entered the following statement:

```
iResult = Application.InputBox _
("Please enter your favorite number:", , , , , , 1)
```

If you forgot even one of the commas, you probably got an error when this statement executed. Passing argument values positionally definitely has its drawbacks. To remedy this, VBA supports *named arguments*. Using named arguments allows you to pass arguments in any order. For example, by using named arguments, you can replace the preceding statement with the following:

```
iResult = Application.InputBox("Please enter your favorite number:", Type:=1)
```

To use a named argument, type the name of the argument as it appears in the syntax, followed by a colon and an equal sign. Follow the equal sign with the value for the argument. The syntax of a statement is shown in the QuickInfo box that displays when you type a statement. It is also available through online Help.

 If QuickInfo does not display, select Tools, Options. Select the Editor tab of the Options dialog box. Place a check next to Auto Quick Info.

5

String Concatenation

If you need to combine strings, use the string concatenation character (&). Listing 5.1 illustrates the use of the string concatenation character.

LISTING 5.1 String Concatenation

```
1: Sub stringstuff()
2:     Dim sName As String
3:     Dim sLongText As String
4:
5:     sName = InputBox("Please enter your name: ")
6:
```

continues

LISTING 5.1   Continued

```
 7:      'The following line of code combines Hello and the value
 8:      'of sName so that it is displayed as a single string
 9:      'in a message box.
10:      MsgBox "Hello " & sName
11:
12:      sLongText = "This is an example of using string "
13:      sLongText = sLongText & "concatenation to combine long "
14:      sLongText = sLongText & "strings." & vbNewLine
15:      sLongText = sLongText & "The vbNewLine constant allows you "
16:      sLongText = sLongText & "to add line breaks to your strings."
17:      MsgBox sLongText
18: End Sub
```

Figure 5.6 shows the result of the string displayed by the line MsgBox sLongText. Using
the concatenation character, you can combine strings contained in literal text, variables,
constants, and so on.

FIGURE 5.6

*String concatenation is
a useful tool for build-
ing message boxes.*

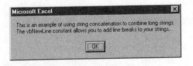

Summary

This hour, you learned a variety of ways to prompt your user for information. The
message box is a great tool for getting a simple Yes/No, OK/Cancel, and other simple
responses. InputBox allows your user to type a response into a dialog box–like interface.

The next hour gives you the tools to test the results received from message boxes and
input boxes. Based on the user's response, your code will be able to select the appropriate action.

Q&A

Q Which should I use, the InputBox function or the InputBox method?

A The InputBox method has the desirable trait of built-in error handling that often
makes it the best choice.

Q What can I do with the value returned from an InputBox?

A You can use the returned value in a message box, place it in a cell, or use it in a
calculation, to name just a few of the things that you can do.

Q Why should I use message boxes?

A They provide a familiar interface through which you can communicate with your users.

Workshop

The quiz questions and exercise are provided for your further understanding. See Appendix A for the answers.

Quiz

1. What is the string concatenation character?
2. What is the data type of the value returned from a message box?
3. What is the data type of the value returned from the InputBox method?
4. What are some of the things that you set for a message box via the *buttons* argument?
5. True or False: In VBA, arguments can only be passed positionally.

Exercise

Create a procedure named YourInfo. This procedure needs to perform the following tasks:

1. Display three input boxes. The first input box should prompt you for your name. The second should prompt for the city you live in, and the third for your age.
2. Display the result of the three input boxes in one message box.

5

HOUR 6

Conditional Logic

In the previous hour, you learned how to prompt a user for a response and then save that response to a variable. What do you do with it next? You'll use the response to make a decision. The issue you need to address is how to handle all the possible responses a user can make to your prompt. This is done with conditional logic and is the focus of this hour.

The highlights of this hour include

- How to control the flow of your application
- Using the If statement
- Using the Select Case statement
- How to display Excel's built-in dialog boxes

Controlling the Flow of Your Application

NEW TERM   Your application displays a message box with Yes and No buttons on it. You
need to decide what to do if the user selects Yes and what to do if the user
selects No. In other words, different statements need to be executed depending on what
the user selects. This is done with conditional statements. A *conditional statement* evaluates whether a condition is True or False, and depending on the result of that evaluation,
one or more statements will execute. You'll probably find yourself frequently using conditional statements in your procedures.

NEW TERM   In your conditional statements, you'll use conditional logic to control program
flow. *Conditional logic* allows you to select different program paths based on a
variable value, user response, function calculation, or property setting. When you use
conditional logic, you create a test and then, based on the results of that test, your program performs an action.

NEW TERM   If, for example, your procedure displays an input box that prompts your user for
the region where she works, you can use conditional logic so that one set of
statements executes if the user works in the Southern region, and another set of statements executes if she works in the Northern region. Or you might have a worksheet that
contains the total number of sales your employees have made. You could create a procedure that calculates commission based on the number of years the person has been with
your company. If the person has been employed fewer than two years, he gets 2% commission. If he has been employed more than 2 years, he gets 4% commission. To do this
type of test, you need to use *comparison operators*. The result of a test using a comparison operator is either True, meaning it met the test condition, or False, meaning it did
not meet the test condition. You might be familiar with comparison operators from working with some of Excel's functions, such as the If function. Table 6.1 lists the available
comparison operators.

Table 6.1   Comparison Operators

Comparison Operator	Meaning
=	Equal to
<>	Not equal to
>	Greater than
> =	Greater than or equal to
<	Less than
< =	Less than or equal to

Sometimes you'll need to test whether a value meets multiple conditions. You might need, for example, to test whether an employee has been employed more than 5 years and is a manager to calculate vacation time. To do this, use logical operators to combine test condition requirements. Table 6.2 lists VBA's logical operators.

Table 6.2   Logical Operators

Logical Operator	Meaning
And	If both conditions are True, the result is True.
Or	If either condition is True, the result is True.
Not	If the conditional expression is False, the result is True. If the conditional expression is True, the result is False.
Xor	If one and only one of the conditions is True, the result is True. If both are True or both are False, the result is False.

The If Statement

The first conditional statement you are going to work with is the If...Then...Else statement. The syntax for this statement is as follows:

```
If condition Then
[statements]
[ElseIf condition-n Then
[elseifstatements] ...
[Else
[elsestatements]]
End If
```

The condition is a required part of the syntax. This is where you enter the condition that is to be tested. If the condition tests to True, the statements listed after the word Then execute.

If you want to test a second condition within the same If statement, you can add one or more optional ElseIf clauses to the If statement. VBA tests the condition listed after the If first. If that condition tests False, VBA goes to the next condition to be tested in the ElseIf clause and continues to do so until a condition is tested to be True. If none of the conditions tests as True, VBA proceeds to the End If statement, unless you have an Else clause. The statements that follow the optional Else clause execute if none of the conditions in the If statement tests as True. The following exercise gives you an opportunity to experiment with the If statement:

6

1. Open a new workbook.

2. Create the sheet shown in Figure 6.1.

FIGURE 6.1

This worksheet is the foundation of your new application.

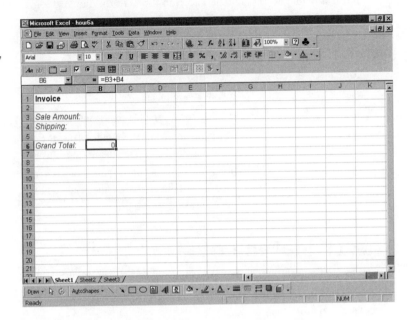

3. In cell B6, enter the formula B3+B4. This calculates the grand total.

4. Press Alt+F11 to open the Visual Basic Editor.

5. Right-click ThisWorkbook in the Project Explorer.

6. Select Insert, Module to add a module to the workbook.

7. Create a new procedure called Shipping.

8. Enter the following code for the Shipping procedure:

```
Dim iResponse As Integer

iResponse = MsgBox("Does this sale need to be shipped?", vbYesNo)

If iResponse = vbYes Then
    Range("B4").Value = 10
Else
    Range("B4").Value = 0
End If
```

9. Go the worksheet you created in step 2.

10. Add a command button to the worksheet. The Assign Macro dialog displays.

11. Select Shipping and click OK. Your procedure is assigned to the button.

12. Highlight the text on the newly added button. Press Delete to remove the text. Type `Calculate Total`. This is now the button's caption.

13. Click outside the button to deselect it. The complete worksheet should look similar to the one shown in Figure 6.2.

FIGURE 6.2

The completed worksheet.

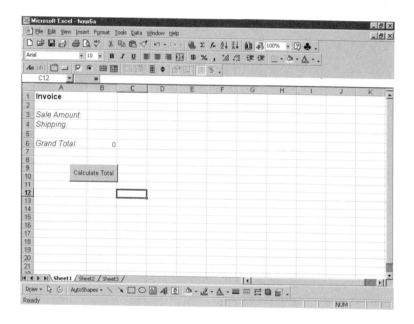

14. Enter `120` in cell B3 for the amount of the sale.

15. Click the Calculate Total button. A message box displays asking you whether this sale needs to be shipped (see Figure 6.3).

16. Click the Yes button. `10` is placed in cell B4. This is because of the `If` statement in your procedure.

17. Click the Calculate Total button again.

18. Click the No button in response to the message box. This time a zero is placed in cell B4.

6

FIGURE 6.3

This message box asks you about shipping.

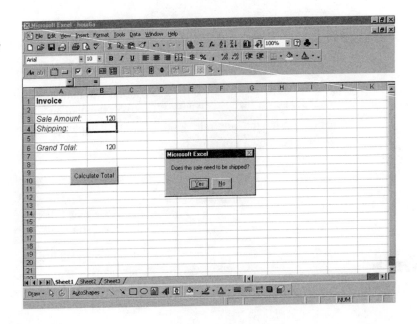

This simple example shows you how useful conditional logic can be. Before continuing, however, take a moment to review the code from this exercise. The complete procedure is shown in Listing 6.1.

LISTING 6.1 The Shipping Procedure

```
 1: Public Sub Shipping()
 2:     Dim iResponse As Integer
 3:
 4:     iResponse = MsgBox("Does this sale need to be shipped?", vbYesNo)
 5:
 6:     If iResponse = vbYes Then
 7:         Range("B4").Value = 10
 8:     Else
 9:         Range("B4").Value = 0
10:     End If
11:
12: End Sub
```

The first thing you did in this procedure was declare a variable:

```
Dim iResponse As Integer
```

This variable is used in the procedure to hold the response from the message box, as shown in the next line of code:

```
iResponse = MsgBox("Does this sale need to be shipped?", vbYesNo)
```

The message box generated by this statement has two buttons on it: Yes and No. The value of the iResponse variable is tested by the If statement.

```
If iResponse = vbYes Then
    Range("B4").Value = 10
Else
    Range("B4").Value = 0
End If
```

If iResponse is equal to vbYes, meaning that the user clicked on the Yes button, 10 is entered into cell B4. Otherwise, 0 is entered into cell B4.

You can create much more complicated If statements than the one previously illustrated. You can even put If statements within If statements. The following steps take you through creation of a more complex If statement. In this scenario, the commission rate takes three factors into consideration. The first factor is whether the item is on sale. If the item isn't on sale, all salespersons get a minimum of 2% commission. If the item is on sale, everyone gets 1%. The second factor is the number of years the person has been with the company. The final factor has to do with department. People who work in the furniture department get an additional 1%.

NEW TERM When an If statement is within another If statement, it is said to be an *embedded If statement*.

1. Add a new worksheet to your workbook.
2. Create the worksheet shown in Figure 6.4.
3. Go to the Visual Basic Editor.
4. Insert a new procedure named Commission.
5. Enter the following code in the procedure:

```
Dim sngCommission As Single
sngCommission = 0.02

If Range("B2") = "No" Then
    sngCommission = 0.02

    If Range("B3").Value >= 5 And Range("B3") < 10 Then
        sngCommission = sngCommission + 0.01
    ElseIf Range("B3").Value >= 10 Then
        sngCommission = sngCommission + 0.02
    End If
```

6

```
        If Range("B1").Value = "Furniture" Then
            sngCommission = sngCommission + 0.01
        End If

    Else
        sngCommission = 0.01
    End If

    Range("B5").Value = sngCommission
```

FIGURE 6.4

This worksheet is used to calculate the commission rate.

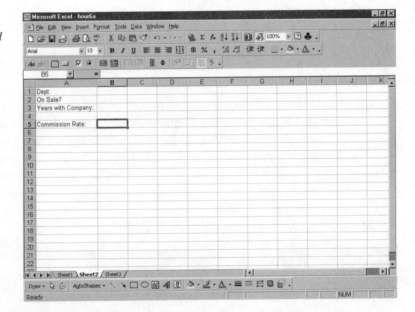

6. Go to your worksheet and add a command button. Assign the Commission procedure to the button.

7. Edit the text on the button so that its caption is Calculate Comm.

8. Click outside the button to deselect it.

9. Enter Furniture in cell B1. Be sure to enter the text exactly as shown in this step.

10. Enter No in cell B2. Be sure to enter the text exactly as shown in this step.

11. Enter 10 in cell B3.

12. Click the command button. The commission should be calculated as .05 because the item wasn't on sale, was from the furniture department, and the person had worked there for 10 or more years.

This exercise used a much more complicated If statement. The complete procedure is listed in Listing 6.2.

LISTING 6.2 The Commission Procedure

```
 1: Public Sub Commission()
 2:     Dim sngCommission As Single
 3:
 4:     If Range("B2") = "No" Then
 5:         sngCommission = 0.02
 6:
 7:         If Range("B3").Value >= 5 And Range("B3") < 10 Then
 8:             sngCommission = sngCommission + 0.01
 9:         ElseIf Range("B3").Value >= 10 Then
10:             sngCommission = sngCommission + 0.02
11:         End If
12:
13:         If Range("B1").Value = "Furniture" Then
14:             sngCommission = sngCommission + 0.01
15:         End If
16:
17:     Else
18:         sngCommission = 0.01
19:     End If
20:
21:     Range("B5").Value = sngCommission
22:
23: End Sub
```

As usual, you started the procedure by declaring a variable, in this case sngCommission. sngCommission is used to hold the running total being generated for the commission rate. The first test is whether or not the item is on sale:

```
If Range("B2") = "No" Then
    sngCommission = 0.02
```

Cell B2 contains either Yes if the item is on sale or No if it isn't. If it isn't on sale, the minimum commission is 2%. If it is on sale, the commission is 1%:

```
Else
    sngCommission = 0.01
End If
```

If the item isn't on sale, two other tests occur:

```
If Range("B3").Value >= 5 And Range("B3") < 10 Then
    sngCommission = sngCommission + 0.01
ElseIf Range("B3").Value >= 10 Then
    sngCommission = sngCommission + 0.02
End If
```

6

```
If Range("B1").Value = "Furniture" Then
    sngCommission = sngCommission + 0.01
End If
```

The first If statement listed in the preceding code tests to see how long an employee has been with the company. The second test determines whether the item is from the furniture department. These If statements were embedded in the primary If statement in this procedure.

When you went through the exercise to create this procedure, you were specifically instructed to type No. To see why, complete these steps:

1. Go to the worksheet with the Calculate Comm. button on it. Note that the commission rate is calculated to be .05.

2. Enter no (all lowercase) in cell B2.

3. Click the Calculate Comm. button. What is the commission calculated to be? It is .01. Why?

4. Return to the Visual Basic Editor and look at the Commission procedure. Look specifically at the first If statement that says If Range("B2") = "No". You might have guessed by now that the If statement is case sensitive. To get around this make the following changes to the procedure. Changes are bold:

```
Public Sub Commission()
    Dim sngCommission As Single
    sngCommission = 0.02

    If UCase(Range("B2")) = "NO" Then
        sngCommission = 0.02

        If Range("B3").Value >= 5 And Range("B3") < 10 Then
            sngCommission = sngCommission + 0.01
        ElseIf Range("B3").Value >= 10 Then
            sngCommission = sngCommission + 0.02
        End If

        If UCase(Range("B1").Value) = "FURNITURE" Then
            sngCommission = sngCommission + 0.01
        End If

    Else
        sngCommission = 0.01
    End If

    Range("B5").Value = sngCommission

End Sub
```

5. Return to the worksheet and click the Calculate Comm. button. The procedure should correctly execute.

The UCase function takes the contents of a string and converts them to all uppercase. By doing this, you can work around the case sensitivity of the If statement.

Select Case

Take a look at the code in Listing 6.3. This listing contains an If statement that tests a value and determines a grade.

LISTING 6.3   A Detailed If Statement with Multiple Tests

```
 1: If Range("A3") >= 90 Then
 2:     MsgBox "You got an A on the test!"
 3: ElseIf Range("A3") < 90 And Range("A3") >= 80 Then
 4:     MsgBox "You got a B on the test."
 5: ElseIf Range("A3") < 80 And Range("A3") >= 70 Then
 6:     MsgBox "You got a C on the test."
 7: ElseIf Range("A3") < 70 And Range("A3") >= 60 Then
 8:     MsgBox "You got a D on the test."
 9: Else
10:     MsgBox "You failed."
11: End If
```

This statement contains a lot of ElseIfs and can be a little hard to read. An alternative to the If statement is the Select Case statement. Select Case statements are easier to read than If statements and are better designed to work with a multiple-test situation. Listing 6.4 shows the code converted to a Select Case statement.

LISTING 6.4   A Select Case Example

```
 1: Select Case Range("A3")
 2:     Case Is >= 90
 3:         MsgBox "You got an A on the test!"
 4:     Case 80 To 89
 5:         MsgBox "You got a B on the test."
 6:     Case 70 To 79
 7:         MsgBox "You got a C on the test."
 8:     Case 60 To 69
 9:         MsgBox "You got a D on the test."
10:     Case Else
11:         MsgBox "You failed."
12: End Select
```

6

As you can see from the listing, Select Case statements are easier to read in a multiple-test situation. The syntax of the Select Case statement is as follows:

```
Select Case testexpression
[Case expressionlist-n
[statements-n]] ...
[Case Else
[elsestatements]]
End Select
```

Listing 6.5 shows another example of a Select Case statement. When separating values by a comma, you are in essence implying an Or select. For example, Case "Florida", "Texas" is interpreted as Florida or Texas by the Select Case statement.

LISTING 6.5   Another Select Case Example

```
 1: 'Select Case to determine shipping cost.
 2: Select Case State
 3: Case "New York"
 4:     cShipping = 5.00
 5: Case "Georgia", "South Carolina", "Ohio"
 6: cShipping = 4.00
 7: Case "Florida", "Texas"
 8:     cShipping = 3.00
 9: Case "Alabama", "Washington", "California", "Illinois"
10:     cShipping = 2.00
11: Case Else
12:     cShipping = 1.00
13: End Select
```

To use the comparison operators, you need to use the Is or To keyword. The Is keyword is used when you want to compare the test expression to the expression listed after the Is keyword. The To keyword defines a range of values.

Using Built-in Excel Dialog Boxes

Now that you know how to control the flow of your application, you can actually do something with the response your user gives you to a message box. For example, if you are asking your user whether she wants to save her work, you will want to display a Save dialog. Excel has approximately 200 built-in dialog boxes. You can access all of these built-in dialog boxes using VBA. The syntax for displaying a built-in dialog box is as follows:

```
Application.Dialogs(xlDialogConst).Show
```

To see a list of xlDialogConst values, open the Object Browser. To figure out the name of the xlDialogConst that you need, go to the dialog and look at its title bar. If you wanted to display the Save As dialog box, you would select File, Save As and see that the title bar of this dialog says Save As. The xlDialogConst value always starts with xlDialog and is followed by the name of the dialog, so in this case you would use xlDialogSaveAs. Use the following steps to display a built-in dialog box:

1. Insert a new procedure to your module named SaveNow.

2. Enter the following code for the procedure:

```
Dim iResponse As Integer

iResponse = MsgBox("Do you wish to save your work?", vbYesNo)
If iResponse = vbYes Then
    Application.Dialogs(xlDialogSaveAs).Show
End If
```

3. Go to the sheet in your workbook where you have the Calculate Comm. button.

4. Add another button to the sheet. Assign the SaveNow procedure to the button.

5. Change the button's caption to Save.

6. Click outside the button to deselect it.

7. Click the Save button. A message box displays asking you if you want to save work.

8. Click Yes. The Save As built-in dialog box displays, as shown in Figure 6.5.

FIGURE 6.5

All of Excel's dialog boxes are available for your use.

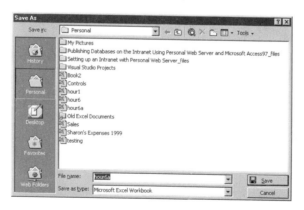

6

9. Click Cancel.

Summary

In this hour, you learned two ways to control the flow of your application: the If statement and the Select Case statement. Using these statements in conjunction with the comparison operators, you can add decision making to your application.

This hour also showed you how to display the built-in Excel dialog boxes. This saves you time by providing you with more than 200 dialog boxes and gives your user a familiar interface to work with.

Q&A

Q If the decision I need to make has several possible outcomes, which is better: If or Select Case?

A The Select Case statement would be a better candidate because it is designed to work with multiple outcomes.

Q If I need a File Save, File Print, or other type of dialog box that is already found in Excel, do I have to create my own to use in VBA?

A No, any dialog that Excel has is available for your use.

Workshop

The quiz questions and exercise are provided for your further understanding. See Appendix A for the answers.

Quiz

1. What are the two primary control-of-flow statements?
2. True or False: The If and Select Case statements are case sensitive.
3. What method do you use to display a built-in Excel dialog box?
4. How do you convert a string to all uppercase?

Exercise

First, create a procedure named ClickTest. This procedure needs to display a message box that prompts the user with "Do you wish to continue?", and should have OK and Cancel buttons on it. Use an If statement to test which button was clicked and display a message telling the user what she selected.

Next, create another procedure called `Discount`. Display an input box that prompts for the discount category, which can be 1, 2, 3, or 4. Using a `Select Case` statement, display the amount of discount in a message box. A 1 equals 5%, 2 equals 10%, 3 equals 15%, and 4 equals 20%.

6

HOUR 7

Looping Through Code

If you need to do the same thing to 15 prices, do you want to write the same lines of code 15 times? No! And you don't have to. Instead, you can use loops. Loops allow you to repeat the same code multiple times. In this hour, you'll learn about Do loops and For statements.

The highlights of this hour include

- Implementing a For statement
- Using a Do loop

For...Next Statement

When you write code, you'll find that there are often times when you need to do the same thing multiple times. In a situation where you need to repeat the execution of a set of statements a specific number of times, you'll need to use a For...Next loop. The syntax for the For...Next statement is as follows:

```
For counter = start To end [Step step]
[statements]
[Exit For]
[statements]
Next [counter]
```

For...Next executes a certain number of times based on the *start* and *end* settings. *counter* is an integer variable that is incremented by one, unless otherwise incremented by the optional *step* setting, each time the Next statement is executed. When the value of *counter* is greater than the value of *end*, the loop stops executing. The optional Exit For statement gives you a way to terminate the loop. The Exit For statement is usually placed in an If statement or Select Case statement. To experiment with the For...Next statement, open a new workbook. Save the workbook as Hour 7. Access the Visual Basic Editor by pressing Alt+F11. Now complete the following steps to see a simple example of a For...Next statement:

1. Right-click ThisWorkbook in the Project Explorer and select Insert, Module.

2. Insert a new sub procedure named BeepMe. This is going to be a procedure that simply makes your computer beep a certain number of times.

3. Enter the following code for the BeepMe procedure:

```
Dim iCounter As Integer

For iCounter = 1 To 15
    Beep
Next
```

4. Press F5 to run the procedure. You should hear a long beeping noise.

If you want to experiment with this For statement, you can change the number of times the statement executes by changing the 15 to, for example, 25 or 5 to see the difference. If you refer to the syntax of the For statement, you'll notice that there is an optional Step clause. This cause allows you to control how the For counts. For example, you can set the For statement to count by fives, tens, or whatever suits your needs. You can also count backward by setting the step to -1. Use the following steps to create a For statement that steps backward:

1. Insert a new sub procedure named Countdown. The Countdown procedure is going to display a series of message boxes that will illustrate both the For statement and the optional Step clause.

2. Enter the following code for the Countdown procedure:

```
Dim iCounter As Integer

For iCounter = 1 To 3
    MsgBox "CountUp: " & iCounter
Next

For iCounter = 3 To 1 Step -1
    MsgBox "CountDown: " & iCounter
Next
```

3. Run the procedure. You'll see the first message box, as shown in Figure 7.1. You can see from this message box that the iCounter variable is currently set to 1.

FIGURE 7.1

Looking at the text of this message box, you can see that the counter is set to 1.

4. Click OK as the message boxes display until you see the message box shown in Figure 7.2. The iCounter is set to 3.

FIGURE 7.2

The counter is incremented before each message box is shown.

5. Click the OK button again. Note that the count is moving backward.

6. Continue clicking OK in response to the message boxes until the procedure completes its run.

Now that you've got the hang of the For statement, you are going to create one more procedure that uses a For statement to calculate how much your money would be worth if you placed it in an account that paid 10% interest. Complete the following steps:

1. Insert a new sub procedure named HowMuchMoney.

2. Enter the following code for the HowMuchMoney procedure:

```
Dim iNumberOfYears As Integer
Dim cSavings As Currency
Dim iCounter As Integer

cSavings = InputBox("Enter amount you are placing in the account:")
iNumberOfYears = InputBox("Enter number of years you are saving the money:
")

For iCounter = 1 To iNumberOfYears
    cSavings = cSavings * 1.1
Next
MsgBox "In " & iNumberOfYears & " years you'll have " & _
            Format(cSavings, "0.00") & " dollars."
```

3. Run the HowMuchMoney procedure.

4. Enter 1000 for the amount of money you are saving.

7

5. Enter 10 for the number of years. A message box displays with the amount you will have in 10 years. Can you believe that you'll have $2593.74 in 10 years?

6. Click OK to dismiss the message box.

Using the variable iNumberOfYears to control the number of times the loop is executed, you calculate the final value of cSavings. You might have noticed the use of the Format statement in the HowMuchMoney procedure. The statement Format(cSavings, "0.00") formats the result placed in cSavings to display two decimal places.

> In Hour 9, "Commonly Used Objects," you'll see the HowMuchMoney procedure converted to a function that can be used on a worksheet.

Do Loops

The For statement is great when you know how many times you need to execute a series of statements. To get around this limitation, VBA provides an alternative to the For statement called the Do loop. The Do loop is a conditional loop. There are two kinds of Do statements: Do While and Do Until. Do While repeats a block of statements as long as a particular condition is True. Do Until repeats a block of code until a particular condition becomes True. The syntax for this statement is as follows:

Syntax 1:

```
Do [{While | Until} condition ]
    [statements ]
    [Exit Do]
    [statements ]
Loop
```

Syntax 2:

```
Do
    [statements ]
    [Exit Do]
    [statements ]
Loop [{While | Until} condition ]
```

There is a subtle difference between the two syntax statements for the Do loop. Syntax 1 places the test condition at the beginning of the loop. This means that if the condition isn't met, the block will never execute. Syntax 2 places the condition at the end of the loop. This means the block will always execute at least once. In both statements, you have the optional Exit Do that can be used to exit the loop if necessary. Like the Exit For clause, you typically place the Exit Do clause in an If or Select statement.

Complete the following steps to create a procedure using a Do loop:

1. Insert a new sub procedure named EnterName. The EnterName procedure will continue to prompt a user for their name until the either enter their name or elect to
quit.

2. Enter the following code for the EnterName procedure:

```
Dim sName As String
Dim iResponse As Integer

SName = ""

Do While sName = ""
    sName = InputBox("Please enter your name: ")
    If sName = "" Then
        iResponse = MsgBox("Do you wish to quit?", vbYesNo)
        If iResponse = vbYes Then
            Exit Do
        End If
    End If
Loop
```

> Just as a reminder, when you click Cancel in response to an input box cre-
> ated using the InputBox function, it returns an empty string. If you click
> Cancel in response to an input box created using the Application.InputBox
> method, False is returned.

3. Run the procedure.

4. In response to the input box, press Enter or click Cancel without entering a value
in the input box. A message box displays asking you if you wish to quit.

5. Click No. The input box displays again. Enter your name. The procedure ends.

In Hour 4, "Understanding the Role of Variables and Constants," you were introduced to
the concept of arrays. In that discussion, you were told about dynamic arrays. Dynamic
arrays are arrays whose size can change. Dynamic arrays can be quite useful when
teamed with Do loops. Complete the following steps to create a dynamic array that is
used in conjunction with a Do loop:

1. Insert a new sub procedure named ListOfNames. This procedure is going to let the
user enter names until they select not to continue. Each time the user enters a new
name, an element is added to a dynamic array.

7

2. Enter the following code for the ListOfNames procedure:

```
Dim iCount As Integer
Dim sNames() As String
Dim iResponse As Integer
Dim i As Integer

iResponse = vbYes

Do While iResponse = vbYes
    iCount = iCount + 1
    ReDim Preserve sNames(iCount) As String
    sNames(iCount) = InputBox("Please enter a name:")
    If sNames(iCount) = "" Then
        iResponse = MsgBox("Do you wish to continue?", vbYesNo)
        If iResponse = vbYes Then
            sNames(iCount) = InputBox("Please enter a name:")
        End If
    End If
Loop

For i = 1 To iCount - 1
    MsgBox "Name #" & i & " is " & sNames(i)
Next
```

3. Run the procedure. The first message box displays (see Figure 7.3).

FIGURE 7.3
This input box will display until you select Cancel.

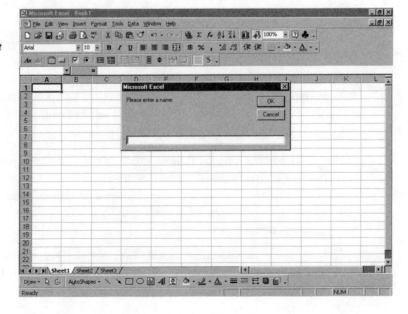

4. Enter Bob for the first name and press Enter.

5. Enter Mary for the second name and press Enter.

6. Enter Tom for the third name and press Enter.

7. Click Cancel. A message box displays asking you if you wish to continue.

8. Click No. A message box displays with the first name, Bob.

9. Click OK. Mary's name is displayed.

10. Click OK. Tom's name displays.

11. Click OK. The procedure is complete.

The strength of the ListOfNames procedure is the fact that you don't have to know how many names are going to be entered before the procedure starts. The complete procedure is shown in Listing 7.1.

LISTING 7.1   The ListOfNames Procedure

```
 1: Sub ListOfNames()
 2:     Dim iCount As Integer
 3:     Dim sNames() As String
 4:     Dim iResponse As Integer
 5:     Dim i As Integer
 6:
 7:     iResponse = vbYes
 8:
 9:     Do While iResponse = vbYes
10:         iCount = iCount + 1
11:         ReDim Preserve sNames(iCount) As String
12:         sNames(iCount) = InputBox("Please enter a name:")
13:         If sNames(iCount) = "" Then
14:             iResponse = MsgBox("Do you wish to continue?", vbYesNo)
15:             If iResponse = vbYes Then
16:                 sNames(iCount) = InputBox("Please enter a name:")
17:             End If
18:         End If
19:     Loop
20:
21:     For i = 1 To iCount - 1
22:         MsgBox "Name #" & i & " is " & sNames(i)
23:     Next
24: End Sub
```

7

The first things to look at in this procedure are the variable declarations:

```
Dim iCount As Integer
Dim sNames() As String
```

```
Dim iResponse As Integer
Dim i As Integer
```

The `iCount` variable is incremented at the beginning of the `Do` loop, and is used to control the size of the array as well as to select array elements. The `sNames` array is a dynamic array that is resized every time the `Do` loop executes. The `iResponse` variable tracks whether or not the user wants to continue entering names. `iResponse` acts as the controlling factor as to whether the loop executes. The `i` integer controls the `For` statement used to display the names. The first thing you do after declaring your variables is initialize the `iResponse` variable:

```
iResponse = vbYes
```

Now that the variable is initialized, you are ready to start the loop:

```
Do While iResponse = vbYes
```

Because `iResponse` is initialized to `vbYes`, the loop is ready to execute. The first thing that is done is to add one to `iCount`. The first time the loop is run, the value of `iCount` becomes 1; the second time, the value is 2, and so on. After `iCount` is incremented, it is used to redimension the `sNames` array. Then the newly added dimension is used to store a new name:

```
iCount = iCount + 1
ReDim Preserve sNames(iCount) As String
sNames(iCount) = InputBox("Please enter a name:")
```

The next thing you need to do is to test to see whether the user selected Cancel or accidentally forgot to enter a name:

```
If sNames(iCount) = "" Then
    iResponse = MsgBox("Do you wish to continue?", vbYesNo)
    If iResponse = vbYes Then
        sNames(iCount) = InputBox("Please enter a name:")
    End If
End If
```

After the loop is completed, you can use a `For` statement to display the names. In this `For` statement, you use the statement's counter to move through the elements in the array:

```
For i = 1 To iCount - 1
    MsgBox "Name #" & i & " is " & sNames(i)
Next
```

Note that the count for the `For` statement is `i=1` to `iCount -1`. You need to subtract one from `iCount` to compensate for the fact that this variable is incremented at the top of the `Do` loop. If you want to see what happens if you don't subtract one, delete the `-1` from this statement and run it again. You'll get an extra message box with a blank name. Now you can see the purpose of not only Do loops, but dynamic arrays as well.

Summary

This hour gave you the opportunity to work with VBA's looping mechanisms. Using the For statement, you saw how to execute the same statements multiple times. Using the Do loop, you saw how to conditionally execute the same statements multiple times.

This hour also expanded your knowledge of arrays, particularly dynamic arrays. Dynamic arrays coupled with loops give you a great way to efficient create and dynamically variables.

Q&A

Q What is the purpose of loops?

A To execute a group of statements a number of times.

Q How do I decide when to put the condition for a Do loop at the top of the loop versus placing it at the bottom of the loop?

A Ask yourself the question, "What is the minimum number of times I want the loop to execute?" If the answer is one, put the condition at the bottom of the loop. If the answer is none, put the condition at the top of the loop.

Workshop

The quiz questions and exercise are provided for your further understanding. See Appendix A for the answers.

Quiz

1. What are the two main types of loops in VBA?
2. What statements allow you to break out of a loop?
3. What are the two types of Do loops?
4. True or False. The condition of a Do loop must be placed at the top of the loop.

7

Exercise

First, create a procedure named EnterHours. Using a For statement, allow your user to enter an employee's hours for five days and then calculate the total number of hours. Display the total in a message box.

Next, create another procedure named Salary. Prompt the user for the hourly wage of the employee. The minimum hourly wage at the company is six dollars. Using a Do loop, continue to display the input box until the minimum amount is entered. Use this rate to calculate the amount of salary based on the number of hours calculated by EnterHours. Display the total in a message box.

Hint: Declare the variable that is to hold the number of hours as a public variable.

Run EnterHours first and then run Salary.

HOUR 8

An Introduction to Objects

Whether or not you realize it, up to this point you've been building a foundation for developing using the VBA language. You've created variables, constants, message boxes, input boxes, conditional logic, and loops. What you haven't done much of is worked directly with Excel. That is about to change. In this hour you'll start working with the specifics of the Excel environment.

The highlights of this hour include

- A discussion of what objects are as they pertain to VBA
- A discussion of objects, properties, and methods
- An overview of Excel's object model
- Using the Range object in VBA code
- Working with known and unknown ranges
- Changing the size or position of the range you are manipulating with code
- Entering values into ranges

What Is an Object?

NEW TERM Before beginning the discussion of objects I want to point out something that might not be obvious to you. VBA is a language, and as such, it has definite constructs. When studying a language, you learn that much of using that language has to do with describing the behavior, action, or appearance of something. That something in the English language is called a noun or subject. In the VBA language the items being described are called *objects*. Objects are the things in the programming environment that you want to control.

Name some of the elements of Excel. Did you come up with things like workbooks, worksheets, cells, ranges, and charts? If you did, you just named some Excel objects.

Objects, Properties, and Methods

NEW TERM Objects are controlled by two things, properties and methods. *Properties* pertain to the characteristics of an object. Changing the value of a property changes the behavior or appearance of the object. Using properties you can, for example, change the color, value, font, or format of a range of cells.

NEW TERM *Methods*, on the other hand, are actions that the objects can perform. An example of this is the Clear method of the Range object.

Going back to our comparison of the English language to VBA, you can say that objects are the nouns of the VBA language, properties are the adjectives, and methods are the verbs.

Just about anything can be described using the terminology of objects, properties, and methods. You can describe yourself, for example. You are a human object. Your properties include Name, Height, Weight, EyeColor, HairColor, and Age. Some of your methods are Sleep, Eat, Run, and Program. What I'm trying to get across here is don't make the concepts of objects, properties, and methods hard; they are really very easy to deal with.

Excel's Object Model

NEW TERM One of the first things you must do when starting to program in Excel using VBA (or in any application that supports VBA, for that matter) is look at Excel's object model. An *object model* describes how objects relate to one another.

Excel has more than 100 objects in its object model, but don't panic thinking you have to learn all these objects. You'll probably find that you work with 20 or fewer objects as you program. To see a list of Excel's objects, complete the following steps:

1. Close all open workbooks so you have an uncluttered environment.

2. Open a new workbook.

3. Press Alt+F11 to open the Visual Basic Editor.

4. Press F1 to invoke Help.

5. Enter the question, What is an object?.

6. Press Enter. Select Microsoft Excel Objects from the list of topics. The detailed object model diagram shown in Figure 8.1 displays.

FIGURE 8.1

Online Help does a great job of describing Excel's object model.

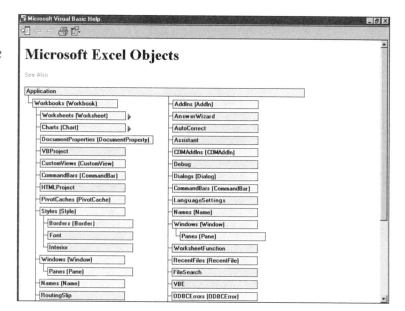

7. Click the arrowhead to the right of Worksheets (Worksheet). This expands this level of the object model (see Figure 8.2).

By looking at this model you can see that the Application object is at the top of the hierarchy. You already used the Application object when you used the InputBox method in Hour 5, "User Input." The next object in the hierarchy you want to look at is the Workbook object, which is equivalent to an Excel file. Being familiar with the Excel environment you won't be surprised to find out that within a workbook are worksheets and that worksheets contain, among other objects, ranges. You know four of the five most used objects in Excel VBA programming!

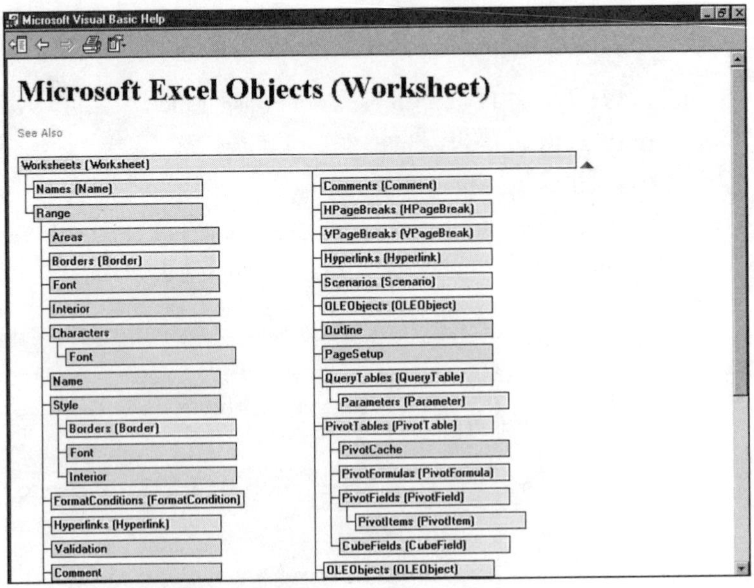

FIGURE 8.2

As you can see, numerous objects are contained within the `Worksheet` *object.*

The Top Five Most-Used Objects

The Top Five Most-Used Objects

Even though there are more than 100 objects in Excel's object model, you'll find that your programming will be focused primarily on the following five objects:

- `Application`
- `Workbook`
- `Worksheet`
- `Range`
- `Chart`

This is not to say that you won't work with other objects, but these five objects are definitely the workhorse objects. The `Application` object represents Excel. Using the `Application` object you control application-wide settings, built-in worksheet functions, and high-level methods, such as the `InputBox` method.

The `Workbook` object refers to an Excel workbook; that is, an Excel file. In the VBA world you don't open a file, you open a workbook. You don't save a file, you save a workbook.

One of the first things you are taught when you are learning Excel is that workbooks contain worksheets. Worksheets are the individual pages of a workbook in which data is stored.

8

A worksheet contains cells. You might think you'll be writing a lot of code that manipulates cell objects, but there is no such thing as a `Cell` object. (There is a `Cells` property, but you'll cover that later.) Instead, you'll be working with the `Range` object. A `Range` object is one or more cells.

Most Excel users use its charting capability, so you'll find yourself working with the `Chart` object. All the things that you can do when you create a chart using the Chart Wizard can be done through VBA code.

You might not realize it, but the controls you worked with in Hour 3, "Working with Controls," are objects too. These include command buttons, option buttons, check boxes, and labels. In Hour 15, "Automating UserForms," you'll work with control objects extensively.

What Does Object Hierarchy Mean?

NEW TERM   When you look at the object model you see that it is designed to look like a hierarchy chart. `Application` is at the top of the hierarchy. Under the `Application` object you'll find, among others, the `Workbook` object. Using VBA terminology, the `Workbook` object is *contained* within the `Application` object. Continuing, the `Worksheet` object is contained in the `Workbook` object, and so on. *Containment* means that objects can contain other objects.

Think of the object model like a Russian nesting doll. When you open the first doll you'll find another contained in the larger doll. Open the second doll and you find yet another doll contained in the second doll, and so on. The object hierarchy works the same way.

Referencing Objects in Code

You might be wondering why you have to know the concept of containment. Containment comes into play when you refer to objects in code. To fully qualify an object's name in code you must "tunnel" through the object model's hierarchy. For example, to refer to the range A1 on Sheet1 in Book1 you would use the following code:

```
Application.Workbooks("Book1").Worksheets("Sheet1").Range("A1")
```

In reality you can drop the `Application` reference in most cases (a readily available exception is `Application.Inputbox`). You can also reference range A1 using the following code:

```
Workbooks("Book1").Worksheets("Sheet1").Range("A1")
```

You don't always have to use the fully qualified object name in code. In some case, such as when a worksheet has just been activated in code, you can get by with a shorter reference:

```
Range("A1")
```

Experience will teach you how much you have to qualify your objects. Qualifying an object is necessary to distinguish it from other objects with the same name. For example, you might have two workbooks, each with a worksheet named Sheet1 in it. In this case you would want a fully qualified name to avoid ambiguity.

Working with Objects in Code

When you are working with objects in code you are doing one of the following three things:

- Setting an object's properties
- Getting an object's properties
- Executing an object's methods

In the next sections, you will explore these a bit more in depth.

Working with Properties

To set an object's properties, use the following basic syntax:

```
Object.propertyname = value
```

The *Object* is the object's name. The *propertyname* refers to the name of the property being changed. The *value* refers to the setting being provided for the property. The name of the object is separated from the property by a period. For example, to set the Range object's Value property, use the following code:

```
Range("A1").Value = 100
```

Getting an object's properties setting is similar to setting a property. The basic syntax is

```
Var_name = Object.propertyname
```

In this syntax, you are reading the object's property setting into a variable or another holder such as another property. If you want to get the setting of a range's Value property, use the following code:

```
Dim sngValue As Single
SngValue = Range("A1").Value
```

You can use a property's setting in a variety of other ways. For example, you can display a property's setting in a message box using the following code:

```
MsgBox "The range's value is " & Range("A1").Value
```

Using Methods

You implement an object's methods by using the following syntax:

```
Object.Method
```

When you execute an object's method you separate the name of the object from the name of the method with a period. For example, to execute a workbook's Open method you would use the following code:

```
Workbooks("VBA Example").Open
```

Some methods have arguments that are either optional or required. For example, the following code saves a workbook with the name Current Budget:

```
ThisWorkbook.SaveAs Filename:= "Current Budget"
```

You might have guessed that methods are sometimes referred to as object-specific procedures and functions. This would explain the fact that some methods have arguments. Some methods even return a value.

Getting Information on Properties and Methods

VBA's help system is geared toward providing you with information on properties and methods. To see an example of this follow these steps:

1. If you don't already have one open, insert a module in the current workbook.
2. In the Visual Basic Editor, type worksheet.
3. Position the insertion point within the word worksheet.
4. Press F1. The Context Help dialog displays (see Figure 8.3).

FIGURE 8.3

The Context Help dialog often displays multiple choices.

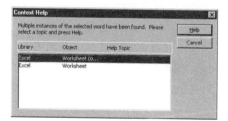

5. Select the item that appears as Worksheet(o...) and click Help. The Worksheet Object help topic displays as shown in Figure 8.4.

FIGURE 8.4

The Worksheet *object's help topic not only describes the object, but also provides information about the object's available properties and methods.*

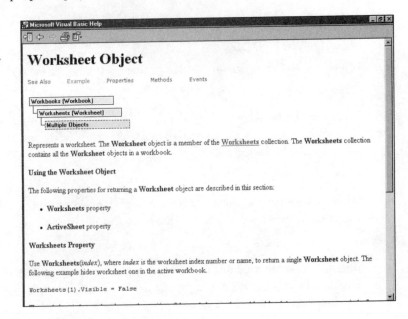

6. Look toward the top of the help topic. You'll find Properties and Methods listed. Click Properties. The Topics Found dialog displays as shown in Figure 8.5.

FIGURE 8.5

Because Properties was selected, the Worksheet's properties are listed.

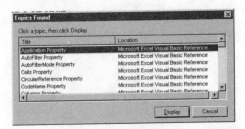

7. At this point if you wanted to get additional information on a property, you could select it and click Display. For the purpose of this exercise, click Cancel to return to the Worksheet Object help topic.

8. Click Methods. The Topics Found dialog displays the available methods.

9. Click Cancel to return to the Worksheet Object help topic.

10. Minimize the Help window. You'll need to return to Help later this hour.

You'll find that as a beginning VBA programmer you'll know what you want to do but not how to do it. Help is a great tool for this type of situation. Locate the object's help topic and view its properties first. Often you'll find the property that you need. If not, try looking at the object's methods as well.

Using Object Variables

NEW TERM When you learned about variable data types, one data type wasn't discussed. The missing variable type is called an *object variable*, which is a variable that points to an object. Because object variables point to objects, they can utilize the properties and methods associated with the object.

Object variables are created like any other variable, using the Dim statement. You can use the generic Object data type or you can use the specific object type. Listing 8.1 shows some examples of object variable declarations.

LISTING 8.1 Object Variable Declarations

```
1: Dim BudgetSheet As Object
2: Dim AnotherBudget As Worksheet
3: Dim WorkingFile As Workbook
4: Dim DeptCodes As Range
```

The first Dim statement used the generic Object data type. This is the least preferred method of object variable declaration. The other Dim statements show the preferred method of object variable declaration. If you know the type of object you are creating, use it in the Dim statement. After the variables are declared, use the Set statement to assign an object reference to the variable. Listing 8.2 shows the usage of the Set statement.

LISTING 8.2 The Set Statement

```
1: Set BudgetSheet = Workbooks("Finance").Worksheets("Budget")
2: Set AnotherBudget = Workbooks("MIS").Worksheets("Budget")
3: Set WorkingFile = WorkBooks("Finance")
4: Set DeptCodes = Workbooks("Budget").Worksheets("Category").Range("A1:A12")
```

After setting the variables to the objects they are referencing, you can use them in code just as you would an object name. Listing 8.3 is an example of code using object variables.

LISTING 8.3 Using Object Variables

```
 1: Sub ObjectVarExample()
 2:    Dim WorkingRange As Range
 3:
 4:    Set WorkingRange = Workbooks("Hour8").Worksheets("Sheet1").Range("A1:D1")
 5:
 6:    WorkingRange.Font.Bold = True
 7:    WorkingRange.Font.Italic = True
 8:    WorkingRange.Font.Name = "Courier"
 9:
10: End Sub
```

You can see in this example that the WorkingRange variable is used in place of the name of the object. As you can already see, this saves you from typing a long, fully qualified name. As you progress through this book, you'll find other uses for object variables.

When programming, I use the rule that if I need to type the same fully qualified name more than twice, I create an object variable to save typing.

Collections

Take a moment and look at one of the fully qualified names you worked with earlier:

```
Application.Workbooks("Book1").Worksheets("Sheet1").Range("A1")
```

NEW TERM   Notice the pluralized words, Workbooks and Worksheets. These are collections. A *collection* is a group of similar objects. Workbooks is a collection. Worksheets is a collection. In the preceding example, Book1 is an element of the Workbooks collection.

In most cases, collections are plural.

There is no Ranges object. One of the things you can do to a collection is add to it. You can't add more ranges because they are already defined and limited by Excel.

To see some of Excel's available collections, follow these steps:

1. Restore the Help window.
2. Select the Contents tab.
3. Expand the Microsoft Excel Visual Basic Reference topic.
4. Select Microsoft Excel Objects. The Microsoft Excel Object model displays.
5. Scroll to the bottom of the Microsoft Excel Objects topic. You'll see that the object model is color-coded. Yellow items are objects and collections. Cyan items are objects only.

The object model diagram provides a great tool for understanding and identifying Excel's collections. When you are finished viewing the object model, close the Help window.

The Add Method

One of the things that collections share in common is the capability to add to them. By adding, I mean creating new elements in the collection. To create a new element in a collection, you use the Add method. For example, to add a new workbook you would use the following code:

```
Workbooks.Add
```

This code is equivalent to going to Excel's File menu and adding a new workbook. To add a new worksheet to a workbook you would use the following code:

```
Worksheets.Add
```

The Count Property

Collections support a useful property called Count. The Count property stores the number of elements in a collection. If you want to know how many worksheets are in a workbook, you would use the following code:

```
Dim iWSCount As Integer
IWSCount = Worksheets.Count
```

You may be wondering why you would use the Count property. Let's say that you are creating an application that contains a worksheet for each business day of the week when the workbook is complete. Using the Count property you could test to see if the workbook contains five worksheets. In that case, you could use code similar to that in Listing 8.4.

LISTING 8.4 Using the Count Property

```
 1: Sub CountWorkSheets()
 2:     Dim iWSCount As Integer
 3:     Dim sMessage As String
 4:
 5:     iWSCount = Worksheets.Count
 6:
 7:     If iWSCount <> 7 Then
 8:         sMessage = "The workbook contains " & iWSCount
 9:         sMessage = sMessage & ". It should contain 7 worksheets."
10:         MsgBox sMessage
11:     End If
12: End Sub
```

Summary

In this hour, you learned about some of VBA's most important concepts: objects, properties and methods. You now know how to use methods and properties to control the behavior and appearance of objects.

From this point forward, you'll be learning new objects and their properties and methods. Using this knowledge, you'll be able to add more and more functionality to your Excel-based applications.

Q&A

Q What features do all objects in Excel share?

A All objects have properties and methods. Properties control the attributes, appearance, and behavior of objects. Methods are the actions that objects can perform.

Q The Excel object model is shown in a tree or hierarchal structure. Why?

A Because of the concept of containment. Some objects are contained by other objects, hence the appearance of the object model.

Workshop

The quiz questions and exercise are provided for your further understanding. See Appendix A, "Answers," for the answers.

Quiz

1. How do you set a property?
2. How do you call a method?
3. What statement do you use to assign an object to an object variable?
4. True or False: Only objects have properties and methods, not collections.
5. How do you create a new element in a collection?

Exercise

Using either the Object Browser or online help, locate the following properties.

For the Application object:

- The directory path where Excel is installed
- The operating system being used
- The name of the registered user of this copy of Excel

For the Workbook object:

- Whether the workbook has been saved

Using this information, you are going to write a new procedure. Insert a new module in the current workbook. Create a new procedure named TellMeMore. The TellMeMore procedure should use the properties you located to display a series of message boxes. The first message box would look similar to that in Figure 8.6. Run your procedure. (Hint: The Application object has a property named ThisWorkbook, which contains the name of the current workbook. This would be useful when generating the message box to display whether or not the workbook has been saved.)

HOUR 9

Commonly Used Objects

Now it's time to really start working with the Excel objects. This hour focuses on three frequently used objects, `Application`, `Workbook`, and `Worksheet`. You'll learn to work with the properties and methods of these objects.

The highlights of this hour include

- The role of the `Application` object in VBA
- Creating and controlling `Workbook` objects
- Using the `Worksheet` object

The `Application` Object

In the previous hour you learned that the `Application` object is the top level of Excel's object hierarchy. What does this mean to you as a programmer? It means that you can use the `Application` object to control application-wide settings and options such as those found in the Tools, Options dialog. To see an example of this, first close all open workbooks and then open a new workbook. Then complete the following steps:

1. Select Tools, Macro, Record New Macro to display the Record Macro dialog. Enter `AppSettings` for the macro name. Select This Workbook for where to store the macro.

2. Click OK to begin recording.

3. Select Tools, Options. The Options dialog displays. Select the View tab. Remove the check from the Status Bar check box.

4. Select the General tab. Check R1C1 Reference Style. Click OK.

5. Stop recording the macro.

6. Select Tools, Options. Select the View tab. Check Status bar.

7. Select the General tab. Remove the check from R1C1 Reference Style. Click OK.

8. Select Tools, Macro, Macros. The Macros dialog displays.

9. Select Edit to view the macro's code. The Visual Basic Editor opens.

Listing 9.1 shows the recorded code of the AppSettings macro.

LISTING 9.1   The AppSettings Procedure

```
 1: Sub AppSettings()
 2:     With Application
 3:         .ReferenceStyle = xlR1C1
 4:         .UserName = "Sharon Podlin"
 5:         .StandardFont = "Arial"
 6:         .StandardFontSize = "10"
 7:         .DefaultFilePath = "C:\WINNT\Profiles\Administrator\Personal"
 8:         .EnableSound = False
 9:         .RollZoom = False
10:     End With
11:     Application.DisplayStatusBar = False
12: End Sub
```

The main thing you should notice about this code is the object that is being manipulated—the `Application` object. This demonstration should give you some idea of importance of this object.

Using Excel's Built-In Functions

The role of the `Application` object is not limited to application-wide settings and options. The `Application` object is also the owner of Excel's built-in functions. If you want to use SUM, AVERAGE, MAX, IRR, or any of the built-in functions from within your VBA procedure, you must use the `Application` object.

Remember, one of the advantages of using Excel as a development platform is its built-in functions. Why not exploit this feature in your VBA code? Complete the following steps to use the AVERAGE and SUM functions in VBA code:

1. Create a new procedure named BuiltIns.

2. Enter the following code for the procedure:

```
Dim sngAnswer As Single

sngAnswer = Application.Average(Worksheets("Sheet1").Range("A1:A4"))
MsgBox "The average for this range is " & sngAnswer

sngAnswer = Application.Sum(Worksheets("Sheet1").Range("A1:A4"))
MsgBox "The sum of this range is " & sngAnswer
```

3. Go to Sheet1 in your workbook.

4. Enter 100 in cell A1, 200 in cell A2, 300 in cell A3, and 400 in cell A4.

5. Run the BuiltIns procedure. The first message box displays with the average of the numbers (see Figure 9.1).

Press Alt+F8 to go to the Macros dialog and run the procedure from there.

FIGURE 9.1

The result displayed in this message box was calculated using one of Excel's built-in functions.

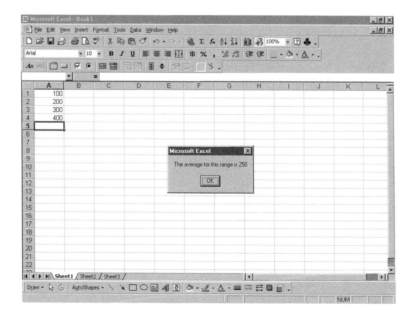

6. Click OK to dismiss the message box. The second message box displays with the result of the sum of the numbers.

7. Click OK to dismiss the message box and complete the procedure.

As you can see from this example, you use any of Excel's built-in functions in your VBA procedures by qualifying the function name with the Application object and providing values to any necessary arguments.

Useful Application Object Properties and Methods

The Application object has several properties and methods that you'll find very useful. Some of its properties include the following:

- ActiveWorkbook—Returns the active workbook.
- ActiveSheet—Returns the active sheet in the active workbook. The sheet returned can be any of the support sheet types, including worksheets and chart sheets.
- ActiveCell—Returns the active cell on the active sheet in the active workbook.
- ThisWorkbook—Returns the workbook in which the executing procedure resides.
- MailSystem—Returns the mail system that is being used by this system. This is a useful property when you are working with mail automation.
- MailSession—Used to test whether the user is logged on to email.
- OperatingSystem—OperatingSystem is a useful property when you are developing for a VBA application that is to be used by both Windows and Mac users. You can use this property to determine which operating system is being used and make any necessary changes.
- Selection—Used to determine what is currently selected. Selections can be cells, charts, graphic objects, and so on.

You've already worked with one of the Application object's methods, InputBox. The InputBox method enables you to display an input box and specify the type of data to be returned. Other useful methods of the Application object include the following:

- MailLogon and MailLogoff—Used in conjunction with the MailSystem and MailSession properties, the MailLogon and MailLogoff methods enable you to log a user on and off email.
- Quit—The Quit method is used to terminate Excel.
- Run—The Run method is t used to execute Excel 4.0 macros.

The Workbook Object

You already know that the Workbook object represents an Excel file. Because of this, you probably can immediately think of the types of things you'll need to do with the Workbook object: open, save, print, and close. Rather than starting with the properties of this object, let's start with some of its most-used methods:

- Activate—The Activate method is used to activate the workbook.
- Close—The Close method closes the workbook.
- Save—The Save method saves the workbook.

> If the workbook has not been saved before and the Save method is executed, the book is saved with its current name. This means it will be saved as, for example, Book1.

- SaveAs—The SaveAs method saves the workbook. The difference between this method and the Save method is that the SaveAs method has several useful optional arguments, including Filename, FileFormat, Password, WriteResPassword, and ReadOnlyRecommended.
- PrintOut—The PrintOut method is used to print the entire workbook.
- PrintPreview—The PrintPreview method displays the workbook in Print Preview.

There are a few workbook properties that you'll use as well. Like the Application object, the Workbook object supports the ActiveSheet property. If you need to find the directory location of a workbook, use the Path property. An extremely useful property of the Workbook object is the Saved property. This property returns a value of True if it has been saved, meaning all changes have been saved. If your changes to the workbook have been made and not saved, False is returned.

The one thing not covered yet in this discussion is how to create a new workbook object. In other words, what is the VBA code equivalent to clicking Excel's New toolbar button? You already know the answer to the question from your work in Hour 8, "An Introduction to Objects." You use the Add method. Remember that you use the Add method whenever you add a new object to a collection. In the next exercise you are going to create a workbook, print it, save it, and close it.

1. Create a new procedure named `WorkbookExample`.

2. Enter the following code for the procedure:

```
Dim wbNewWorkbook As Workbook
Set wbNewWorkbook = Workbooks.Add
wbNewWorkbook.Worksheets("Sheet1").Range("A1").Value = 100
wbNewWorkbook.SaveAs "Hour9"
wbNewWorkbook.Close
MsgBox "The workbook is closed."
```

3. Run the program. You might not see much going on.

4. When the message box displays letting you know that the workbook is closed, click OK.

5. Open the workbook. (If you are in the Visual Basic Editor you'll need to go to the Excel application window and open the workbook using the File menu.)

6. You'll see a value of 100 in cell A1, letting you know that this is, in fact, the workbook you created using your procedure.

After that procedure you should be feeling like a genuine Excel developer! Now you are going to examine the lines that made up this procedure. Listing 9.2 shows the complete procedure.

LISTING 9.2   The `WorkbookExample` Procedure

```
1: Sub WorkbookExample()
2:     Dim wbNewWorkbook As Workbook
3:     Set wbNewWorkbook = Workbooks.Add
4:     wbNewWorkbook.Worksheets("Sheet1").Range("A1").Value = 100
5:     wbNewWorkbook.SaveAs "Hour9a"
6:     wbNewWorkbook.Close
7:     MsgBox "The workbook is closed."
8: End Sub
```

You started this procedure by creating an object variable.

```
Dim wbNewWorkbook As Workbook
```

This object variable comes into play when the new workbook is created:

```
Set wbNewWorkbook = Workbooks.Add
```

This statement creates the workbook by adding a new element to the `Workbooks` collection. At the point of creation, Excel assigns it a name like Book1 or Book2. You can't guarantee what the name of the workbook will be. To work around this issue, assign it to the object variable and use the object variable to refer to the new workbook in code.

The next thing the procedure does is place a value in cell A1 just so that you can have some data in the workbook:

```
wbNewWorkbook.Worksheets("Sheet1").Range("A1").Value = 100
```

Finally, you perform the `Workbook` methods of `SaveAs` and `Close`. The message box is added as an easy way of knowing when everything is finished:

```
wbNewWorkbook.SaveAs "Hour9a"
wbNewWorkbook.Close
MsgBox "The workbook is closed."
```

And you are finished. You've created, saved, and closed your first Excel workbook using VBA code!

> After you save the workbook with a name, you can either refer to it by that name or continue to refer to by using the object variable. It's just a matter of your preference.

The Worksheet Object

Now that you know how to work with the `Workbook` object you are ready for the `Worksheet` object. Take a moment like you did with the `Workbook` object and think of the types of things you do with worksheets as an Excel user. You probably select them, name them, insert new worksheets in a workbook, copy worksheets, and delete worksheets. Now that you know what you want to do with the `Worksheet` object, you need to know the properties and methods to accomplish these tasks.

You will primarily use a couple of properties when working with worksheets. One is the `Name` property. Setting the `Name` property is the VBA equivalent of double-clicking a sheet's tab and entering a new name. For example, to change the name of a sheet to Budget you would use the following code:

```
ActiveSheet.Name = "Budget"
```

If you wanted to do some formatting to the entire worksheet, how would you select all the cells on a worksheet? You would do this by using the `Cells` property. If you wanted to set the font for all the cells on a sheet, you could use the following code:

```
Worksheets("Sheet1").Cells.Font.Name = "Arial"
```

You might need the following three Worksheet object methods:

- Activate—This method activates the sheet.
- CheckSpelling—As its name implies, the CheckSpelling method is used to check the spelling of the contents of the worksheet.
- Delete—If you need to delete a sheet, use the Delete method.

It's pop quiz time. How do you insert a worksheet in a workbook? If you said by using the Add method, you are correct! To insert a worksheet and change its name, follow these steps:

1. Create a new procedure named MyNewWorksheet.
2. Enter the following code for the procedure:
   ```
   Dim wsNewWorksheet As Worksheet

   Set wsNewWorksheet = Worksheets.Add
   wsNewWorksheet.Name = Format(Date, "mmmm d, yyyy")
   ```
3. Run the procedure.
4. If you are in the Visual Basic Editor when you run the procedure, go to the Excel application window to see the newly added worksheet (see Figure 9.2).
5. Save the workbook as Hour9, and close it.

FIGURE 9.2

Notice the name of the worksheet you added. It is the same as today's date.

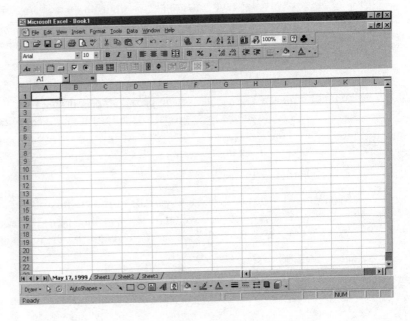

This code shared some similarities with the code you used to create a workbook. Just as you did in that code, you started by creating an object variable and using it in conjunction with the Add method so that you could refer to the object in code using the object variable's name:

```
Dim wsNewWorksheet As Worksheet
Set wsNewWorksheet = Worksheets.Add
```

After the page is inserted, you can use the Name property:

```
wsNewWorksheet.Name = Format(Date, "mmmm d, yyyy")
```

This line of code uses an interesting approach to selecting a name—it uses today's date as the name. The Format function enables you to control the format or appearance of the date. In this case, the date is formatted as month, day, year.

> Many developers like to incorporate the current date into a file or sheet name to avoid duplicate names.

Summary

In this hour you got a lot of experience working with some of Excel's primary objects: Application, Workbook, and Worksheet. With the Application object you now know how to set application-wide settings and options and use Excel's built-in functions. Using the Workbook object, you can create a new Excel workbook file and add and manipulate worksheets in workbooks. In this hour you also had more of an opportunity to work with properties and methods.

In the following hour you are going to work with another of Excel's key objects, the Range object. When you use the Range object, you'll find yourself doing the hard-core work of an Excel developer.

Q&A

Q Am I going to have to learn a lot of objects to be able to work with VBA?

A No, you probably will work with less than 20 objects. If you need to work with an object that you aren't familiar with, don't forget two tools: online help and recording a macro.

Q Why would Excel itself be treated as an application?

A Certain things only apply to Excel as an application. You can control settings and options for the entire Excel environment, such as viewing the formula bar or controlling recalculation. Because of this and other reasons, Excel itself is an object in the form of the Application object.

Q Why do you use the `Add` method to create both workbooks and worksheets?

A Because you are adding elements to collections. In one case you are adding a `Workbook` object to the `Workbooks` collection; in another case you are adding a `Worksheet` object to the `Worksheets` collection.

Workshop

The quiz questions and exercise are provided for your further understanding. See Appendix A, "Answers," for the answers.

Quiz

1. How would you use the `MAX` function in VBA to determine the largest number in the range A1:C5?

2. Which object is the outer-most level in the object hierarchy?

3. What method do you use to create either a new `Workbook` object or a new `Worksheet` object?

4. Using VBA code, how do you remove a worksheet from a workbook?

5. Which property returns the workbook in which the current procedure is located? Which object has this property?

6. True or False: You cannot run an Excel 4.0 macro in VBA.

Exercise

Create a new procedure named Hour9Lab. This procedure must perform the following tasks:

- Create a new workbook.
- Add a new worksheet to the workbook.
- Name the newly added sheet using your first name.
- Save the workbook as Hour9Lab.

Run the procedure. Go to Hour9Lab and add some values in the worksheet you added to the workbook. Create another procedure named SaveHour9. This procedure should test whether the workbook has been saved. If it hasn't been saved, save it and display a message saying it has been saved. If it has been saved, display a message box telling you it has already been saved. Run the procedure.

HOUR 10

The Range Object

Probably the single most frequently used object in VBA code is the Range object. The Range object is the real workhorse in the world of Excel objects. As an Excel user, you spend most of your time interacting with ranges. In this hour you'll learn a variety of techniques for working with ranges.

The highlights of this hour include

- Understanding the role of the Range object
- Using the With statement
- Using the For Each statement
- Analyzing several procedures that use the Range object

The Range Object

As an Excel user, you primarily interact with the cells on a worksheet. In VBA this translates to the Range object. Of all Excel's objects, the Range object is the one you'll work with the most if you are a typical programmer. Because of this, in this hour you will learn more about the Range object.

A `Range` object can be any of the following things:

- A single cell
- A selection of cells
- Multiple selections
- A row or column
- A 3D range

Range **Object Properties**

As you did with the other objects, you are going to start by learning about some of the `Range` object's properties and methods. The following are some useful properties:

- `Address`—The `Address` property returns the current location of the range.
- `Count`—The `Count` property is used to determine the number of cells in a range.
- `Formula`—Returns the formula used to calculate the display value.
- `Offset`—The `Offset` property is useful for moving from one range to another.
- `Resize`—Enables you to resize the currently selected range.
- `Value`—Returns the value of the range.

This list in no way comes close to the true number of `Range` object properties; the `Range` object's properties actually number in the dozens. The following steps enable you to experiment with some of the `Range` object's properties. Begin by closing all workbooks and opening a new workbook. Then start by creating a new worksheet:

1. Enter 100 in cell B1. Enter 200 in cell B2. Enter 300 in cell B3.
2. Select cell B4 and enter `=SUM(B1:B3)`.
3. Press Alt+F11 to open the Visual Basic Editor and Insert a new module in the current workbook.
4. Create a new procedure called `RangeProperties`.
5. Enter the following code for the procedure:

```
ThisWorkbook.Worksheets("Sheet1").Range("A1").Activate
ActiveCell.Offset(2, 2).Activate
MsgBox "The current active cell is " & ActiveCell.Address

MsgBox "The value of B4 is " & Range("B4").Value
MsgBox "The formula of B4 is " & Range("B4").Formula
```

6. Go to Sheet1 of your workbook and run the `RangeProperties` procedure. The first message box appears, telling you that the active cell is C3 (see Figure 10.1).

FIGURE 10.1

The Address *property is used to create the text for this message box.*

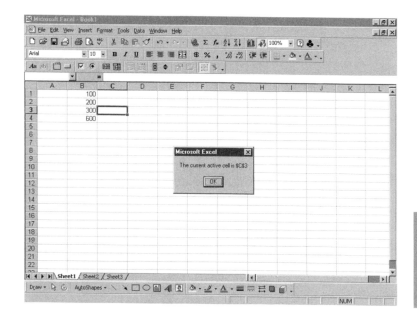

7. Click OK. The next message box displays with the value of cell B4.

8. Click OK. The final message box displays with cell B4's formula.

9. Click OK to dismiss the message box.

Did you pick up on some of the subtle differences in the information displayed? To be sure that you are comfortable with the code you used in this example, take a moment to review what you did. Listing 10.1 shows the completed procedure.

LISTING 10.1   The RangeProperties Procedure

```
1: Sub RangeProperties()
2:     ThisWorkbook.Worksheets("Sheet1").Range("A1").Activate
3:     ActiveCell.Offset(2, 2).Activate
4:     MsgBox "The current active cell is " & ActiveCell.Address
5:
6:     MsgBox "The value of B4 is " & Range("B4").Value
7:     MsgBox "The formula of B4 is " & Range("B4").Formula
8: End Sub
```

The first thing you did in this procedure is activate cell A1:

```
ThisWorkbook.Worksheets("Sheet1").Range("A1").Activate
```

After this cell was activated, you used the `Offset` method to move to cell C3 and display the newly activated cell's address in a message box:

```
ActiveCell.Offset(2, 2).Activate
MsgBox "The current active cell is " & ActiveCell.Address
```

The `Offset` property enables you to move to another range location. The syntax for this property is

```
rangename.Offset(RowOffset, ColumnOffset)
```

The optional `RowOffset` and `ColumnOffset` arguments control the direction of movement. In the procedure, you set the `RowOffset` to 2 and the `ColumnOffset` to 2, which is how you ended up in cell C3.

The next thing you did was display the value of the cell and then the formula of the cell:

```
MsgBox "The value of B4 is " & Range("B4").Value
MsgBox "The formula of B4 is " & Range("B4").Formula
```

These two lines did an excellent job of illustrating the difference between the `Value` property and the `Formula` property. The `Value` property returns what is displayed in the cell. The `Formula` property returns what is actually in the cell.

Range Object Methods

The `Range` object also has numerous methods, including the following:

- `Activate`—Activates a range.
- `Clear`—Clears the contents of a range.
- `Copy`—Copies the contents of the range on the Clipboard.
- `Cut`—Places the contents of the range on the Clipboard.
- `PasteSpecial`—Pastes the contents of the Clipboard to the range.
- `Select`—Selects a range.

Using the With Statement

Now that you are familiar with the most frequently used objects in Excel, it's time to learn about a construct that is geared toward making working with objects easier. One of the common tasks when working with range objects is setting a variety of formatting properties. Listing 10.2 shows an example of code that is used to perform a variety of formatting to a range object.

LISTING 10.2   The Range Formatting Code

```
 1: Range("A1:A6").NumberFormat = "#,##0.00"
 2: Range("A1:A6").Font.Name = "Courier New"
 3: Range("A1:A6").Font.FontStyle = "Regular"
 4: Range("A1:A6").Font.Size = 11
 5: Range("A1:A6").Font.Strikethrough = False
 6: Range("A1:A6").Font.Superscript = False
 7: Range("A1:A6").Font.Subscript = False
 8: Range("A1:A6").Font.OutlineFont = False
 9: Range("A1:A6").Font.Shadow = False
10: Range("A1:A6").Font.Underline = xlUnderlineStyleNone
11: Range("A1:A6").Font.ColorIndex = xlAutomatic
```

If you were to type the code in Listing 10.2, you would quickly tire of typing
`Range("A1:A6")` over and over. You could use an object variable to reference
`Range("A1:A6")` but you would still have to type the variable's name over and over.
VBA provides a way to avoid this—the `With` statement. The `With` statement is used to
set multiple properties or execute multiple methods for the same object. Listing 10.3
shows the same code using the `With` statement.

10

LISTING 10.3   The With Statement Example

```
 1: With Range("A1:A6")
 2:      .NumberFormat = "#,##0.00"
 3:     With .Font
 4:          .Name = "Courier New"
 5:          .FontStyle = "Regular"
 6:          .Size = 11
 7:          .Strikethrough = False
 8:          .Superscript = False
 9:          .Subscript = False
10:          .OutlineFont = False
11:          .Shadow = False
12:          .Underline = xlUnderlineStyleNone
13:          .ColorIndex = xlAutomatic
14:     End With
15: End With
```

Although the `With` statement in this listing didn't reduce the number of code lines, it did
reduce the amount of typing required. The following is the syntax for the `With` statement:

```
With object
    [statements]
End With
```

The *object* in this syntax is the object being manipulated by the properties and methods listed in the *statements* section. Each line in the *statements* section begins with a period, as you'll see if you refer to Listing 10.3. Also notice in Listing 10.3 that you can nest With statements. In that listing, a With statement for the Font object was nested within the With statement of the Range object. Listing 10.4 illustrates a With statement that utilizes properties and methods.

LISTING 10.4   A With Statement Containing Properties and Methods

```
1: Sub WithWorksheet()
2:     With ThisWorkbook
3:         .SaveAs "WithExample"
4:         MsgBox "Save Status: " & .Saved
5:     End With
6: End Sub
```

Using the For Each Statement

Whereas the With statement is used to execute multiple statements for the same object, the For Each statement executes the same statements for multiple objects. The For Each statement enables you to repeat statements for each element in a collection.

> The For Each statement can also be used with arrays.

The following is the syntax for the For Each statement:

```
For Each element In group
    [Statements]
    [Exit For]
    [Statements]
Next
```

Notice that this syntax supports the Exit For clause. Like the other Exit clauses, it is typically placed in an If statement. If, for example, you needed to change the value of each cell in a range, you would use the code in Listing 10.5.

LISTING 10.5   The For Each Statement Example

```
1: Sub ForExample()
2:     Dim x As Range
3:
```

```
4:      For Each x In ThisWorkbook.Worksheets("Sheet1").Range("A1:A6")
5:          x.Value = x.Value + 10
6:      Next
7: End Sub
```

Range Object Code Examples

When I teach classes, I frequently hear from the programmers in my class that the best way for them to learn is by seeing examples of code, hence this section. In this part of the hour you are going to see a variety of code examples that use the Range object. The code examples have been selected because they are commonly used by programmers.

The first code example changes the formatting in every row of a range. This is a popular thing to do with very long worksheets to make them easier to view when printed. In this example, you are assuming that you have a worksheet similar to the one shown in Figure 10.2. Notice that the first row contains headings. The rows need to start being bolded on the third row. The procedure to accomplish this task is shown in Listing 10.6.

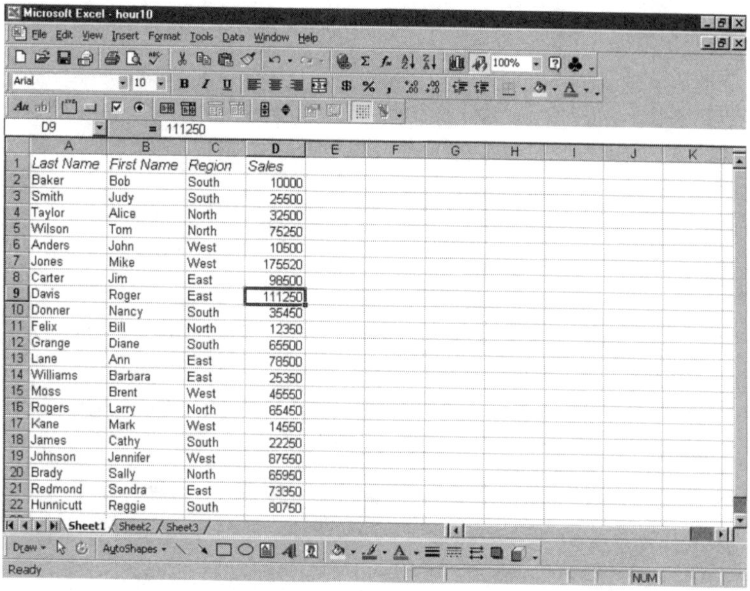

10

FIGURE 10.2

This worksheet is going to be modified as a result of the BoldEveryOther *procedure.*

LISTING 10.6 Using the Row Object and the For Next Statement

```
1: Sub BoldEveryOther()
2:     Dim iCounter As Integer
3:
4:     For iCounter = 3 To ThisWorkbook.Worksheets("Sheet1"). _
Range("A1:C25").Rows.Count Step 2
5:         ThisWorkbook.Worksheets("Sheet1").Range("A1:C25"). _
Rows(iCounter).Font.Bold = True
6:     Next
7:
8: End Sub
```

The main key to this procedure is the For Next statement. Notice that the iCounter is set initially to 3. This is to start the bold process on the third row. The Step is set to 2 so that every other row is bold. Figure 10.3 shows the worksheet after the procedure has run.

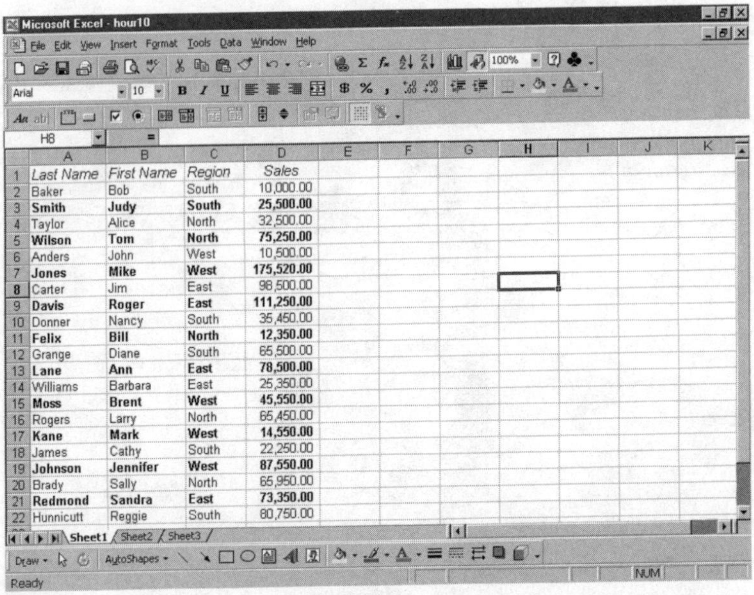

FIGURE 10.3

You can see that after the EveryOtherRun procedure runs, the range has the desired formatting.

You might have thought to yourself that the code shown in this hour is great if you know the address of the range you are working with, but what if you don't know the size of the range? A classic example of this occurs when you import data into a worksheet from another application such as a database. You might not know how many rows are going to be returned. The code in Listing 10.7 shows an example of selecting a range with an unknown size.

LISTING **10.7** Selecting a Range with an Unknown Size

```
1: Sub SelectRange()
2:     ThisWorkbook.Worksheets("Sheet1").Range("A1").Activate
3:     ActiveCell.CurrentRegion.Select
4:     MsgBox "The address of the selected range " & Selection.Address
5: End Sub
```

The key element of the SelectRange procedure is the CurrentRegion property. This returns the region bounded by the first empty row and column. By selecting the CurrentRegion, you don't have to know the size of the range.

The final procedure that you are looking at is one that performs a copy-and-paste operation. In the code in Listing 10.8 you'll see that whatever is selected is copied and then pasted to another location on the sheet.

LISTING **10.8** Copying and Pasting a Range

```
1: Sub CopyAndPaste()
2:     Selection.Copy
3:     Range("F3").Select
4:     ActiveSheet.Paste
5:     Application.CutCopyMode = False
6: End Sub
```

The Selection.Copy statement places the selected range on the Clipboard. The next step is to move to the desired destination for the copied range. There you use the Paste method to move the copied range from the Clipboard to the new location. Finally, you set the Application object's CutCopyMode property to False. If you don't do this, the marquee (the moving dashed line) remains around the orginal text and the status bar contains instructions to move to the destination.

Summary

You should be comfortable working with the Range object at this point because you've worked with several properties and methods in a variety of procedures.

You also worked with two VBA constructs that are geared toward working with objects. The With statement is used to set multiple procedures and execute multiple methods for the same object. The For Each statement executes the same statements for multiple objects.

In the final part of this hour you saw several procedures that manipulated Range objects. These procedures were provided so that you could see examples of Range object usage.

Q&A

Q Why isn't there a Range collection?

A One of the requirements of a collection is that it can be added to. The number of cells (that is, ranges) on a worksheet has been predefined by Microsoft, and there is no way you can add more cells to a worksheet. Because of this, there is no Range collection.

Q How does the For statement differ from the For Each statement?

A Let's start by discussing what they have in common. They both execute the same statement multiple times. Now the question is, how are they different? The number of times statements are executed by the For statement is controlled by a numeric starting point and a numeric ending point. The number of times statements are executed by the For Each statement is controlled by the number of objects or array elements being manipulated.

Workshop

The quiz questions and exercise are provided for your further understanding. See Appendix A, "Answers" for the answers.

Quiz

1. True or False: In VBA, a range always refers to multiple cells.
2. Which Range object property is useful for accessing one range based on the address of another range?
3. If you want to increase the value of each cell in a range, which statement would you use to do this with the least code?
4. Which property enables you to select an unknown range based on the location of another range?
5. How would you find out how many cells there were in a range?
6. What property is used to remove the contents of a range?
7. You must set several properties for the same object. What is the most efficient way to do this?

Exercise

Open a new workbook. Enter the following values in the first sheet of the workbook:

Cell	Value
A1	Item
A2	Widget
A3	Gidget
A4	Gizmo
A5	Junk
A6	Stuff
B1	Price
B2	15
B3	5
B4	3
B5	7
B6	9

Create a procedure named ReducePrices. This procedure must decrease the value of the cells in Range(B2:B6) by 5. If a price is equal to or less than zero, make it and the item name red and bold. If any cells in the range are equal to or less than zero, display a message box letting the user know that there is a problem before ending the procedure. Run and test your procedure.

HOUR 11

Working with the Visual Basic Editor

Now that you are familiar with the syntax of the language, you are probably curious about some of the features of the Visual Basic Editor. There are numerous features of the editor that are designed to make coding easier and faster to do. In this hour, you'll work with these features, including toolbars, online help, and the Object Browser.

The highlights of this hour include

- Working with the Visual Basic Editor's toolbars
- Tips for browsing your code
- Getting the most out of online help
- The how and why of the Object Browser
- Setting the Visual Basic Editor's options

Using the Visual Basic Editor's Toolbars

Up to this point, you've used just a few of the buttons found on Visual Basic Editor's Standard toolbar. This toolbar contains buttons to execute the most frequently used commands. You might not realize it when you first look at it, but the toolbar is segmented by type of commands.

The first section of buttons (see Figure 11.1) relates to workbooks in that by using these buttons, you can return to Excel, add items to the current project, and save your work.

FIGURE 11.1

The View Microsoft Excel, Insert, and Save buttons of the Visual Basic Editor's Standard toolbar.

The next section of buttons (see Figure 11.2) relates to editing functions. These buttons are used to cut, copy, and paste text. In this section is also a button for finding text.

FIGURE 11.2

The Cut, Copy, Paste, and Find buttons of the Visual Basic Editor's Standard toolbar.

The third section of the toolbar (see Figure 11.3) has two buttons, Undo and Redo. Think of these as your "Oops!" buttons.

FIGURE 11.3

The Undo and Redo buttons of the Visual Basic Editor's Standard toolbar.

Next, you have what I call the testing and design buttons (see Figure 11.4). The first three buttons in this section allow you to run, pause, and end a procedure's execution. The final button in this section places a UserForm in Design mode.

FIGURE 11.4

The Run, Pause, End, and Design buttons of the Visual Basic Editor's Standard toolbar.

The next section (see Figure 11.5) of the Visual Basic Editor Standard toolbar is used to view the different sections of the Visual Basic Editor. These buttons allow you to display the Project Explorer, the Properties window, the Object Browser, and the Toolbox.

FIGURE 11.5

The Project Explorer, Properties Window, Object Browser, and Toolbox buttons of the Visual Basic Editor's Standard toolbar.

Finally, you have the Visual Basic Help button (see Figure 11.6). This Help button works the same as the Help button you see throughout Microsoft applications.

FIGURE 11.6

The Help button of the Visual Basic Editor's Standard toolbar.

Another toolbar that comes in handy when working with the Visual Basic Editor is the Edit toolbar. The tools on this toolbar affect and augment the editing environment of the Visual Basic Editor. The buttons found on the Edit toolbar are

- **List Properties/Methods**

  When clicked, this button shows a list of properties and methods.

- **List Constants**

  Displays the system constants that apply to the current argument.

- **QuickInfo**

  Displays the QuickInfo box that provides syntax information.

- **Parameter Info**

  Displays applicable parameter information.

- **Complete Word**

  Initiates VBA's complete word feature that allows you to type part of a reserved word and have the editor enter the rest.

- **Indent**

  Indents the selected text.

- **Outdent**

  Outdents the selected text.

- **Toggle Breakpoint**

  Places a breakpoint at the selected line of code.

> For more information on breakpoints, go to Hour 12, "Debugging Your VBA Code."

- **Comment Text**

  Converts the selected text to a comment. This is used during the debugging and testing phase of application development as a way of skipping segments of code.

- **Uncomment Text**

  Returns selected text to code.

- **Toggle Bookmark**

  Marks the current line as a bookmark. A *bookmark* is a line that you want to mark for easy reference.

- **Next Bookmark**

  Moves to the next bookmark.

- **Previous Bookmark**

  Moves to the previous bookmark.

- **Clear All Bookmarks**

  Removes all the bookmarks from the text.

Browsing Code

One of the nice features of working with the Visual Basic Editor is that if you are famil-iar with the navigation keys in Microsoft Word, you can apply that knowledge. Table 11.1 lists some of the navigation keys.

TABLE 11.1 Navigation Keys

To Go To	Press This Key
Beginning of line	Home
End of line	End
Beginning of module	Ctrl+Home
End of module	Ctrl+End
Next word	Ctrl+Right Arrow
Previous word	Ctrl+Left Arrow
Next procedure	Ctrl+Up Arrow
Previous procedure	Ctrl+Down Arrow

11

If you are looking for a specific word or phrase, you can use the Visual Basic Editor's Find feature. Find can be accessed through the Edit menu, by clicking the Find button located on the Standard toolbar, or by pressing Ctrl+F. An extension of the Find feature is Replace. Replace is used to locate a word or phrase and replace it with other text.

 You can press F3 to access the Replace command.

Another browsing feature of the Editor is bookmarks. Bookmarks allow you to mark text so that it is easier to locate. This can be of particular use when testing and debugging code. If you suspect that you have multiple errors in your code, you can mark them using bookmarks. You can also use bookmarks to mark areas of code that need to be inserted by another team member. Or you can mark areas of code that need to be updated or upgraded.

Using Online Help

You've already used a couple of VBA's help features. Now take a few moments to become more familiar with VBA's help features by completing the following steps:

1. Select Help, Microsoft Visual Basic Help. The Assistant starts and prompts you to enter a question (see Figure 11.7).

FIGURE 11.7

The Assistant, which can be a variety of shapes, is the initial interface to Visual Basic Help.

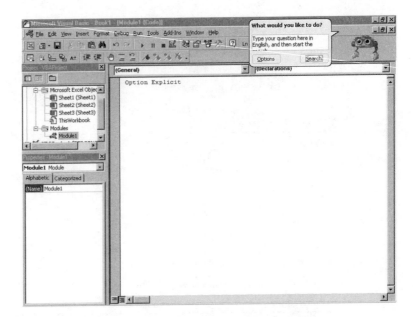

2. Enter the question How do I create a new workbook? and press Enter.

3. Select Creating a New Workbook. The Creating a New Workbook help topic displays (see Figure 11.8).

FIGURE 11.8

Selecting a topic from the Assistant leads you into the appropriate help topic.

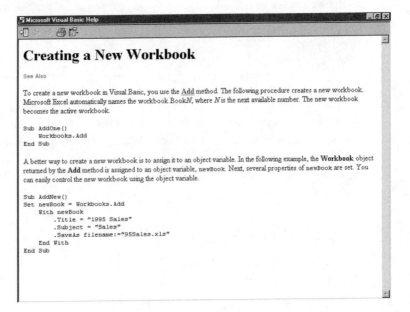

Visual Basic's Help provides numerous examples of code. You can copy sample code from Help and paste it into your own procedures using the following steps:

1. Click the word Add (located toward the top of the topic and displayed as underlined text). Underlined text links you to another topic—in this case, the Add method.

2. Click the word Example located at the top of the help topic. Sample code displays (see Figure 11.9).

FIGURE 11.9

Sample code is a great learning tool.

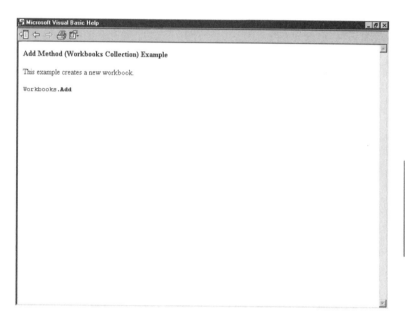

3. Highlight the line Workbooks.Add.
4. Right-click the highlighted line. Select Copy from the menu displayed.
5. Close the Help window.
6. Add a new module to this workbook.
7. Create a new procedure named NewBook.
8. Paste the sample code into your new procedure. This is a nice time-saving tool, too.

Even though the code example used in this exercise wasn't extensive, you get the basic idea. If you see code you like in Help, use it!

In my opinion, context-sensitive help is the best help feature VBA provides. You enter into the Editor the object, property, method, or function that you want to find information on and press F1. You are taken to the appropriate help topic.

There are several other features that you might not immediately identify as help features. These include

- **List Member**

  This feature displays a list that contains information on what is logically needed to complete the statement being entered.

- **Quick Info**

  This is a small pop-up box that displays information about functions and their parameters as you type.

- **Data Tips**

  This displays in a small box the value of the variable over which your cursor is placed. This feature is only available in Break mode.

 Break mode is discussed in detail in Hour 12, "Debugging Your VBA Code."

Using the Object Browser

The Object Browser gives an easy-to-use interface to browse through all the available objects in your project. You can see the objects' properties, methods, and events. You can also see the procedures and constants that are available from any object libraries referenced by your project. There are several ways to access the Object Browser:

- Click the Object Browser button on the Standard toolbar.
- Select View, Object Browser.
- Press F2.

I personally like to use the Object Browser as a learning and help tool. The Object Browser is a great way to become familiar with the properties and methods of an object. You can also access Help via the Object Browser. Complete the following steps to use the Object Browser:

1. Press F2 to display the Object Browser (see Figure 11.10).

Figure 11.10

The Object Browser catalogs objects, properties, methods, and events.

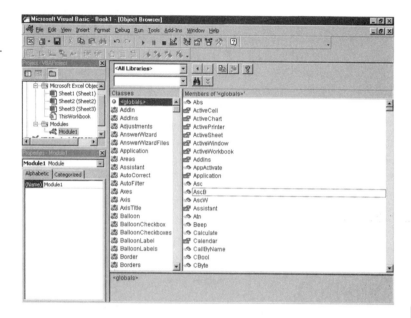

2. Locate the Range object and select it.

3. Scroll through the methods (referred to as functions by the Object Browser) and properties available for the Range object.

4. Select Activate.

5. Press F1. The Activate Help topic displays.

6. Close Help.

7. Close the Object Browser.

Setting Options

The Visual Basic Editor environment can be customized by using the Options dialog. Through this dialog, you can control Editor settings, the format of the Editor, general settings, and docking settings. Use the following steps to become familiar with the settings available through the Options dialog:

1. Select Tools, Options. The Options dialog displays.

2. Select the Editor tab. The Editor tab is used to set code and window settings. This is where you can turn on and off features such as Auto Quick Info and Auto Syntax Check.

3. Select the Editor Format tab. The Editor Format tab allows you to control the colors used for the different types of text in the Editor. You can also choose different font styles and font sizes. You might want to change some of the colors used by the Editor if you are working on a laptop because the difference between blue and black is not significant on older machines. If you are visually challenged, you can enlarge the text displayed.

4. Select the General tab. This tab contains settings that affect the overall Editor environment. The Form Grid settings are used to control the grid available when designing UserForms. You can also control the settings in Edit and Continue, Error Trapping, and Compile.

5. Select the Docking tab. The Docking tab is used to control which items in the Visual Basic Editor are dockable.

6. Click Cancel to close the dialog.

Summary

Now that you've spent a few hours coding in VBA, you can better appreciate the tools and features presented in this hour. As you now know, the online help system doesn't just explain the syntax of statements—it gives you working examples of them. And you know that the Object Browser is a wonderful tool for exploring objects, methods, properties, and events.

Even little things make your life easier. Navigation keys, toolbars, and options all give you control over how you work with the Visual Basic Editor's environment.

Q&A

Q How can I use Help if I don't even know the name of the property I'm looking for?

A No problem! You can either look up the object you are working with in Help and then cruise through its properties, or you can locate the object in the Object Browser and look for a suitable property there.

Q I don't like the Courier font used by the Editor. Am I stuck with it?

A No, by selecting Tools, Options you display the Options dialog. Select the Editor Format tab and select another font.

Workshop

The quiz questions and exercise are provided for your further understanding. See Appendix A, "Answers," for the answers.

Quiz

1. Name three ways to get to online help.

2. The Object Browser is a great source for listing objects, events, properties, and _____.

3. What keys do you press to go to the beginning of a module?

4. _____ is a small pop-up box that displays information about functions and their parameters as you type.

5. Where do you go to control the use of features such as Auto Quick Info and Auto Syntax Check?

6. True or False: The examples provided through online help are viewable only— meaning that they cannot be copied and placed in your own code.

Exercise

Using whatever tool you prefer (Help or the Object Browser), locate the following information:

The method used to perform a spell check (Hint: Check the Application object): _____

Property that contains the location where Excel is installed: _____

Property that tells you if a workbook has been saved: _____

Method used to force manual calculation: _____

Property used to hide (make invisible) a worksheet: _____

Method used to empty the contents of a range: _____

11

HOUR 12

Debugging Your VBA Code

In the olden days of macro development, debugging could be described as follows: run the macro, have the macro fail, guess what happened. This is no longer the case. The Visual Basic Editor provides a feature-rich development environment that includes many of the same debugging tools found in higher-end development tools.

The highlights of this hour include

- Understanding what testing and debugging your application means
- Pausing your application's execution
- Interacting with your application using the Immediate window
- Viewing line-by-line execution of your procedures
- Using watches to track variable and property values

The Testing and Debugging Phase of Application Development

NEW TERM   After you get your procedure written, *testing* is the process of running your procedure and trying to guess everything your user can do to your procedure. For example, during testing, you do things like enter a variety of values, click different buttons, and make different selections. The point of testing is to ensure that the expected result occurs. You are also looking for the unexpected, such as an incorrect result being returned from a calculation. Your goal is to determine whether entering a certain value or performing a particular action will result in the premature termination of the procedure. When the unexpected and undesirable occurs in a procedure, it is called a *bug*.

There are things that you as a programmer can do to minimize these types of mistakes in your procedures. This is the time when I get on my soapbox! I know it is tempting to jump in and immediately start writing code. But if you'll spend time carefully designing and documenting the goals and requirements of your application, you can eliminate some problems with your application. By understanding the goals and features of the application, you have a clearer picture of what is expected of the application. This is particularly important if you are developing for a client other than yourself. You don't want to waste time developing code that doesn't do what the client wants. By spending a little time up front in the analysis of your application, you can save a lot of time in the end.

Another tool you have at your disposal is a naming convention. A consistent naming convention for variables and objects helps you not only debug your application, but also makes it easier to support and maintain your application. A variety of naming conventions are presented throughout this book.

> See Hour 3, "Working with Controls," for naming conventions for controls. See Hour 4, "Understanding the Role of Variables and Constants," for naming conventions for variables and constants.

While we are talking about supporting and maintaining code, don't forget to comment your code. By commenting your code, you make it easier to understand why you wrote code a particular way. You might be wondering how to decide what to comment. I recommend assuming that you will not be the one supporting the application in the future. Add the type of comments you would want to see in an application you were supporting but did not write.

While completing some of the exercises in this book, you have probably accidentally typed something in wrong. If this is the case, you saw a message box display when you pressed Enter. This message box told you that there was a syntax error (see Figure 12.1). This is because, as a default, the Visual Basic Editor checks each statement for syntax errors when you press Enter. You can turn the Auto Syntax Check feature on and off through the Option dialog's Editor tab.

FIGURE 12.1

The Visual Basic Editor gives you immediate feedback about syntax errors.

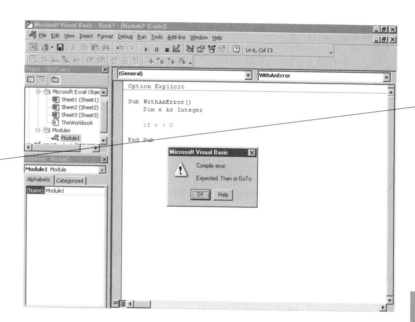

NEW TERM Another type of error you might encounter is a runtime error. A *runtime error* is any error that makes an application stop running. Sometimes this is the fault of the programmer. For example, you might mistype the name of an object in your procedure. VBA won't catch this type of mistake until you run your procedure. A runtime error can also result from a user action that you can't control or even predict. For example, a runtime error could occur when a user doesn't provide a value for a function you wrote.

The final type of error that can occur is a *logic error*. The Visual Basic Editor won't point this type of error out to you because there's nothing wrong with the language of the statement. The problem is that the code doesn't do what you wanted it to do. That means something is wrong with the logic of the statement. You'll find that most of your debugging effort deals with logic errors.

12

Debugging

NEW TERM The process of locating errors is called *debugging*. Because VBA is a feature-rich development environment, you have several debugging tools at your disposal. These tools include

- The Immediate window
- Watch expressions
- Breakpoints
- Stepping through code

Before beginning the debugging process, you need some code to debug. Use the following steps to create a procedure that contains a bug:

1. Close any open workbooks.
2. Open a new workbook.
3. Press Alt+F11 to go to the Visual Basic Editor.
4. Insert a new module in this workbook.
5. Create a new procedure named Buggy.
6. Enter the following code for the Buggy procedure:

```
Dim response

response = Application.InputBox("Enter your name: ")
If response = "" Then
    MsgBox "Procedure cancelled."
    Exit Sub
Else
    MsgBox "Your name is " & response
End If
```

7. Run the procedure. When prompted, type your name and press Enter. The message box displays, containing your name. So far, everything seems to be working as expected.
8. Click OK to dismiss the message box.
9. Press F5 to run the procedure again.
10. Click Cancel in response to the input box. What happened? You get a message box telling you that your name is False! You would have expected a message box telling you that the procedure was cancelled.
11. Click OK to dismiss the message box.

This procedure definitely returned an unexpected result. You might have already guessed the problem, but don't solve it yet. You are going to use this procedure to experiment with debugging techniques.

Placing Your Procedure in Break Mode

NEW TERM When debugging a procedure, you really need to deal with every line of the procedure. Often you have a general idea of where the problem lies. To facilitate isolating the problem area, VBA provides a variety of ways to pause the procedure at a certain point. This is called placing the procedure in Break mode. *Break mode* temporarily suspends the execution of the procedure. By placing a procedure in Break mode, you can examine the current values of variables and properties, and apply other debugging techniques. When your procedure is in Break mode, you can perform the following actions:

- Edit the code of the application
- Look at the values of variables, properties, and statements
- Enter different value for variables and properties
- Run Visual Basic statements using the Immediate window

NEW TERM In the Buggy procedure, you know that the error occurs somewhere after the InputBox statement. This makes the line containing the InputBox statement a good candidate line for a location to pause the procedure. The way you pause a procedure at a specific location is called a *breakpoint*. There are several ways to set a line of code as a breakpoint:

- Select a statement to use as a breakpoint and select Debug, Toggle Breakpoint from the menu.
- Select a statement to use as a breakpoint and press F9.
- Select a statement to use as a breakpoint and click the margin indicator bar of the Code window.

You can only set a breakpoint on a line of executable code. You can't set a breakpoint on a line containing nonexecutable code. This includes comments, variable and constant declaration statements, and blank lines. When a line has been set as a breakpoint, it changes color based on your current Editor Format settings, and a dot is placed beside that line in the margin indicator bar, as shown in Figure 12.2.

12

FIGURE 12.2

Breakpoints are visually easy to identify in the Code window.

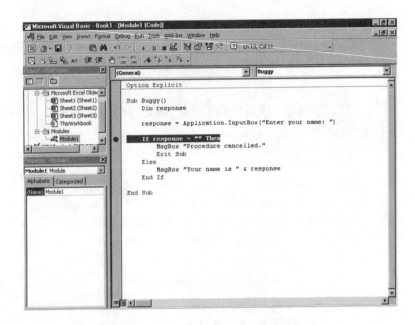

These same three actions can also be used to remove a breakpoint. This is because breakpoints are toggle items. If you've placed several breakpoints in your application and want to remove them all at once, select Debug, Clear All Breakpoints or press Ctrl+Shift+F9.

You need to set a breakpoint after the line of code that uses the InputBox statement in the Buggy procedure. Use the following steps to do this:

1. Position the insertion point anywhere in the line after the one with the InputBox statement.

 2. Click the Toggle Breakpoint button—located on either the Edit toolbar or the Debug toolbar—or press F9. You'll see the line of code changes color, and a dot displays in the margin indicator bar.

After you set your breakpoint, you are ready to use other debugging tools to find a solution to the bug. By the way, you are not limited to just one breakpoint in your procedure. You can have as many as you feel you need. Now run your procedure and see how the breakpoint affects it, using the following steps:

1. Run the Buggy procedure.

2. Type your name in response to the input box and press Enter. The Visual Basic Editor displays and the current line of code is highlighted, as shown in Figure 12.3. Take a look at the title bar for the Visual Basic Editor window. You'll see that the word break is placed there to let you know that you are in Break mode.

Figure 12.3

When the breakpoint is reached, you are shown the code in the Visual Basic Editor.

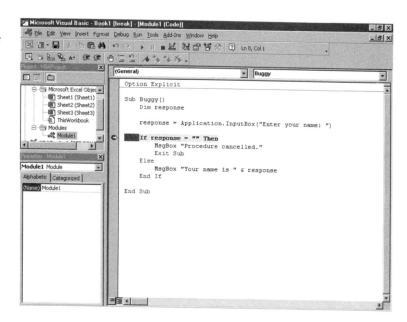

Now that you are in Break mode, you can look at the value of the response variable to see if it is what you expected. One way to do this is to simply move your pointer over the variable's name. A small box pops up containing the current value of the variable (see Figure 12.4). You can see that the value of this variable is what you would expect. You are going to need to do a little more debugging to find the problem.

Figure 12.4

The Visual Basic Editor provides immediate feedback of the value of a variable or property setting.

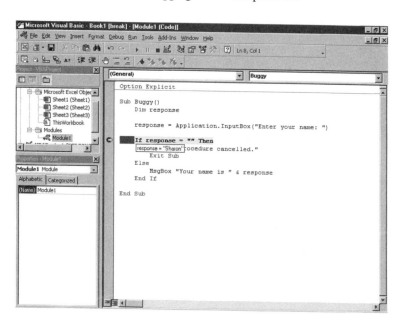

12

There are other ways of identifying the value of a variable or property. In the next section of this hour, you'll learn to use the Immediate window, which you can use to interact directly with your variable and property settings. Later in this hour, you'll learn to use watches to track variable and property settings.

Using the Immediate Window

The Immediate window, which can be seen at the bottom of Figure 12.5, gives you a window into the world of your procedure's property and variable values. The Immediate window allows you to do a variety of tasks, including

- Printing variable and property values while a procedure is running
- Changing the value of a variable or property while a procedure is running
- Viewing debugging output while an application is running
- Calling a procedure as you would in program code
- Typing new statements and immediately executing them, allowing you to experiment with different code scenarios
- Copying and pasting existing code lines into the Immediate window and executing them

FIGURE 12.5

The Immediate window might not appear to be much, but it is actually a useful debugging tool.

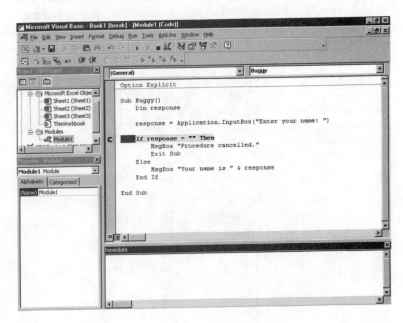

Displaying Values in the Immediate Window

As you saw earlier, when you're running an application, you can learn the value of a variable by positioning your pointer above the variable name while in Break mode. Another way to identify the value of a variable (or a property) is by using the Immediate window. What you are going to do is display the desired value in the Immediate window. There are three ways to display values to the Immediate window. You can use the `Print` method in the Immediate window. You can use a question mark (?) in the Immediate window. The ? is actually shorthand for the `Print` method. Another way to display a value in the Immediate window is to add a `Debug.Print` statement directly in a procedure.

The `Print` method (or the question mark) gives you another way to test the value of variables and properties. To print the value of the `Response` variable in the Immediate window, use the following steps:

1. If the procedure is in Break mode, reset the procedure by using the Run menu or by clicking the Reset toolbar button.

2. Press F5 to run the application. In response to the input box, click the Cancel button.

3. If you don't see the Immediate window when you are returned to the Visual Basic Editor, press Ctrl+G. This displays the Immediate window. You can also display the Immediate window using the View menu.

4. To print the value of `Response` in the Immediate window, click the Immediate window to activate it. Type the following line:

   ```
   ? Response
   ```

You could have also typed `Print Response`, which is equivalent to `? Response`.

If you want to execute a statement that has previously been entered in the Immediate window, just move the insertion point to that line and press Enter.

5. Press Enter. The value of `Response` is shown on the next line of the Immediate window. In this case, you see the value is `False` (see Figure 12.6).

FIGURE 12.6

The Immediate window is another tool for displaying values.

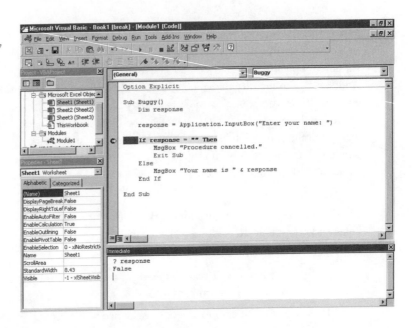

6. Earlier, you were told that you can use the Immediate window to enter a value for a variable or property. At this point, you might want to test the logic of your procedure. Because your procedure is looking for an empty string, why not see what happens when an empty string is provided? Type the following line in the Immediate window:

```
Response = ""
```

7. Press Enter. This resets the value of the Response variable to an empty string. You should be getting an idea of what the problem is.

8. Select Run, Reset to end the procedure.

The disadvantage to this approach is that that you have to find a point in the procedure's execution where you can access the Immediate window. In the previous exercise, you did this by using a breakpoint. If you don't want to pause the procedure's execution, but do want to know the value of a property or variable, you can use the Debug.Print statement. This statement is added directly to a procedure and sends text to the Immediate window. You can look at the printed debugging text after the application runs. To include the Debug.Print statement with the Buggy procedure, complete the following steps:

1. Select Debug, Clear All Breakpoints to remove any breakpoint that's currently set.

2. Delete the text from the Immediate window.

3. Modify the Buggy procedure so that it matches the following (changes are in bold):

```
Public Sub Buggy()
```

```
        Dim response

        response = Application.InputBox("Enter your name: ")
        Debug.Print "Value of response is " & response
        If response = "" Then
            MsgBox "Procedure cancelled."
            Exit Sub
        Else
            MsgBox "Your name is " & response
        End If
    End Sub
```

4. Run the procedure by pressing F5.

5. Type your name in response to the input box and press Enter.

6. Click OK to dismiss the message box.

7. Run the Buggy procedure again.

8. Click Cancel in response to the input box. Click OK to dismiss the message box.

9. Return to the Visual Basic Editor.

When you look at the contents of the Visual Basic Editor, you'll see two lines of text (see Figure 12.7). The first line was created the first time you ran the procedure. The second line was created the last time you ran the procedure. You can immediately see an advantage of using the Debug.Print statement in that you get results that are viewable after the procedure runs.

FIGURE 12.7

Debug.Print *gives you a printed history of values in the Immediate window.*

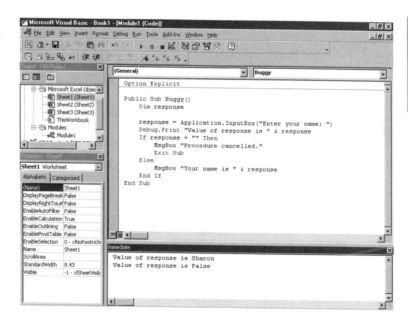

12

Stepping Through Your Code

In most cases, you are going to be debugging the logic and flow of your procedures. In this case, it is helpful to know in what order the lines of your procedure execute. This is particularly useful when debugging an If statement or a Select statement. To do this, you are going to step through code—meaning that you are going to watch as each line executes.

There are two types of steps: Step Into and Step Over. Both stepping methods allow you to see line-by-line execution of the application so you can trace the flow of logic statements and look at variable and property values.

There's just one difference between the two types of stepping. If you're debugging a procedure that calls one or more other procedures and you do not want to step through any called procedures, use Step Over. Step Over does not do line-by-line execution of called procedures. On the other hand, if you want to observe line-by-line execution of all statements, including the statements in any called procedures, use Step Into.

You don't usually step through an entire procedure. Usually you set a breakpoint at the point in your procedure where you are having the problem. Then you begin to step from there. To step through your procedure, complete the following steps:

1. Remove the Debug.Print statement from the procedure.

2. Set a breakpoint at the line after the InputBox statement. Press F5 to run the procedure.

3. Press Cancel in response to the input box. You are returned to the procedure because of the breakpoint. The procedure is ready to execute the If statement. What you want to have happen is that the first condition will test as True.

4. Press F8 to step to the next code line. Notice that the next line that executes is the Else clause, not the Procedure Cancelled message box (see Figure 12.8). This is what we call a really big clue!

5. Click F5 to continue the run of the procedure. Click OK to dismiss the message box.

FIGURE 12.8

As lines execute while stepping through a procedure, the current line is identified with an arrow in the margin indicator bar.

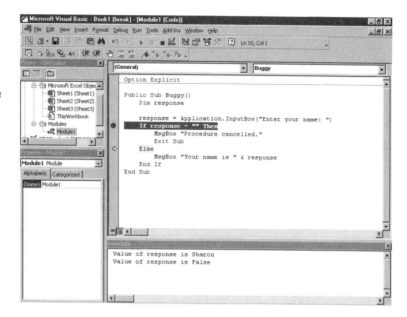

Using Watches

NEW TERM

You probably know what the problem is at this point. Before you correct the problem, however, try one more debugging technique called watch expressions. *Watch expressions* are user-defined expressions that enable you to look at the values set for a variable or an expression. A watch expression can be any valid Visual Basic expression.

There are three types of watch expressions:

- **Watch Expression**

  Used to monitor an expression without affecting the execution of the application.

- **Break When Value Is True**

  Used if you want to see, for example, when Response becomes equal to " ".

- **Break When Value Changes**

  If you use this option, the procedure execution breaks when the value of the expression changes.

12

To use a watch expression to provide the value of response, follow these steps:

1. Remove all breakpoints.

2. Highlight response in the Buggy procedure.

3. Select Debug, Add Watch to display the Add Watch dialog box (see Figure 12.9).

FIGURE 12.9

*The Add Watch dialog
lets you create the
three types of watches.*

4. Because the variable was highlighted when you selected Debug, Add Watch, its name is already in the Expression text box.

   The items in the Context frame allow you to control where this variable is a watch expression. Because this is a variable with local scope, no changes need to be made to these items.

5. Select the Break When Value Changes option button.

6. Click OK.

If you want to quickly create a watch expression, highlight the expression in the Code window and select Debug, Quick Watch or press Shift+F9. This only creates watch expressions, meaning that you can't use this technique to create a watch with the Break When the Value Changes or Break When the Value Is True option.

7. Press F5 to run the application.

8. Click Cancel in response to the input box. The procedure is placed in Break mode because of the watch expression. The Watches window displays in the Visual Basic Editor (see Figure 12.10).

FIGURE 12.10

The Watches window lists any watches you have defined and their value.

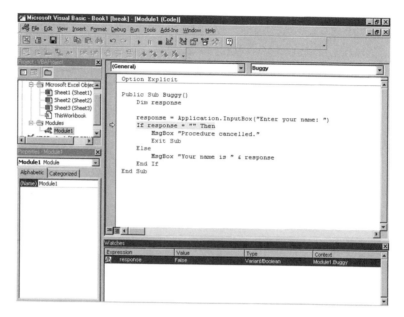

9. Press F5 to continue the execution of the application. Click OK to dismiss the message box.

Now that you are through with the watch and are ready to correct your procedure, you can delete the watch using the following steps:

1. Select Debug, Edit Watch. The Edit Watch dialog displays (see Figure 12.11).

FIGURE 12.11

Use the Edit Watch dialog to modify and delete existing watches.

2. response is listed in the Expression box because it is the only watch. Click Delete. The watch is removed.

12

Correcting the Error

At this point, you're definitely ready to correct the error in the Buggy procedure. The problem is that the InputBox method returns False when the Cancel button is selected, rather than an empty string like its cousin the InputBox function does. The corrected procedure is shown in Listing 12.1.

LISTING 12.1 The Corrected Buggy Procedure

```
 1: Public Sub Buggy()
 2:     Dim response
 3:
 4:     response = Application.InputBox("Enter your name: ")
 5:     If response = False Then
 6:         MsgBox "Procedure cancelled."
 7:         Exit Sub
 8:     Else
 9:         MsgBox "Your name is " & response
10:     End If
11: End Sub
```

By testing to see whether response equals False, you solve the problem.

Summary

For a long time, professional developers looked down on application automation languages, considering them to be the realm of users. One of the reasons for this attitude is the lack of debugging tools. As you now can see, VBA has addressed this issue. Its feature-rich debugging tools meet the needs of the casual and professional developer.

Q&A

Q What if I just want to run part of a procedure?

A Place a breakpoint at the point you wish to break or pause the procedure. This is what a breakpoint is used for.

Q Why would I use a watch instead of using the Print statement in the Immediate window?

A The advantage of a watch over the Immediate window is that it can be set before the procedure runs and is continuously tracked through the procedure's run. Watches can also be used to break the procedure for testing.

Workshop

The quiz questions and exercise are provided for your further understanding. See Appendix A, "Answers," for the answers.

Quiz

1. What mode occurs when you reach a breakpoint?

2. How do you determine the order in which the procedure code is executed?

3. How do you display the value of properties and variables in the Immediate window?

4. Name a way other than a breakpoint to pause the application.

5. True or False: When a procedure is placed in Break mode, its variable's values aren't available for your viewing.

6. Name the two forms of stepping through code execution.

7. True or False: Watches never affect program execution.

Exercise

Create the following procedure:

```
Sub Hour12Exercise()
    Dim sWhichState As String

    sWhichState = InputBox("Enter the state for shipping: ")

    Select Case sWhichState
        Case "FL"
            MsgBox "Shipping is 3.50."
        Case "NY"
            MsgBox "Shipping is 5.00."
        Case "OH"
            MsgBox "Shipping is 2.00."
        Case "CA"
            MsgBox "Shipping is 6.00."
        Case Else
            MsgBox "We don't ship there."
    End Select

End Sub
```

Run the procedure and enter Ny in response to the input box. Use one of the debug procedures presented in this hour to find out why you got an unexpected response.

12

Hour **13**

Error Handling

In the previous hour, you learned that debugging is the process of dealing with all the problems you can predict and correct. But what about things you can't control and can't predict? Unless your application is very small, there's no way for you to predict every possible thing that can happen while your application runs. You cannot control the operating system or hardware platform, and you definitely cannot control the user.

The highlights of this hour include

- What is error handling?
- Setting an error trap
- Writing error-handling routines
- Providing an exit from an error handler
- Creating a centralized error handler

Error Handling

NEW TERM To handle unexpected occurrences, you need to write an error handler. An *error handler* is a routine for trapping and dealing with errors in your procedure. Developing an error handler can be broken down into three steps:

1. **Set an error trap.**

   When you set an error trap, you are telling the procedure where to go to when an error occurs.

2. **Write an error-handling routine.**

   The error-handling routine is where the procedure goes if there is an error.

3. **Provide an exit from the error-handling routine.**

   In other words, what do you want the program to do after the error is handled?

Step One—Setting an Error Trap

Setting an error trap tells VBA where to go and this is done with the `On Error` statement. Only one error trap at a time can be enabled in a given procedure. This is not to say that your procedure can only have one `On Error` statement, but if you have more than one `On Error` statement in your procedure, the one that has been executing most recently is the one in effect.

NEW TERM There are two different ways of handling errors. One way is to perform in-line error handling. *In-line error handling* has the instruction for dealing with the error within the `On Error` statement. To perform in-line error handling, use one of the following statements:

- **`On Error Resume`**

  If a runtime error occurs, execution resumes at the statement that caused the error.

- **`On Error Resume Next`**

  If a runtime error occurs, execution resumes at the statement after the one that caused the error.

> To disable an error handler, use an `On Error GoTo 0` statement in the procedure after the initial `On Error` statement. Disabling an error handler is useful if you're testing the procedure and don't want error handling to occur.

In-line error handling is not the recommended or preferred method of error handling. The preferred way of error handling is to use an error trap that jumps to an error-handling routine. This approach gives you the flexibility to respond to a variety of errors.

To set an error trap that jumps to an error-handling routine, use the On Error GoTo *line* statement, where *line* represents the line label preceding the error-handling code. To create a line label, you type a name for the line and follow it with a colon. Line labels in VBA need to be on lines by themselves. Listing 13.1 shows the basic outline of a procedure that contains an error-handling routine.

LISTING 13.1   A Basic Outline of a Procedure Containing an Error-Handling Routine

```
 1: Sub WithErrorHandler()
 2:     On Error GoTo ErrorHandler
 3:     'The body of the procedure goes here.
 4:     .
 5:     .
 6:     .
 7:     'The next statement, Exit Sub or Exit Function (whatever is
 8:     'appropriate), goes before the line label for the error handler.
 9:     'This is done so that if there are no errors, the error-
10:     'handling routine is skipped.
11:     Exit Sub
12: 'The next line is the line label for the error-handling
13: 'routine.
14: ErrorHandler:
15:     'The code for the error handler goes here.
16:     .
17:     .
18:     .
19: End Sub
```

Step 2—Writing the Error-Handling Routine

13

When an error occurs, VBA looks for the line label and begins to execute at that point in the procedure. The code for the error-handling routine evaluates the error that was generated and determines a course of action. This evaluation process is done with either an If statement or a Select statement. You should always include an Else clause in these statements to handle all unanticipated errors.

Step 3—Providing an Exit from the Error Handler

You might be wondering what you'll use with your condition for the error handler's `If` or `Select` statement. You'll be testing the value of the `Err` object's `Number` property, which is the object's default property. The `Err` object contains information about runtime errors. Its `Number` property can be used to return the numeric value specified by the error that occurs. After you've determined what the error is, you have four options:

- `Resume`   Return to the statement that caused the error.
- `Resume Next`   Return to the line after the one that caused the error.
- `Resume line`   Go to a line label in the procedure.
- `End`   End the procedure or application.

Putting It All Together

Now that you know the theory of creating an error handler, you are ready to put it into practice. Add a new module in this workbook. To create a procedure that has an error handler, perform the following steps:

1. Create a new procedure named `ErrorExample`.

2. Enter the following code in the procedure:

```
Dim sngValue As Single, sngDivideBy As Single, sngAnswer As Single
Dim iResponse As Integer
On Error GoTo ErrorZone
sngValue = InputBox("Enter the number you wish to divide: ")
sngDivideBy = InputBox("Enter the number you wish to divide by: ")
sngAnswer = sngValue / sngDivideBy
MsgBox "The answer is " & sngAnswer

Exit Sub
ErrorZone:
    Select Case Err
        Case 7
            MsgBox "Out of Memory" & _
                    Chr(13) & "Close nonessential applications."
            Resume
        Case 35 To 51
            MsgBox "Contact the Help Desk."
        Case 11
            MsgBox "You can't divide by zero."
        Case Else
            MsgBox "Unrecoverable error. Exiting application."
            End
    End Select
```

3. Run the procedure. Enter 10 in response to the first input box.

4. Enter 0 in response to the second input box. When you press Enter, you'll see an error message display. This is because you tried to divide by zero, which causes an error.

5. Click OK to dismiss the message box.

You can use the Error function to display the text associated with the error that has occurred. To modify your procedure to use the Error function, complete the following steps:

1. Modify the ErrorExample procedure to match the one listed below (changes are in bold):

```
Private Sub ErrorExample()
    Dim sngValue As Single, sngDivideBy As Single, sngAnswer As Single
    Dim iResponse As Integer
    On Error GoTo ErrorZone
    sngValue = InputBox("Enter the number you wish to divide: ")
    sngDivideBy = InputBox("Enter the number you wish to divide by: ")
    sngAnswer = sngValue / sngDivideBy
    MsgBox "The answer is " & sngAnswer

Exit Sub
ErrorZone:
        Select Case Err
            Case 7
                MsgBox "Out of Memory" & _
                            Chr(13) & "Close nonessential applications."
                Resume
            Case 35 To 51
                MsgBox "Contact the Help Desk."
                Exit Sub
            Case 11
                MsgBox "An error has occurred: " & Error
            Case Else
                MsgBox "Unrecoverable error. Exiting application."
                End
        End Select
End Sub
```

2. Run the procedure. Enter 5 in response to the first input box.

3. Enter 0 in response to the second input box. When you press Enter, you'll see an error message display with the text associated with the error message (see Figure 13.1).

13

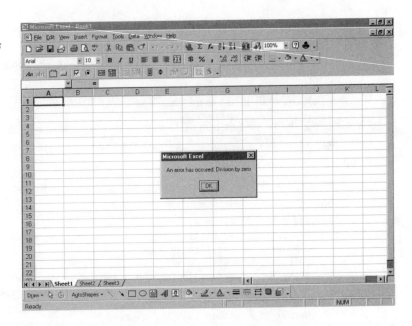

FIGURE 13.1
This message box uses text generated by the Error *function.*

4. Click OK to dismiss the message box.

You might be thinking to yourself, "I really don't want to write an error-handling routine for each of my procedures." You don't have to. In the next section you will learn how to create a centralized error handler.

Creating a Centralized Error Handler

NEW TERM   Rather than including an error-handling routine in each of your procedures, you can create a centralized error handler. A *centralized error handler* is a separate function that processes each error that's generated and then, based on the error number, initiates an action. Each of your procedures that you want to have error handling still requires an On Error statement. This statement branches to an area of the application that has a Select Case statement to process the results returned by the centralized error handler. There are five possible cases for this Select Case statement:

- Perform a Resume
- Perform a Resume Next
- Perform a Resume *line*
- Exit the procedure
- End the application

For each error, a value ranging from 1 through 5 is returned from the centralized error handler function to the local procedure. The local procedure uses the returned value to initiate an action. The best way to understand this process is to do it. To add a centralized error handler, use the following steps:

1. Add a module to this workbook and create a function named HandleErrors. Be sure to make it a function.

2. Type the following code for this function:

```
Function HandleErrors(iErrNum) As Integer
    Select Case iAction
    Case 5
        'Invalid procedure call
        MsgBox Error(iErrNum) & " Contact Help Desk."
        iAction = 2
    Case 7
        'Out of memory
        MsgBox "Close all unnecessary applications."
        iAction = 1
    Case 11
        'Division by zero
        MsgBox "Zero is not a valid value."
        iAction = 1
    Case 48, 49, 51
        'Error in loading DLL
        MsgBox iErrNum & " Contact Help Desk."
        iAction = 5
    Case 57
        'Device I/O error
        MsgBox "Insert Disk in Drive A."
        iAction = 1
    Case Else
        MsgBox "Unrecoverable Error."
        iAction = 5
    End Select

    ErrorHandler = iAction
End Function
```

3. Locate the ErrorExample procedure (it is in a module other than the current one).

4. Modify this procedure to match the following (changes are in bold):

```
Private Sub ErrorExample()
    Dim sngValue As Single, sngDivideBy As Single, sngAnswer As Single
    Dim iResponse As Integer
    On Error GoTo ErrorZone
    sngValue = InputBox("Enter the number you wish to divide: ")
    sngDivideBy = InputBox("Enter the number you wish to divide by: ")
    sngAnswer = sngValue / sngDivideBy
    MsgBox "The answer is " & sngAnswer
```

13

```
Exit Sub
ErrorZone:
    'This Select statement uses the value returned
    'from the HandleErrors function for its condition.
    Select Case HandleErrors(Err)
    Case 1
        Resume
    Case 2
        Resume Next
    'This procedure doesn't need Case 3 which is resuming to a line.
    Case 4
        Exit Sub
    Case 5
        End
    End Select
End Sub
```

5. Run the procedure.

6. Enter 8 in response to the first input box.

7. Enter 0 in response to the second input box. An error has occurred.

8. Click OK to dismiss the message box.

By branching to a centralized error handler function and then performing the Resume, Resume Next, or other necessary statement in the local procedure, you're assured that VBA resumes in the correct location.

This approach also allows for custom code, such as a message, to be placed in the local procedure's error routine. This code needs to be placed in all procedures where you want to support error handling.

You only need to create the centralized error handler function once. Copy and paste this function in your future applications.

Summary

Debugging can find only predictable errors. To deal with the unpredictable and the unavoidable, you need to use error handling. By enabling error handling, you make your application more stable and robust. If your application contains several procedures, you might want to implement a centralized error handler.

Q&A

Q If I need to force an error, how would I do that?

A You can use the `Raise` function to force an error. This is useful during the testing process, and in some cases might be useful in the final application, as well.

Q I have a procedure that is called by another procedure. The procedure doesn't have an error handler, but the calling procedure does. What happens if there is an error?

A If a procedure is called by another procedure and doesn't have an error handler, VBA will look for an error handler in the calling procedure.

Workshop

The quiz questions and exercise are provided for your further understanding. See Appendix A, "Answers," for the answers.

Quiz

1. What are three main steps to creating an error handler?
2. Name the object and its property that are used to return the error number.
3. Which statement returns you to the line that caused the error?
4. What character do you place at the end of a line to make it a line label?
5. What statement would you execute to skip a line that caused an error?
6. True or False. Each procedure must have its own error handling routine.
7. Which logical construct is best to use when creating an error handler?

Exercise

Create the following procedure:

```
Sub ProcWithError()
    Workbooks.Open "C:\nosuchfile.wkb"
End Sub
```

Add code to implement an error handler that displays a message and resumes on the next line of the procedure.

13

HOUR 14

Working with UserForms

You know lots of syntax. You know how to test and debug an application. You know how to handle errors. What's next? Actually, you are going to return to the user interface for a while. At this point, you are going to start working with UserForms as a way to customize your application's interface.

You are going to be creating an application to track expenditures made by guests at a hotel. When a guest uses the golf course or tennis court, requests extra towels at the pool, and so on, an entry is made into this application. The user will not be interacting directly with a worksheet in this application. Instead, the user will be inputting information via a custom dialog box that you are going to create in this hour.

The highlights of this hour include

- Adding and running UserForms
- Placing controls on a UserForm
- The importance of your controls' tab order
- Implementing accelerator keys

Adding a UserForm to Your Application

In Hour 3, "Working with Controls," you placed controls directly on a worksheet. This is a nice approach when you want your users to interact with a worksheet, but what if you are trying to shield them from the Excel environment? What if you are trying to create an application that has a customized interface? Then you want to use UserForms.

NEW TERM   *UserForms* become the custom windows and dialog boxes of your application. They contain controls that are used to get information from a user. To add a UserForm to an application, complete the following steps:

> In older versions of Excel, UserForms were called dialog sheets.

1. Close all open workbooks.
2. Open a new workbook.
3. Press Alt+F11 to access the Visual Basic Editor.
4. Right-click ThisWorkbook in the Project Explorer.
5. Select Insert, UserForm from the menu. A UserForm is added to your workbook, as shown in Figure 14.1.

FIGURE 14.1

A newly added UserForm looks like an empty dialog box.

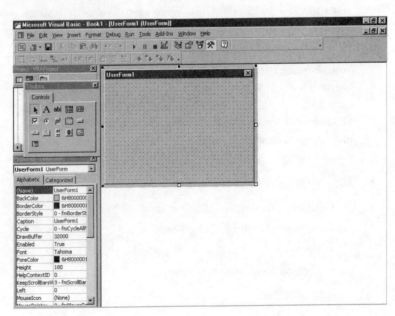

The newly added UserForm appears as a gray box with a title bar. This is your foundation for building a custom dialog box, and you will look at its properties and how to run it next.

Setting a UserForm's Properties

The first step to working with UserForms is to set some property values. The first thing you want to set for the UserForm or any object is the Name property. The Name property controls how the UserForm is referred to in code. When the UserForm is first created, it is assigned a name, such as UserForm1, by Excel. Can you imagine trying to keep track of several forms using names such as UserForm1, UserForm2, UserForm3, and so on?

A recommended naming prefix for UserForms is frm. frm is used as shorthand for form.

After setting the Name property, the next thing to do is to set the UserForm's Caption property. The Caption property controls the text in the form's title bar. To set these properties, use the following steps:

1. If the Properties window is not displayed, press F4. Figure 14.2 shows the Properties window with the UserForm's properties listed.

FIGURE 14.2

You have the option of viewing properties alphabetically or by categories.

2. Select the Name property. This property is found at the top of the alphabetical properties listed and is shown as (Name).

3. Enter frmGuestExpenses.

4. Select the Caption property.

5. Enter Guest Expenses. Notice that as you type Guest Expenses into the Caption property, the title bar of the UserForm changes.

14

So far, the only change to the form you can see is its title bar. There are numerous other properties that you can set for a UserForm, but these two are the only ones needed at this point.

Running the UserForm

Even though there isn't any code associated with the form, you can run it. Running a UserForm means seeing it display as it would in your application. Use the following steps to run the UserForm:

1. Click the UserForm to select it.
2. Press F5. The UserForm displays in Run mode, as shown in Figure 14.3. Notice that the grid that displays when you are working with the UserForm in the Visual Basic Editor does not display when you run the form.

FIGURE 14.3

An example of a running UserForm.

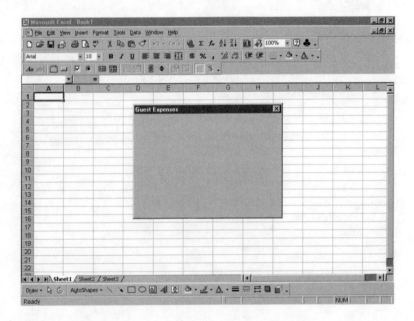

3. Close the UserForm using the Close button on the form's title bar.
4. Return to the Visual Basic Editor.

As you saw from these steps, you get a bonus when using UserForms. You don't have to write code for a form's Close button. That's handled for you.

Adding Controls to Your UserForm

Adding controls to a UserForm is very much like placing controls on a worksheet. You simply select the control you want to work with from the Toolbox and, using your mouse, draw the control on the form.

> When placing controls on a worksheet, you used the Forms toolbar. Here you are going to use the Toolbox.

> See "The Different Types of Controls" in Hour 3 for more information on the different types of controls and their uses.

You are going to be creating a form that tracks miscellaneous guest expenses at a hotel. The form, when it is completed, will look like the one in Figure 14.4.

FIGURE 14.4

The completed Guest Expenses form.

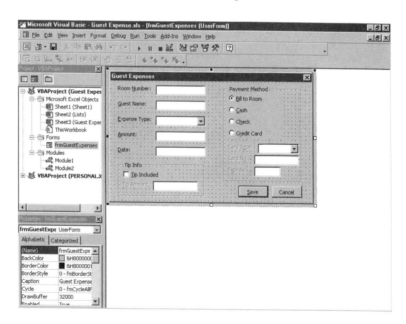

As you can see from Figure 14.4, this form uses a variety of controls. You are now ready to place these controls on your form using the following steps:

1. If the Toolbox is not displayed, select View, Toolbox.
2. Select the Label control from the Toolbox.

14

3. Using Figure 14.4 as a guide, place the label toward the upper-left corner of the form.

4. If the Properties window is not open, press F4. Set the Label control's (Name) property to lblRoomNumber and its Caption property to Room Number:.

5. Select the Text control from the Toolbox. Place a text box beside the label. Set the (Name) property to txtRoomNumber.

6. Using Figure 14.4 as a guide, continue creating the following controls using the properties in Table 14.1. When working with frames, draw the frame first and then place the controls in the frame. Also, don't worry about making the alignment and size of your controls perfect. You are going to learn some techniques to make that process easier.

TABLE 14.1 frmGuestExpenses Controls

Control Type	Name Property	Caption Property
Label	lblGuestName	Guest Name:
Text box	txtGuestName	
Label	lblExpenseType	Expense Type:
List box	lstExpenseType	
Label	lblAmount	Amount:
Text box	txtAmount	
Label	lblDate	Date:
Text box	txtDate	
Frame	fraPayment	Payment Method
Option button	optBillToRoom	Bill to Room
Option button	optCash	Cash
Option button	optCheck	Check
Option button	optCreditCard	Credit Card
Label	lblCardType	Card Type:
List box	lstCardType	
Label	lblCardNumber	Card No.:
Text box	txtCardNumber	
Label	lblExpires	Expires:
Text box	txtExpires	
Command button	cmdSave	Save
Command button	cmdCancel	Cancel

Control Type	Name *Property*	Caption *Property*
Frame	fraTips	Tip Info
Check box	chkTipIncluded	Tip Included
Label	lblTipAmount	Tip Amount:
Text box	txtTipAmount	

7. Save the workbook as Guest Expenses.

I know creating controls can be a little tedious, but they are obviously necessary. During the remainder of this hour, you'll work with other properties and techniques to make the form and its controls look better.

Setting Additional Properties

In the previous exercise, you set the (Name) property for all the controls and the Caption property for some of the controls. Now you are going to set some additional properties.

Command Button Properties—Default and Cancel

The first controls you are going to set additional properties for are the command buttons. Your form has two command buttons: Save and Cancel. The Save button will eventually have the job of validating data and, if valid, writing the data to a worksheet. Think about how you enter data. You probably go from field to field and when you are done, you press Enter. Pressing Enter on this UserForm accomplishes nothing. You have to set a property so that when a user press Enter, it is as if the Save button were clicked. To do this, you need to set the Save button's Default property to True. Only one command button on a form can have the Default property equal to True.

On most forms when you press Enter, it performs a cancel. On your form, you need to set the Cancel property of the Cancel button to be True.

You also want these to make these two buttons the same size. To do this, use the Make Same Size toolbar button by completing the following steps:

1. Click the Save button to select it.

2. Hold down the Ctrl key and click the Cancel button. This selects both the buttons at the same time.

3. From the UserForm toolbar, select the down arrow beside the Make Same size button.

If you don't see the Userform toolbar, right-click on a toolbar and select Userform from the menu.

4. Select Both.

The buttons resize based on the size of the Cancel button. The last button selected acts as the template for the other selected buttons.

Setting an Option Button's `Value` Property and Aligning Controls

The next group of controls you are working with are the option buttons. Notice the order of the option buttons on the form—Bill to Room is first, followed by Cash, and so on. This order was selected because it is assumed that most people bill expenses to their room. The second most-frequently used payment method is Cash, and the order continues down. You now can see that when designing a form that uses option buttons, you try to order them in order of most used to least used. You also need to set one of the option buttons as the default option. To do this, set the `optBillToRoom` option button's `Value` property to `True`.

You also want to align your option buttons so that they align on the left side. Use the following steps to do this:

1. Click the Bill to Room option button.
2. Ctrl+click the remaining option buttons.
 3. Click the down arrow button next to the Align toolbar button found on the UserForm toolbar.
4. Select Lefts. The controls now are aligned on their left side.

If other controls in the Payment Method frame need to be aligned, perform the alignment at this time.

Disabling Controls

There are a couple of controls that are needed only if other controls are selected. For example, you don't need the Tip Amount text box unless the Tip Included check box has a check in it. And you don't need the controls that pertain to a credit card unless the Credit Card option button is selected. To make this more obvious to your user, you can disable these controls, which makes them unavailable for use, and they appear to be grayed out. Then if the appropriate control is selected, you can enable these controls. Set the `Enabled` property equal to `False`.

Working a Little More on the Form's Appearance

Now take a few moments to align controls and resize them using the techniques presented in this hour. Use Figure 14.5 as a guide.

> Another property you might want to set when working with controls is the ControlTipText property. If a value is entered in this property, it displays as the ToolTip that is shown when a user positions the pointer over a control.

Assigning Tab Order to Controls

Run your UserForm now. Start pressing your Tab key. You might notice that the Tab key doesn't select the controls in the exact order you might have expected. For example, using the Tab key, you'll select the payment method controls before you'll select the tip controls. Also, the Save and Cancel buttons are not the last controls to be selected. This is because the tab order of the controls is based on the order in which they were created. If you don't have the desired tab order on the form, it's up to you to correct it using the TabIndex property. The TabIndex property controls the tab order for the controls on a form. The number for the TabIndex property starts with 0.

Your first reaction to setting the TabIndex property is to start with the first button and begin numbering 0, 1, 2, 3, and so on. There is another approach you might prefer. Start by selecting the last control in your desired tab order. Set its TabIndex to 0. Select the next-to-last control in the desired tab order (be sure to include labels and frames), and set its TabIndex property to 0. Continue backward, setting each control's TabIndex property to 0. What happens is that when you set one control's TabIndex to 0, it increments all the other TabIndex property values by 1. That's why you work backward! Take a few moments to correct your tab order. After you have the TabIndex properties set, run the UserForm.

Assigning Accelerator Keys to Controls

You are almost done with the interface portion of your form. Run your form. Do you notice anything missing? You probably do if you prefer to use your keyboard rather than a mouse. The form as it stands doesn't have any accelerator keys (also known as keyboard access characters). To add accelerator keys, you need to use the Accelerator property. Enter the letter found in the control's caption that you want to use for the accelerator key. After it is set, the letter entered for the Accelerator property is underlined in the control's caption (see Figure 14.5). Table 14.2 shows a list of recommended Accelerator property values for this form.

14

NEW TERM   An *accelerator key* is used in conjunction with the Alt key on the PC platform or
           Command key on the Macintosh to access a control. For example, if there were a
control that had the letter B as its accelerator key, you could press Alt+B to access the
control.

FIGURE 14.5

Users who prefer to use the keyboard instead of the mouse appreciate accelerator keys.

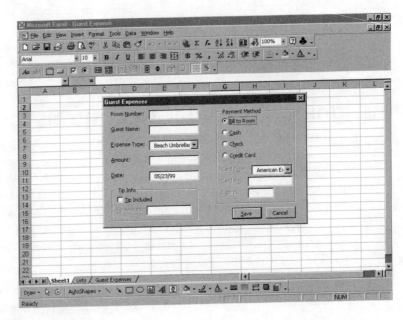

TABLE 14.2   Accelerator Keys

Control	Accelerator Key
lblRoomNumber	N
lblGuestName	G
lblExpenseType	E
lblAmount	A
lblDate	D
chkTipIncluded	T
lblTipAmount	i
optBillToRoom	B
optCash	C
optCheck	h
optCreditCard	r
lblCardType	y

Control	Accelerator Key
lblCardNumber	o
lblExpires	x
cmdSave	S

Summary

In this hour, you created a UserForm that is now ready for automating. You added a UserForm to your application, placed controls on the form, and set properties for the controls. The final result is a professional-looking custom dialog box.

In the next hour, you are going to write the code necessary to automate this form. You'll write code to validate the user's input to the form and to write the values of the form to a worksheet.

Q&A

Q Why would I want to use a UserForm rather than place controls on a worksheet?

A You might want to place controls directly on a worksheet if you need only a couple of controls. If you need several controls, a UserForm is a better solution. The other advantage of a UserForm is its professional appearance. Placing controls directly on a worksheet tends to make your application look more "home grown."

Q Am I just limited to one UserForm per application?

A No, you can add dozens of forms to your application if you want. Obviously, the more sophisticated the application, the more forms are needed.

Workshop

The quiz questions and exercise are provided for your further understanding. See Appendix A, "Answers," for the answers.

Quiz

1. True or False: The grid displays on a UserForm when you run it.
2. Which property is used to set an accelerator key for a control?
3. How do you identify a command button as the one to execute when you press Enter?

14

4. Which property do you set to select an option button?

5. True or False: Aligning controls requires setting properties.

6. What happens when you set a command button's Cancel property to True?

7. What sets the initial tab order for controls on a form?

Exercise

In this exercise, you are going to be creating the form shown in Figure 14.6. Name the form frmSplash and set its Caption to Welcome to Guest Expenses! Table 14.3 shows needed property settings.

FIGURE 14.6

The completed form for Hour 14's exercise.

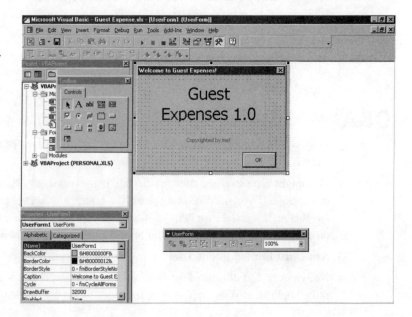

TABLE 14.3   Property Settings

Control Type	*Name*	Caption Property	*Other Properties*
Label	lblTitle	Guest Expenses 1.0	Font size to 26 points, TextAlign to fmTextAlignCenter
Label	lblCopyRight	Copyrighted by Me!	ForeColor to blue
Button	cmdOK	OK	Default to True, Cancel to True

To set the font information for the label, locate and select the Font property. Click the selection button and make your choices using the Font dialog.

14

Hour 15

Automating UserForms

Automating a UserForm can be broken into several parts. You have to decide how you want the form to look when it loads, determine how the controls are to behave, test whether user values are acceptable, and write the data to a worksheet. These are the tasks you'll perform in this hour.

The highlights of this hour include

- How and where to initialize your UserForm's values
- Using VBA code to display UserForms
- Controlling a UserForm's behavior while it is running
- Performing data validation
- Moving the form's values to a worksheet

Initializing Values in UserForms

When you display a form, you want certain things to happen as it loads. For example, your users would probably appreciate it if you placed today's date in the Date text box. To do this, you are going to place code in the UserForm_Activate procedure. The UserForm_Activate procedure executes when the form is activated. The `UserForm_Activate` procedure is where you place code to initialize values for the control on a form.

One of the things that you are going to do in this procedure is use a range of cells to populate a list box. You need values for the Expense Type list box and the Card Type list box. Complete the following steps to enter these values:

1. Go to the current workbook and go to Sheet2 of the workbook. Rename the sheet to Lists.

2. Go to cell A1 and enter `Expense Categories`.

3. Starting in cell B2, enter the following values:

   Cell B2: `Beach Umbrellas`

   Cell B3: `Bike Rental`

   Cell B4: `Golf Lesson`

   Cell B5: `Golf, 18 holes`

   Cell B6: `Golf, 9 holes`

   Cell B7: `Pool Towels`

   Cell B8: `Tennis Court`

   Cell B9: `Tennis Lesson`

4. Select Range B2:B9 and name it Expenses.

> To name a range of cells, select the range. Select the Name box at the left end of the formula bar and type the name for the cells. Press Enter.

5. Go to cell E1 and enter `Credit Card Types`.

6. Starting in cell F2, enter the following values:

   Cell F2: `American Express`

   Cell F3: `Diner's Club`

   Cell F4: `Mastercard`

   Cell F5: `Visa`

7. Select Range F2:F5 and name it CardType.

8. Save the workbook.

9. Press Alt+F11 to return to the Visual Basic Editor.

The next step in the process it to provide initial values and settings for some of the controls on the form. To initialize values in your UserForm, complete the following steps:

1. Double-click the gray background of the UserForm. The Code window opens (see Figure 15.1). The UserForm_Click procedure displays.

FIGURE 15.1

The Code window is used to create and modify code for UserForms.

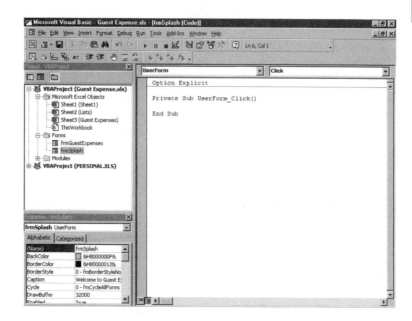

2. You don't want to write code for the UserForm_Click procedure. You need to select the Activate event instead. To do this, click the down arrow button beside the list box toward the top of the Code window that has Activate in it. This is called the Event box. Locate and select Activate. The UserForm_Activate procedure displays.

3. Enter the following code for the UserForm_Activate procedure:

```
With lstExpenseType
    .RowSource = "Expenses"
    .ListIndex = 0
End With

txtDate.Text = Format(Now, "mm/dd/yy")

With lstCardType
    .RowSource = "CardType"
    .ListIndex = 0
End With
```

4. Press F5 to run the procedure. The UserForm displays as shown in Figure 15.2. Notice that the list boxes are populated and that today's date is entered in the Date text box.

FIGURE 15.2

Using the form's Activate *event, you can automatically provide values and settings for your user.*

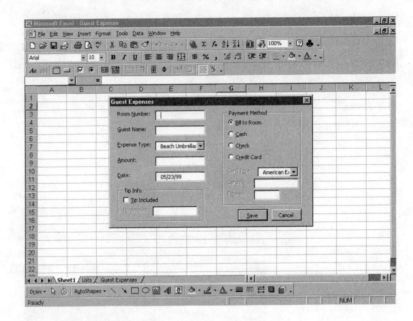

5. Close the form and return to the Visual Basic Editor.

The key to initializing values in a form is to use the form's Activate event as shown in these steps. Using similar code, you can initialize option button values, check box values, list box sources, text box entries, and label captions. In the UserForm_Activate procedure, you worked with list boxes and a text box. Listing 15.1 shows the complete UserForm_Activate procedure.

LISTING 15.1   UserForm_Activate Procedure

```
1: Private Sub UserForm_Activate()
2:     With lstExpenseType
3:         .RowSource = "expenses"
4:         .ListIndex = 0
5:     End With
6:
7:     txtDate.Text = Format(Now, "mm/dd/yy")
8:
9:     With lstCardType
10:         .RowSource = "CardType"
```

```
11:          .ListIndex = 0
12:      End With
13: End Sub
```

15

The `With` statements both dealt with list boxes. Using the first `With` statement as an example, you can see that two properties were set:

```
With lstExpenseType
    .RowSource = "expenses"
    .ListIndex = 0
End With
```

The `RowSource` property refers to the range where the list of values needed to populate the list box is located. It's best to use a named range when you are using cell values to populate a list box just because it makes it easier on you.

The `ListIndex` property determines which item in the list box's list of values is displayed. Index numbering for the first item starts at 0.

The other object type that was initialized by the `UserForm_Activate` procedure was a text box:

```
txtDate.Text = Format(Now, "mm/dd/yy")
```

The `Now` function is used to return the current date, and the `Format` function places it in mm/dd/yy format.

Displaying UserForms

You might be wondering how you display a UserForm other than running it from the Visual Basic Editor. You are going to write a simple procedure to do it. You can assign the procedure to a variety of objects such as a command button, a toolbar button, and a menu item.

> For more information on working with toolbars, see Hour 16, "Toolbars."
> Form more information on working with menus, see Hour 17, "Menus."

Because assigning procedures to toolbar buttons and menu items hasn't been discussed yet in this book, you are going to assign the procedure that displays the form to a button. The procedure that displays the dialog box will have only one line of code in it:

```
frmGuestExpenses.Show
```

The Show method of the UserForm loads the form in memory and displays it. To create this procedure, use the following steps:

1. If you aren't already there, go to the Visual Basic Editor and add a new module to this workbook.

2. Create a new procedure named ShowGuestExpenses.

3. Enter the following code for the procedure:

   `frmGuestExpenses.Show`

4. Go to Sheet1 of your workbook and add a command button to the worksheet.

 To add a command button, you need to have the Forms toolbar displayed.

5. When prompted by the Assign Macro dialog, select ShowGuestExpenses.

6. Set the caption of the button to Show Guest Expenses and Click outside the button to deselect it.

7. Click the button to display the form. The form displays. Notice that the list box controls and the Date text box are initialized.

8. Close the form and ave the workbook.

As you now know, displaying a form is very easy to do using the Show method. The ShowGuestExpenses procedure is used to display the form from a toolbar button and a menu item later in this book.

Controlling Form Behavior

After you display the form, you might need it to take on different behaviors. For example, when you place a check in the Tip Included check box, you want the Tip Amount text box to be enabled. You also want the controls associated with credit card information to be enabled if the Credit Card option button is selected. To do this, you are going to place code in the appropriate control's Change event procedure. The Change event occurs when the control's Value property changes. Because you are working with a option button (Credit Card) and a check box (Tip Included), you want to enable the associated controls if the Value property is True. Complete the following steps to enter code to enable controls:

1. If you are not already there, go to the Visual Basic Editor and open the `frmGuestExpenses` form.

2. Double-click the Tip Included check box to open the Code window.

3. Select Change from the Code window's Event list box and enter the following code for the `chkTipIncluded_Change` procedure:

```
If chkTipIncluded.Value = True Then
    lblTipAmount.Enabled = True
    txtTipAmount.Enabled = True
Else
    lblTipAmount.Enabled = False
    txtTipAmount.Enabled = False
End If
```

4. Located in the upper-left corner of the Code window is a list box that currently has `chkTipIncluded` selected. Click the down arrow for this list box. Locate and select `optCreditCard`.

5. Select Change from the Event list box. The `optCreditCard_Change` procedure displays in the Code window.

6. Enter the following code for the `optCreditCard_Change` procedure:

```
If optCreditCard.Value = True Then
    lblCardType.Enabled = True
    lstCardType.Enabled = True
    lblCardNumber.Enabled = True
    txtCardNumber.Enabled = True
    lblExpires.Enabled = True
    txtExpires.Enabled = True
Else
    lblCardType.Enabled = False
    lstCardType.Enabled = False
    lblCardNumber.Enabled = False
    txtCardNumber.Enabled = False
    lblExpires.Enabled = False
    txtExpires.Enabled = False
end if
```

7. Go to Sheet1 of your workbook and click the command button on the worksheet. The form displays (see Figure 15.3).

8. Place a check in the Tip Included check box. The Tip Amount controls are enabled.

9. Select the Credit Card option button. The credit card controls are enabled as shown in Figure 15.4.

FIGURE 15.3

When the form initially displays, several controls are disabled.

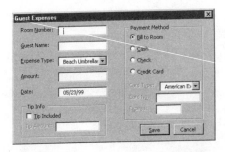

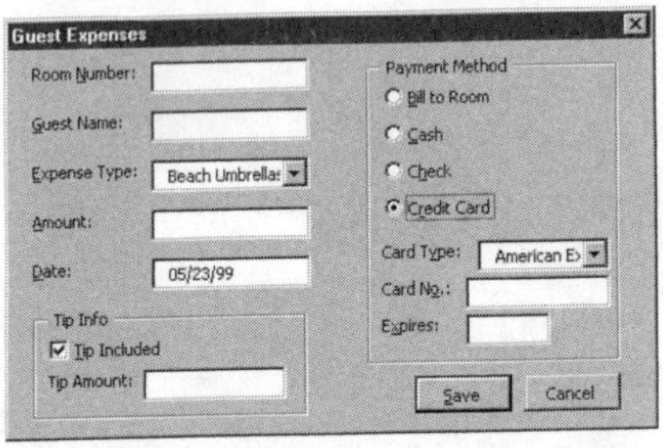

FIGURE 15.4

Using the Change *event of a control, you can enable other controls.*

10. Close the form and save the workbook. Return to the Visual Basic Editor.

Basically, what you did in the Change event procedure was test the Value property. If it was set to True, you set the Enabled property of the appropriate controls to True. Otherwise, you set the Enabled property to False.

You are not limited to working with the Enabled property. You can set any property that can be set at runtime including Text, Value, and Caption.

Data Validation

After the user enters information into the form, she is going to click the Save button. What happens next? The code associated with the Save button needs to do two things: make sure the data is valid, and if the data is valid, write the data to a worksheet. Let's start with validating data.

When you validate data, you make sure it is valid in the context of your application. A text box will accept anything that you can enter from a keyboard. This doesn't mean the data is valid. Looking at the Guest Expenses form, there is only one control that you are going to validate data for: txtRoomNumber. For the purpose of example, this hotel's room numbers start at 101 and end at 730. This doesn't mean that you don't need any other code in your validation routine. You need to add code that ensures required fields have entries. The required fields are Room Number, Expense Type, Amount, and Date. Payment Method is also required, but option buttons take care of themselves by their own nature.

But wait, there's more validation to be done. If the Tip Included check box is checked, the Tip Amount data is required. Also, if the Credit Card option button is selected, the associated credit card information is required.

Now that you've identified what needs to go into the code associated with the Save button, you are ready to write the procedure using the following steps:

1. Display the UserForm in the Visual Basic Editor.

2. Double-click the Save button. The cmdSave_Click procedure displays.

3. Enter the following code for the cmdSave_Click procedure:

```
If Val(txtRoomNumber.Text) < 101 Or Val(txtRoomNumber.Text) > 730 Then
    MsgBox "Invalid room number."
    txtRoomNumber.SetFocus
    Exit Sub
End If

If txtGuestName.Text = "" Then
    MsgBox "Please enter guest's name."
    txtGuestName.SetFocus
    Exit Sub
End If

If chkTipIncluded.Value = True Then
    If txtTipAmount = "" Then
        MsgBox "If tip is included you must enter amount."
        txtTipAmount.SetFocus
        Exit Sub
    End If
End If

If txtAmount.Text = "" Then
    MsgBox "Please enter amount."
    txtAmount.SetFocus
    Exit Sub
End If

If IsNumeric(txtAmount.Text) = False Then
    MsgBox "Amount must be a number."
    txtAmount.SetFocus
    Exit Sub
End If

If txtDate.Text = "" Then
    MsgBox "You must enter a date."
```

```
        txtDate.SetFocus
        Exit Sub
    End If

    If optCreditCard.Value = True Then
        If txtCardNumber = "" Then
            MsgBox "Please enter a card number"
            txtCardNumber.SetFocus
            Exit Sub
        End If
        If txtExpires.Text = "" Then
            MsgBox "Please enter the card's expiration date."
            txtExpires.SetFocus
            Exit Sub
        End If
    End If

    Unload Me
```

4. Go to Sheet1 and click the command button. The form displays.

5. Click the Save button. A message box displays telling you that you must enter a room number (see Figure 15.5).

FIGURE 15.5

One of the many possible error message box that can be generated by the cmdSave_Click *procedure.*

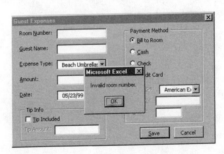

6. Click OK to dismiss the message box. Enter 121 and click the Save button. Another message box displays. Click OK to dismiss the message box.

7. Enter your name as the guest's name. Enter 20 for the amount.

8. Click the Tip Included check box. A message box displays letting you know that you need to enter the tip amount. Click OK to dismiss the message box.

9. Enter 2 for the tip amount and click Save. The form is no longer displayed.

You probably saw a definite pattern to the code you created for the cmdSave_Click procedure. Basically, you tested either the Text or Value property of a control. Listing 15.2 has one of the If statements used in the procedure.

LISTING 15.2   Testing the Room Number Entry

```
1: If Val(txtRoomNumber.Text) < 101 Or Val(txtRoomNumber.Text) > 730 Then
2:     MsgBox "Invalid room number."
3:     txtRoomNumber.SetFocus
4:     Exit Sub
5: End If
```

15

This If statement makes sure that the room number is between 101 and 730. Notice the use of the Val function. The contents of the Value property are actually a string. The Val property converts a string to a number. Did you notice that you didn't write code to check whether txtRoomNumber.text was empty? This is handled already by this If statement because empty is less than 101!

The SetFocus method makes the named control the active object on the form. Exit Sub is used after the appropriate control is activated because there's no reason to continue the procedure after an error has been encountered.

This If statement gives you the basic template for validating controls. If there aren't any invalid entries, the form is removed from memory and displayed using the Unload statement.

Using Return Values

There's still one problem with the cmdSave_Click procedure. How do you get the form's entries to a worksheet? You are going to use the contents of the Text and Value properties on the form and apply them to a worksheet. Use the following steps to modify the cmdSave_Click procedure:

1. Go to Sheet3 of your workbook. (Add a Sheet3 if your workbook doesn't have one.) Rename Sheet3 as Guest Expenses.
2. Go to the Visual Basic Editor and display the UserForm.
3. Double-click the Save button to display the Code window.
4. Insert the following code before the last statement in the cmdSave_Click procedure. It is very important that this code goes before the Unload Me statement:

```
Worksheets("Guest Expenses").Activate
Range("A2").Select
If Range("A2").Value = "" Then
    Range("A2").Activate
Else
    Range("A2").CurrentRegion.Select
    ActiveCell.Offset(Selection.Rows.Count, 0).Activate
```

```
      End If
With ActiveCell
      .Value = txtRoomNumber.Text
      .Offset(0, 1).Value = txtGuestName.Text
      .Offset(0, 2).Value = lstExpenseType.Text
      .Offset(0, 3).Value = txtAmount.Text
      .Offset(0, 4).Value = txtDate.Text
      If chkTipIncluded.Value = True Then
            .Offset(0, 5).Value = txtTipAmount.Text
      End If
      If optBillToRoom.Value = True Then
            .Offset(0, 6).Value = "Room"
      ElseIf optCash.Value = True Then
            .Offset(0, 6).Value = "Cash"
      ElseIf optCheck.Value = True Then
            .Offset(0, 6).Value = "Check"
      ElseIf optCreditCard.Value = True Then
            .Offset(0, 6).Value = "Credit card"
            .Offset(0, 7).Value = lstCardType.Text
            .Offset(0, 8).Value = txtCardNumber.Text
            .Offset(0, 9).Value = txtExpires.Text
      End If
End With
```

5. Go to Sheet1 in your workbook.

6. Save your workbook. It is always a good idea to save your workbook before running a procedure that enters data in it.

7. Click the Guest Expenses button. Enter 430 for the room number. Enter your name for the guest. Select Golf Lesson as the expense type. Enter 100 for the amount. Place a check in the Include Tip check box. Enter 10 as the tip amount. Select the Credit Card option button. Select Visa as the card type. Enter 112233 for the card number. Enter 1/1/00 for when the card expires. Click Save.

The form's entries are written to the Guest Expenses worksheet, as shown in Figure 15.6. Now take a moment to look at some of the code you entered. The first thing you did was determine where to start entering data on the worksheet:

```
Worksheets("Guest Expenses").Activate
Range("A2").Select
If Range("A2").Value = "" Then
    Range("A2").Activate
Else
    Range("A2").CurrentRegion.Select
    ActiveCell.Offset(Selection.Rows.Count, 0).Activate
End If
```

The Guest Expenses worksheet was activated and then Range A2. Range A2 is your starting point because the first row of this worksheet contains headings. The next step tests to see whether there is a value in Range A2. If not, A2 is your starting point for

15

entry. Otherwise, you have to find the last cell. This is where `CurrentRegion` comes into play. By selecting the current region, you can find out how many rows have already been entered and use that information to locate your entry starting point.

After you get your starting point, you use the `Offset` property to enter values going across the row. If the Credit Card option button is selected, you'll have additional entries to make.

There's just one more thing to do to your form. You need to write the code for the Cancel button using these steps:

1. Go to the Visual Basic Editor and double-click the Cancel button to open the Code window.

2. Enter the following code for the `cmdCancel_Click` procedure:

   ```
   Unload Me
   ```

3. Save the workbook.

If the user clicks Cancel, you want to unload the form so that it is now longer displayed and is removed from memory. In real life, you would probably have a message box asking whether the user is sure that he wants to cancel.

Summary

Now you're done! You've created a full-featured dialog box that performs data validation and returns the values to a worksheet. Congratulations!

In the last hour, you focused on the design of the UserForm. This hour you focused on automating the form. You've seen the entire form automation from start to finish. You know how to display a form, initialize its value, validate the form's input, and write that input to a worksheet.

Q&A

Q How do I know which control property to write to my worksheet?

A Here's a summary for you:

Control	Property
Label	Caption
Text Box	Text
List Box	Text

Control	Property
Combo Box	Text
Option Button	Value
Check Box	Value
Spin Button	Value

Q I placed the values used by my list boxes on a worksheet. What if I don't want my users to change or view these lists?

A You have a copy of options. One is to hide the worksheet via the Format, Sheet menu. Another is to set the sheet's Visible property to False in the workbook's Auto_Open procedure.

Workshop

The quiz questions and exercise are provided for your further understanding. See Appendix A, "Answers," for the answers.

Quiz

1. How do you disable a control?
2. How do you display a form?
3. In which procedure do you place form initialization code?
4. How do you remove a form from memory?
5. If you need to return to a control via code, what method do you use?
6. Where do I store the values used by controls like list boxes?
7. Which list box property controls which list item is displayed?
8. Name a place to put validation code.

Exercise

Create a procedure named ShowSplash. The ShowSplash procedure needs to display frmSplash.

Enter the necessary code for the cmdOK button on frmSplash to display the frmGuestExpenses form.

Go to Sheet1 of the Guest Expenses workbook. Assign ShowSplash to the command button on that form. Run and test your application.

HOUR 16

Toolbars

This hour is broken into two main topics: working with toolbars manually and working with toolbars using code. Toolbars are important to most users as an interface with Excel's commands. You can create your own toolbar buttons and assign your procedures to them. This gives your user a familiar and convenient way to execute your macros.

The highlights of this hour include

- Manually adding buttons to toolbars
- Creating new toolbars without code
- Working with toolbars using code

Modifying Toolbars Manually

I'm always surprised to find out how few users of Excel know how to create new toolbars and how to add buttons to toolbars. Toolbars are arguably the most visual part of the Excel application window. Up to this point, you've used two techniques for executing your procedures (not counting the F5 key or the Run menu). You've executed a macro after it has been assigned to a control. You've also executed a macro by selecting Tools, Macro, Macros. If you don't to want to use a control to execute a menu, and you are tired of going to the Tools menu to run a macro, you can assign a procedure to a toolbar button.

The first thing you are going to do is add a toolbar button to an existing toolbar. Microsoft provides you with several images you can use for the face of your toolbar button or you can create your own image. Use the following steps to add a toolbar button to a toolbar and assign a macro to the button:

1. Open the Guest Expenses workbook.

2. Right-click a toolbar and select Customize from the pop-up menu. The Customize dialog box displays (see Figure 16.1).

FIGURE 16.1

The Customize dialog box is used to customize toolbars and menus.

3. Select Macros from the Categories list box on the Commands tab. In the Commands list box, you'll see the Custom Button entry.

4. Drag the Custom button to one of your existing toolbars. As you move over the toolbar, you'll notice a black bar following your movement on the toolbar. This black bar denotes where the toolbar button will be placed if you release your mouse button.

5. After you are satisfied with the location of your new toolbar button, release your mouse. The button is added to the toolbar, as shown in Figure 16.2.

6. Right-click the new toolbar button. Select Name from the pop-up menu. Enter Guest Expenses for the name of the button. The name entered is used for the button's ToolTip.

7. Right-click the new button again. Select Change Button Image. A selection of button images displays (see Figure 16.3). Select the image you want. The button's image is changed to match your selection.

FIGURE 16.2

The default image for a new macro button is a smiley face.

New button

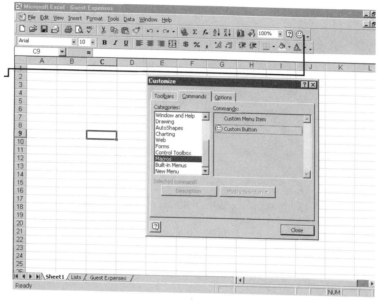

FIGURE 16.3

Excel provides you with several images for your macro buttons.

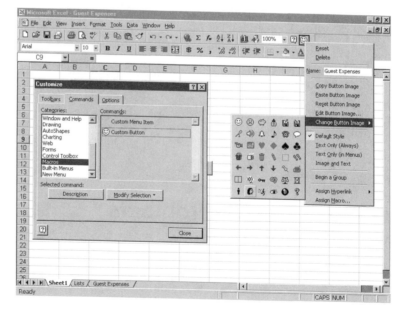

16

8. Right-click the new button again. Select Assign Macro. Assign ShowGuestExpenses to the button.

9. Close the Customize dialog.

10. Click the new Guest Expenses toolbar button. The Guest Expenses form displays.

11. Click Cancel to dismiss the form.

Now you need to find out about the problem with what we just did. This toolbar button is now available to all workbooks. This means that if you were in another workbook and clicked this button, the Guest Expenses dialog would display. In reality, you would only assign macros or procedures to toolbar buttons using this techniques if they were supposed to be used in all workbooks. For example, the macros and procedures located in your PERSONAL workbook would be good candidates for toolbar button assignments.

Because of this issue, you probably want to delete the toolbar button. To do so, complete the following steps:

1. Right-click a toolbar and select Customize from the pop-up menu.

2. Now that the Customize dialog is open, you can delete a button. Drag the Guest Expenses toolbar button back to the Customize dialog. This removes the toolbar button from the toolbar.

3. Close the Customize dialog.

If you've made several changes to your built-in toolbars and want to undo them all, go to the Toolbars tab of the Customize dialog. Select from the Toolbars list box the toolbar from which you want to remove all changes. Click the Reset button. The toolbar is reset and is now as it was when you installed Excel.

Creating Custom Toolbars

You aren't limited to adding toolbar buttons to just the existing toolbars. You can also create custom toolbars. You might want to, for example, create a custom toolbar that can be used to execute all the macros and procedures for your application. Later this hour, you'll learn how to show and hide toolbars, which means you can have control over when the toolbar is available, and therefore when the toolbar buttons are available. To create a new custom toolbar, complete the following steps:

1. Right-click a toolbar.

2. Select Customize from the pop-up menu.

3. Select the Toolbars tab.

4. Click New. The New Toolbar dialog displays.

5. Enter MyToolbar for the name of the new toolbar and press Enter.

6. Click Close to dismiss the dialog box.

The new toolbar appears as a small gray box, as shown in Figure 16.4. As you add toolbar buttons to the toolbar, it will grow in size. Add toolbar buttons to a custom toolbar using the same technique that you used earlier in this hour.

16

FIGURE 16.4

When a toolbar is first created, it is empty.

New, empty toolbar

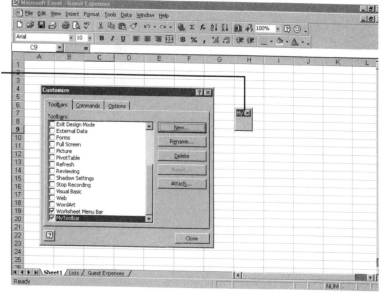

Working with Toolbars in Code

Toolbars can also be created using code. You can create toolbars, add buttons to them, display them, hide them, and delete them all using VBA. There is a major advantage to using code to create and maintain toolbars. Code allows you to create the toolbar when the workbook opens and then to delete the toolbar when the workbook closes. This means that the toolbar and its buttons will only be available while the workbook is open.

Creating a Toolbar

Your first reaction on the subject of how to create a toolbar using VBA code might be to use the Add method to create a new toolbar in the Toolbars collection. You're half right. You are going to use the Add method, but there's no such thing as a Toolbars collection.

Toolbars are grouped with menu bars and shortcut menus and are referred to as CommandBars. Think of CommandBars as a collection of commands and you'll understand why toolbars and menu bars are grouped together. So to create a toolbar, you are going to use the Add method of the CommandBars collection.

After you create a CommandBar, the next step is to add toolbar buttons. To do this you use the Controls collection's Add method. To create a new toolbar with a toolbar button on it, use the following steps:

1. Open the Guest Expenses workbook.

2. Press Alt+F11 to open the Visual Basic Editor.

3. Create a new procedure called CustomTB.

4. Enter the following code for the procedure:

```
Dim ctlGEButton As Object
ThisWorkbook.Activate

Application.CommandBars.Add Name:="GuestTB"
CommandBars("GuestTB").Visible = True
Set ctlGEButton = Application.CommandBars("GuestTB").Controls.Add _
    (Type:=msoControlButton, ID:=2950, Before:=1)
With ctlGEButton
    .FaceId = 2141
    .OnAction = "ShowGuestExpenses"
End With
```

5. Run the procedure. The new toolbar is created.

6. Click the button on the GuestTB toolbar. The Guest Expenses dialog box displays.

7. Click Cancel to dismiss the dialog.

> If you want to run this procedure again, you'll need to delete the GuestTB toolbar by right-clicking a toolbar and selecting Customize. The toolbar can be deleted from the Toolbars tab.

Now it is time to analyze what you did. The first thing you did was create an object variable:

```
Dim ctlGEButton As Object
```

Next, you activate the workbook because the toolbar being created is created for the workbook's use:

```
ThisWorkbook.Activate
```

Next, you created the toolbar and set its `Visible` property to `True` so the toolbar would display:

```
Application.CommandBars.Add Name:="GuestTB"
CommandBars("GuestTB").Visible = True
```

After that, you created a button on the form. You set it to be a control button. The `ID` argument used refers to the button. The Custom Macro button's ID is 2950.

```
Set ctlGEButton = Application.CommandBars("GuestTB").Controls.Add _
    (Type:=msoControlButton, ID:=2950
```

There are several different values you can provide the `Type` argument. The following argument values correspond to the type of toolbar buttons that can be created:

- `msoControlButton`
- `msoControlEdit`
- `msoControlDropdown`
- `msoControlComboBox`
- `msoControlPopup`

Next, you set some of the button's properties, specifically the `FaceID` and `OnAction` properties. The `FaceID` sets the image on the button. The `OnAction` property assigns the macro to the button:

```
With ctlGEButton
    .FaceId = 2141
    .OnAction = "ShowGuestExpenses"
End With
```

You might be wondering how I figured out the number I needed for the `FaceID` property. I used code, of course! I first created a button with the image I wanted to use on GuestTB toolbar. Then I ran the procedure shown in Listing 16.1.

LISTING 16.1   The `FindOut` Procedure

```
1: Sub FindOut()
2:     MsgBox CommandBars("GuestTB").Controls(1).FaceId
3: End Sub
```

If you want a toolbar to be created when you open the workbook, you need to place its code in the `Auto_Open` procedure. You can find out more about the `Auto_Open` procedure in Hour 24, "Running Procedures."

Deleting a Toolbar

If you no longer want a toolbar to be part of the Excel environment, remove it using the `Delete` method. The following steps create the procedure for deleting the GuestTB:

1. Create a new procedure named `DeleteGuestTB`.

2. Enter the following code for the procedure:

```
ThisWorkbook.Activate
CommandBars("GuestTB").Delete
```

3. Run the procedure. The GuestTB is deleted.

Summary

Toolbars are one of the most popular ways for a user to interface with Excel as well as your own applications. You can use Excel built-in features to create custom toolbars or you can use VBA to create, modify, and delete toolbars that are specifically designed to work with your automation solution.

In the next hour, you are going to work with another important part of Excel's interface—the menu system. You'll learn techniques to manipulation the built-in menus and to create a menu from scratch using code.

Q&A

Q When looking at the Object Browser, I can't find an object named `Toolbar`. Why?

A Toolbars are actually a type of object called a `CommandBar`. Another example of a `CommandBar` is a menu bar.

Q What if I don't want to use one of the predefined images for my toolbar? Can I create my own image?

A Yes, Excel provides a button editor. To access the button editor, right-click a toolbar and select Customize. While the Customize dialog box is open, right-click on the button whose image you want to modify. Select Edit Button Image.

Workshop

The quiz questions and exercise are provided for your further understanding. See Appendix A, "Answers" for the answers.

Quiz

1. What collection do toolbars belong to?

2. Which property is used to assign a macro to a toolbar button?

3. Name the collection that toolbar buttons belong to.

4. What method do you use to remove a toolbar?

5. How do you display a toolbar using VBA code?

6. Which property is used to control the image displayed on a toolbar button?

7. True or False. A toolbar automatically displays when it is created.

Exercise

Create a procedure named Hour16Toolbar. This procedure needs to create and display a new toolbar named Hour16 that has 3 buttons on it: New (ID is 2520), Open (ID is 23), and Save (ID is 3).

Create another procedure named DeleteTB that deletes the Hour16 toolbar. Run and test your procedures.

16

HOUR 17

Menus

In the last hour, you learned that toolbars are by definition an alternative method of menu command execution. Now that you know how to modify toolbars, you are probably wondering how to do the same thing to menus. In this hour, you'll be working with menus manually and programmatically.

The highlights of this hour include

- Learning to modify menus manually
- Creating menu bars, menus, and menu items using VBA code
- Displaying and deleting menu bars

Modifying Menus Manually

When you are working with menus, you are actually working with three objects: the container, menus, and menu items. The container, just as it was with toolbars, is called a command bar. It is also called a menu bar. Within the command bar are menus. Examples of menus include File, Edit, and Help. Within menus are menu items. For example, the File menu contains menu items such as Open, Save, and Print.

When working with manually customizing menus, you can add menus and menu items. You can add predefined menus and menu items, or you can create your own custom entries. To create a new menu and menu item that can be used to execute a macro, complete the following steps:

1. Open the Guest Expenses workbook.

2. Right-click the menu bar. Select Customize. The Customize dialog displays.

3. Select the Commands tab. A list of available menu categories and commands displays (see Figure 17.1).

FIGURE 17.1

In the Categories list box, you'll see familiar menus listed.

4. In the Categories list, locate and select New Menu. In the Commands list box, you'll see New Menu.

5. Drag New Menu from the Commands list box. You want to place New Menu between the Data and Window menus. When it is correctly positioned, you'll see a black vertical bar between the two menus.

6. Release your mouse button to drop the menu in its new location. The newly menu is shown in Figure 17.2.

7. After adding the menu, the next step is to rename it. Right-click on New Menu. Select Name. For this menu's name, enter &Guest.

   The & before the G designates the G as the accelerator key for this menu.

8. The next step is to add a new menu item to the Guest menu. Select New Menu again from the Commands list box. Drag it to the Guest menu. When you drag over the Guest menu, a gray box appears below the Guest menu. Drag the new menu into this box. When correctly positioned, a vertical black line appears in this box, as shown in Figure 17.3. Release your mouse button to create the new menu item.

FIGURE 17.2

When a new menu is first added to the menu bar, its caption is New Menu.

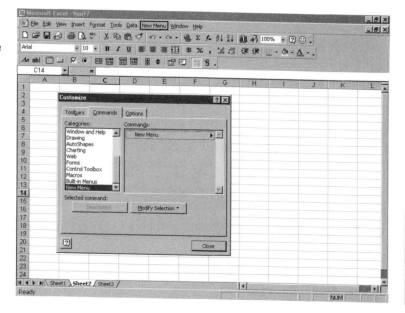

Technically, you could assign a macro to the Guest menu. However, the accepted standard for interface design is that menu items, not menus, execute commands.

FIGURE 17.3

The box that appears below the Guest menu denotes that the menu is currently empty.

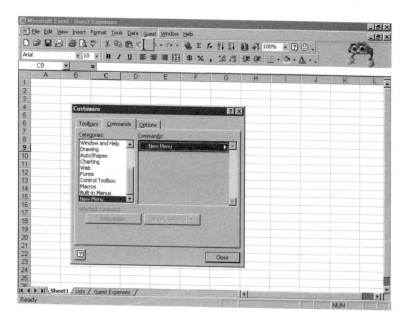

9. Right-click New Menu and select Rename.

10. Enter &Expenses for the name.

11. You are now ready to assign a macro to the Expenses menu item. Right-click Expenses and select Assign Macro. The Assign Macro dialog displays.

12. Select the ShowSplash macro and click OK.

13. Click Close to close the Customize dialog box.

After you close the Customize dialog box, you are ready to use the new menu. Select Guest, Expenses. The Welcome dialog displays. Click OK and then click Cancel. You now have yet another way to start your application!

Working with Menus Programmatically

Adding a menu bar using VBA is very much like a toolbar. As a matter of fact, you add an item to the same collection, called the CommandBars collection. The basic syntax for adding a menu bar is as follows:

```
CommandBars.Add(Name, Position, MenuBar, Temporary)
```

The *Name* argument contains the name of the new command bar. Surprisingly, the *Name* argument is optional. If you don't provide a value for this argument, a default name is assigned to the command bar such as Custom 1.

Position is another optional argument. This allows you to select the position or type of the new command bar.

Because you are creating menu bars, you need to set the *MenuBar* argument to True. Setting this argument to True replaces the active menu bar with the new command bar. The default value is False.

The last argument, *Temporary*, is also optional. Set this to True to make the new command bar temporary. Temporary command bars are deleted when the container application is closed. The default value is False. You might want to set this to True in your own applications so that you don't leave stray menu bars in the environment.

You are going to start your menu bar exploration by creating a menu and displaying it instead of the Worksheet menu. To create a custom menu close any open workbooks and open a new workbook. The access the Visual Basic Editor by pressing Alt+F11. Insert a module in this workbook. Complete the following steps:

1. Create a new procedure named MyFirstMenubar.

2. Enter the following code for the procedure:

```
Dim mybar As CommandBar

Set mybar = CommandBars.Add(Name:="Hour17", _
    Position:=msoBarTop, MenuBar:=True, temporary:=True)
mybar.Visible = True
CommandBars("Worksheet Menu Bar").Visible = False
```

3. Create another procedure named UndoMyMenu.

4. Enter the following code for the procedure:

```
CommandBars("Hour17").Delete
```

5. Go to your workbook. Create a command button on Sheet1. Assign MyFirstMenubar as its macro. Set its caption to My Menu.

6. Create another command button. Assign UndoMyMenu as its macro. Set its caption to Default Menu.

17

7. Click the My Menu button. A blank menu displays instead of the default worksheet menu, as shown in Figure 17.4.

FIGURE 17.4

The gray bar at the top of this window is actually an empty menu bar.

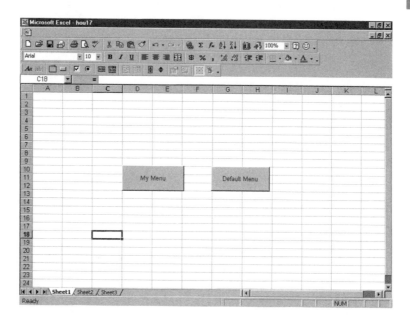

8. Click the Default Menu button. The Worksheet menu returns.

By completing the previous steps you have seen how to display custom and built-in menus. Not only did you display a custom menu but you created the custom menu using Vba code. Listing 17.1 shows the complete procedure for `MyFirstMenu`. Take a moment to study the code used.

LISTING 17.1   The `MyFirstMenu` Procedure

```
1: Sub MyFirstMenu()
2:     Dim mybar As CommandBar
3:
4:     Set mybar = CommandBars.Add(Name:="Hour17", _
           Position:=msoBarTop, MenuBar:=True, temporary:=True)
5:     mybar.Visible = True
6:     CommandBars("Worksheet Menu Bar").Visible = False
7:
8: End Sub
```

The first thing you did in this procedure was create an object variable that is set during the `Add` method that creates the menu bar:

```
Dim mybar As CommandBar

Set mybar = CommandBars.Add(Name:="Hour17", _
    Position:=msoBarTop, MenuBar:=True, temporary:=True)
```

After the menu bar is created, you display it by setting its `Visible` property to `True`. You also set the `Visible` property of the Worksheet menu bar to `False` so that it doesn't display:

```
mybar.Visible = True
CommandBars("Worksheet Menu Bar").Visible = False
```

That's all there is to creating the menu bar. When you no longer want the menu bar, you use the `Delete` method to discard it. The next step is to add menus to your menu bar.

Adding Menus and Menu Items

The next step in menu creation is to add menus and menu items. To do this, you'll use the `Add` method of the `Controls` collection:

```
NameOfMenu.Controls.Add(Type, Id, Parameter, Before, Temporary)
```

As you probably guessed, `NameOfMenu` needs to be replaced with the name of the menu bar you are adding the menu to. The `Type` argument's value needs to be `msoControlPopup` for menus.

The value of the *Id* depends on what type of menu you are adding. If it is a custom menu, the value needs to be 1. If it is a built-in menu, the value of *Id* needs to be the integer that specifies the desired menu. How do you find out what this integer is? Actually, the easiest way is to begin recording a macro and add the menu that you want to the menu bar. The recorded menu will have the integer value you need.

> To add a built-in menu to a menu bar, right-click the menu bar and select Customize. Go to the Commands tab. In the Categories list box, locate and select Built-in Menus. After it is selected, the built-in menus are shown in the Commands list box. Drag the desired menu to the menu bar. The menu is added to the menu bar and includes all of its menu items.

17

The *Parameter* argument is optional, and its value is dependent on the type of menu you are working with. If it is a built-in menu, you probably don't need to provide a value for this argument. If it is a custom menu, you can use this argument to send information to Visual Basic procedures. You can also use it to store information about the control.

The optional *Before* argument's value is a number that represents the position of the new control on the menu bar. The menu (or menu item) is inserted before the control at the provided position. If you don't provide a value for this argument, the menu or menu item is added at the end.

If you want the menu or menu item to be temporary, set the value of the optional *Temporary* argument to `True`. The todefault value for this argument is `False`.

> If you want to add a menu to the active menu bar, use the `CommandBars` collection's `ActiveMenuBar` property to return the name of the active menu bar. An example of using this property is
>
> ```
> Set CurrMenuBar = CommandBars.ActiveMenuBar
> ```

Sometimes you might want to customize your menu so you can launch a simple procedure. The next exercise will show you how to do this. You will be adding the File menu and a custom menu to the Hour 17 menu bar. First, you need to modify the MyFirstMenu procedure to add menus to the commandbar. Then you'll add a menu item to the menu. Modify the `MyFirstMenu` so that it matches the one in Listing 17.2. (Note: Changes are in bold.)

LISTING 17.2   The Modified MyFirstMenu Procedure

```
 1: Sub MyFirstMenu()
 2:     Dim mybar As CommandBar
 3:     Dim mymenu As Object
 4:     Dim mymenuitem As Object
 5:
 6:     Set mybar = CommandBars.Add(Name:="Hour17", _
                Position:=msoBarTop, MenuBar:=True, _
 7: Temporary:=True)
 8:
 9:     mybar.Controls.Add Type:=msoControlPopup, ID:=30002, Before:=1
10:
11:     Set mymenu = mybar.Controls.Add(Type:=msoControlPopup, _
12:         Temporary:=True)
13:     mymenu.Caption = "Hour 17"
14:
15:     Set mymenuitem = mymenu.Controls.Add(Type:=msoControlButton, ID:=1)
16:     mymenuitem.Caption = "Macro Demo"
17:     mymenuitem.Style = msoButtonCaption
18:     mymenuitem.OnAction = "ShowMe"
19:
20:     mybar.Visible = True
21:     CommandBars("Worksheet Menu Bar").Visible = False
22: End Sub
```

You need to create a new procedure. For this example, name it, ShowMe. Enter the following code tofor this procedure:

```
MsgBox "It Works!"
```

Now return to Sheet1 of your workbook, and run the program by clicking the My Menu button. Your menu bar now has menus, as shown by Figure 17.5.

Select the Hour 17 menu, and then select Macro Demo. The message box displays. Click OK to dismiss the message box. Next, click the Default Menu button to return the Worksheet menu bar, and save your workbook as Hour 17.

Taking a moment to analyze the changes to the MyFirstMenu procedure. You will see that you created two new object variables:

```
Dim mymenu As Object
Dim mymenuitem As Object
```

The next new line in the procedure added the File menu. To get the value for the ID property, I recorded a macro that added the File menu. The File menu is the first menu on this menu bar, so its Before argument's value is 1:

```
mybar.Controls.Add Type:=msoControlPopup, ID:=30002, Before:=1
```

FIGURE 17.5

The menu bar is no longer empty.

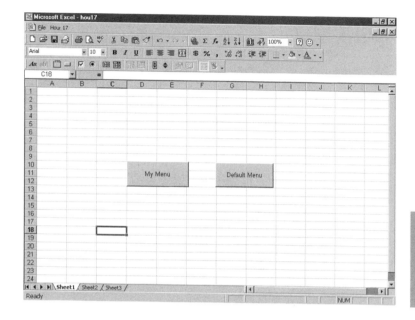

The next menu added is a custom menu:

```
Set mymenu = mybar.Controls.Add(Type:=msoControlPopup, _
Temporary:=True)
mymenu.Caption = "Hour 17"
```

After adding the custom menu, a custom menu item is added:

```
Set mymenuitem = mymenu.Controls.Add(Type:=msoControlButton, ID:=1)
```

The custom menu items needs several properties set. The Caption property is the text displayed for the menu item. The Style is set to msoButtonCaption because it is a menu item that has only display text. Menu items don't have icons associated with them. The OnAction property is set to the procedure that needs to run when the menu item is selected:

```
mymenuitem.Caption = "Macro Demo"
mymenuitem.Style = msoButtonCaption
mymenuitem.OnAction = "ShowMe"
```

Now you know how to add a menu and menu item to your menu bar. Whether you are adding a menu or menu item, you are working with the Controls collection. The trick is understanding which object you are adding the control to. In the case of a menu, you are adding a control to the menu bar. In the case of a menu item, you are adding a control to a menu.

Summary

The key to working with menus using VBA code is the `Add` method. To create a menu bar, a menu, or a menu item, you are using the `Add` method. You worked with two collections in this hour: the `CommandBars` collection and the `Controls` collection. As you now know, working with menus is very similar to working with toolbars. The differences come into play with argument values and property settings.

Q&A

Q **When working with toolbars, I used the `CommandBars` collection and the `Controls` collection. I'm doing the same thing with menus. Why?**

A As far as Excel (and Office, for that matter) is concerned, menu bars and toolbars are both members of the `CommandBars` collection. Menus, menu items, and toolbar buttons are all members of the `Controls` collection. This actually makes sense if you think of it. Menu bars and toolbars are containers for controls that are used to execute commands.

Q **What if I wanted to make a menu or menu item unavailable during my application's run? How would I do that?**

A By setting the menu or menu item's `Enabled` property to `False`, of course!

Workshop

The quiz questions and exercise are provided for your further understanding. See Appendix A, "Answers," for the answers.

Quiz

1. What method do you use to create a menu?
2. What property of a custom control (menu item) do you assign a procedure to?
3. What type of control is a menu?
4. How do you get rid of a menu using VBA code?
5. What dialog box must be open for you to modify menus?
6. When creating a command bar using the Add method, what property is used to automatically delete the command bar when the container application is closed?
7. How to you display a menu bar?

Exercise

Using VBA code, create a custom menu named Exercise17 that contains the File, Edit, and Help menus, and display the newly created menu bar. Create another procedure that deletes the Exercise17 menu. Add another sheet to your workbook if needed. On Sheet2, add two command buttons: one to execute the procedure that creates the menu bar and another to execute the procedure to delete the menu bar. Run and test your procedures.

17

Hour **18**

Charts

One of the most popular features of Excel is its charting abilities. Obviously, you'll want to use this feature in your own applications. In this hour, you'll record the steps of chart creation and then modify the generated code using the Visual Basic Editor.

The highlights of this hour include

- Recording the chart creation process
- Editing the recorded code
- Executing the code you modified
- Creating a more sophisticated chart example

Creating Charts

As a user of Excel, you are probably familiar with creating a chart. Basically, if you know how to create a chart, you have the skills you need to automate a chart. "Why?" you might ask. Because you are going to record most of the process and then tweak the recorded code as necessary.

Using the Chart Wizard and the Macro Recorder

The first thing you need to do after you know what you want to chart is to turn the macro recorder on. You are going to create the desired chart and make any necessary format changes. Then, turn the macro recorder off and look at your code. Let's create a pie chart. First, make sure you have closed all workbooks. Next, open a new workbook and enter the data from Table 18.1.

TABLE 18.1 Data to Be Charted

Cell	Value
A1	Item
A2	Apples
A3	Bananas
A4	Oranges
A5	Lemons
A6	Pears
B1	Sales
B2	1250
B3	795
B4	1400
B5	1000
B6	1550

Go ahead and make the cells A1 through B1 bold. The completed worksheet is shown in Figure 18.1.

Next, select range A1:B6 and go to Tools, Macro, Record New Macro. Name the macro MyPieChart and store it in this workbook. You are now ready to begin recording the macro.

First, start your Chart Wizard and select Pie for the Chart type. Follow steps 2 and 3 by clicking Next and then selecting the Data Labels tab. Select Show Percent and click Next to show the last dialog in the Chart Wizard.

Your chart is now finished, but you should customize and rename the chart by selecting the chart's title, which is Sales. Right-click the title and select Format Chart Title.

FIGURE 18.1

This worksheet's data will be used to create a chart.

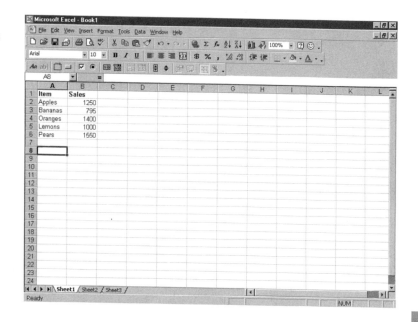

Select the Font tab and make the font 14 points, bold, and italic. After you close the Format dialog, stop recording the macro. You should see the completed chart as shown in Figure 18.2.

FIGURE 18.2

This pie chart was created using the Chart Wizard.

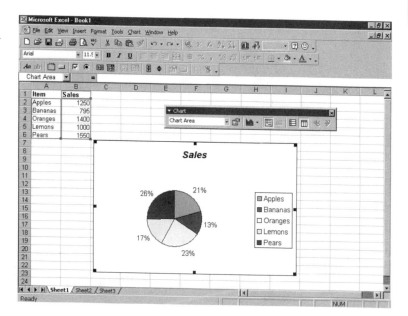

That was easy! Now you need to learn how to edit what you just recorded to maximize what the macro does for you.

Editing the Recorded Code

You can now go to the Visual Basic Editor and see your code by pressing Alt+F11. You might need to expand the current workbook in the Project Explorer and open the Module folder to locate the procedure. Listing 18.1 shows the complete recorded macro.

LISTING 18.1   The MyPieChart Procedure

```
 1: Sub MyPieChart()
 2:     Charts.Add
 3:     ActiveChart.ChartType = xlPie
 4:     ActiveChart.SetSourceData _
 5:         Source:=Sheets("Sheet1").Range("A1:B6"), PlotBy:= xlColumns
 6:     ActiveChart.Location Where:=xlLocationAsObject, Name:="Sheet1"
 7:     ActiveChart.ApplyDataLabels _
            Type:=xlDataLabelsShowPercent, LegendKey:=False _
 8:         , HasLeaderLines:=True
 9:     ActiveChart.ChartTitle.Select
10:     Selection.AutoScaleFont = True
11:     With Selection.Font
12:         .Name = "Arial"
13:         .FontStyle = "Bold Italic"
14:         .Size = 14
15:         .Strikethrough = False
16:         .Superscript = False
17:         .Subscript = False
18:         .OutlineFont = False
19:         .Shadow = False
20:         .Underline = xlUnderlineStyleNone
21:         .ColorIndex = xlAutomatic
22:         .Background = xlAutomatic
23:     End With
24: End Sub
```

The very first action recorded translated into the Add method on the Charts collection:

Charts.Add

This lets you know immediately the collection and the object type you've created. After it is created, the rest of the recorded macro sets properties and executes methods. The ActiveChart referred to in the procedure is a property of the Application object that returns the currently active chart. The ChartType property is set to xlPie (line 3), which is the Excel constant value for a pie chart. You can see in this code (line 4) that the SetSourceData method is executed next and the source is your selected range. The Location method in this example is used to place the chart on the current sheet. Finally, the chart's ApplyDataLabels method is executed and passed the necessary argument values to show percentages by the pie sections.

The next object that is manipulated in this procedure is ChartTitle. ChartTitle is first selected and then its font is changed. Notice that even though you only changed the size and made it bold and italic, all font options on the dialog box were recorded in the macro in lines 9–22.

Executing the Modified Chart Code

You've now recorded and modified the code. To see what happens if the macro is executed again, complete the following steps:

1. Select range A1:B3.
2. Run the MyPieChart macro. Did you notice that even though you had just three rows selected, you got the pie chart for all six rows?
3. Delete all the pie charts on the worksheet.
4. Take a look at the MyPieChart procedure. The reason you are getting all six row charts, no matter what you have selected, is because of the following statement:
   ```
   ActiveChart.SetSourceData _
               Source:=Sheets("Sheet1").Range("A1:B6"), PlotBy:= _
       XlColumns
   ```
5. At the top of the MyPieChart procedure, enter the following lines of code:
   ```
   Dim rCurrentRange As Range
   Set rCurrentRange = Selection
   ```
6. Replace Sheets("Sheet1").Range("A1:B6") in this statement with rCurrentRange. The corrected line should appear as
   ```
   ActiveChart.SetSourceData Source:=rCurrentRange, PlotBy:= _
       XlColumns
   ```
7. Return to your workbook.
8. Select Range A1:B3. Run the MyPieChart macro. The resulting pie chart has just two pie sections (see Figure 18.3).

18

FIGURE **18.3**

By using the Selection property, you can make your procedure more flexible.

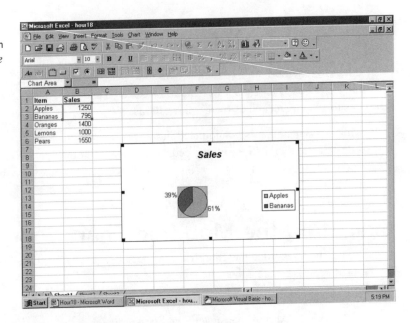

A More Sophisticated Chart Example

The next chart code example will analyze the selection made and determine whether its type should be pie or column. If the selected data has two columns, it is going to be a pie chart. If it has more than two columns, it is going to be a column chart. Complete the following steps:

1. Enter the following values from Table 18.2 in your worksheet:

TABLE **18.2**   Pie Chart Data

Cell	Value
C1	2nd Qtr
C2	1000
C3	1150
C4	875
C5	1270
C6	1395

2. Make C1 bold. Also change the value of B1 to 1st Qtr.

3. Delete any charts on the sheet and select Range A1:C6.

4. Select Tools, Macro, Record New Macro. Name the macro MyColumnChart and store it in this workbook. Click OK to begin recording.

5. Click the Chart Wizard toolbar button. The Chart Wizard begins.

6. Select Column as the Chart type. Click Finish to create the chart.

7. Stop recording the macro.

You now have two macros, MyPieChart and MyColumnChart. You are going to combine these two procedures into another new procedure that will pick the appropriate chart type based on the number of columns in the selected range. Press Alt+F11 to go to the Visual Basic Editor and create a new procedure named MyChart. Enter the code for the MyChart procedure:

```
Dim rCurrentRange As Range
Set rCurrentRange = Selection

If Selection.Columns.Count = 2 Then
```

To save yourself some time go to the MyPieChart procedure and copy the following lines:

```
Charts.Add
ActiveChart.ChartType = xlPie
ActiveChart.SetSourceData Source:=rCurrentRange, PlotBy:= _
    XlColumns
ActiveChart.Location Where:=xlLocationAsObject, Name:="Sheet1"
ActiveChart.ApplyDataLabels Type:=xlDataLabelsShowPercent, LegendKey:=False _
    , HasLeaderLines:=True
```

> Don't forget that the standard shortcut keys for cut (Ctrl+X), copy (Ctrl+C), and paste (Ctrl+V) work in the Visual Basic Editor.

18

Paste these lines on a blank line following the If statement in the MyChart procedure. On a new line after the pasted code in the MyChart procedure, enter the following:

```
ElseIf Selection.Columns.Count > 2 Then
```

Go to the MyColumnChart procedure and copy the following lines:

```
Charts.Add
ActiveChart.ChartType = xlColumnClustered
ActiveChart.SetSourceData Source:=Sheets("Sheet1").Range("A1:C6")
ActiveChart.Location Where:=xlLocationAsObject, Name:="Sheet1"
```

Paste these lines on a blank line following the `ElseIf` statement in the `MyChart` procedure. In the ActiveChart.SetSourceData line that you just pasted, replace Sheets("Sheet1").Range("A1:C6") with rCurrentRange. On a new line after the pasted code in the `MyChart` procedure, enter the following:

```
Else
    MsgBox "Selection is not suitable for a chart."
    Exit Sub
End If

With ActiveChart
    .HasTitle = True
    .ChartTitle.Characters.Text = "Sales"
    .ChartTitle.Select
End With
```

Now copy the following lines from the `MyPieChart` procedure:

```
Selection.AutoScaleFont = True
With Selection.Font
    .Name = "Arial"
    .FontStyle = "Bold Italic"
    .Size = 14
    .Strikethrough = False
    .Superscript = False
    .Subscript = False
    .OutlineFont = False
    .Shadow = False
    .Underline = xlUnderlineStyleNone
    .ColorIndex = xlAutomatic
    .Background = xlAutomatic
End With
```

Paste the copied lines on a blank line after the `End With` statement in the `MyChart` procedure. The completed procedure is shown in Listing 18.2.

LISTING 18.2   The Completed MyChart Procedure

```
 1: Sub MyChart()
 2:     Dim rCurrentRange As Range
 3:     Set rCurrentRange = Selection
 4:
 5:     If Selection.Columns.Count = 2 Then
 6:         Charts.Add
 7:         ActiveChart.ChartType = xlPie
 8:         ActiveChart.SetSourceData Source:=rCurrentRange, PlotBy:= _
 9:             xlColumns
10:         ActiveChart.Location Where:=xlLocationAsObject, Name:="Sheet1"
11:         ActiveChart.ApplyDataLabels _
```

```
                    Type:=xlDataLabelsShowPercent, LegendKey:=False _
12:                    , HasLeaderLines:=True
13:        ElseIf Selection.Columns.Count > 2 Then
14:            Charts.Add
15:            ActiveChart.ChartType = xlColumnClustered
16:            ActiveChart.SetSourceData Source:=rCurrentRange
17:            ActiveChart.Location Where:=xlLocationAsObject, Name:="Sheet1"
18:        Else
19:            MsgBox "Selection is not suitable for a chart."
20:            Exit Sub
21:        End If
22:
23:        With ActiveChart
24:            .HasTitle = True
25:            .ChartTitle.Characters.Text = "Sales"
26:            .ChartTitle.Select
27:        End With
28:
29:        Selection.AutoScaleFont = True
30:        With Selection.Font
31:            .Name = "Arial"
32:            .FontStyle = "Bold Italic"
33:            .Size = 14
34:            .Strikethrough = False
35:            .Superscript = False
36:            .Subscript = False
37:            .OutlineFont = False
38:            .Shadow = False
39:            .Underline = xlUnderlineStyleNone
40:            .ColorIndex = xlAutomatic
41:            .Background = xlAutomatic
42:        End With
43:
44: End Sub
```

18

Basically, by using copy and paste, you combined two procedures into one. The only real trick to this was the addition of the If statement. The If statement tests the selection's Count property's value to determine the number of columns being charted. The If statement creates a pie chart if there are two columns selected, creates a column chart if more than two columns are selected, and displays a message if there is only one column selected:

```
If Selection.Columns.Count = 2 Then
    'code for pie chart
ElseIf Selection.Columns.Count > 2 Then
    'code for column chart
Else
    MsgBox "Selection is not suitable for a chart."
    Exit Sub
End If
```

After the chart is created, the rest of the procedure adds a title to the chart and formats it. To experiment with this procedure go to your workbook, and delete any charts on Sheet1. Select Range A1:C6. Run the MyChart macro. The resulting chart is shown in Figure 18.4.

FIGURE 18.4

Because the selection contained more than 2 columns, a column-style chart was created.

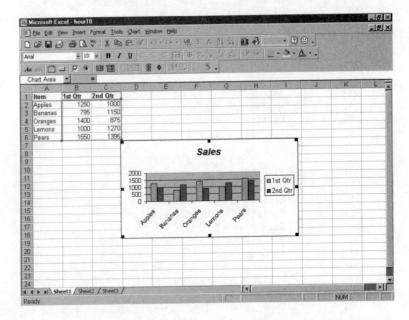

Now delete the chart and select Range A1:B5. Run the MyChart macro. This time, a pie chart is created. Save the workbook as Hour18.

Summary

This hour focused on chart creation. You learned about the `Charts` collection and the `Chart` object, as well as several of their properties and methods.

In this hour, you actually did very little coding. You recorded a couple of macros and then made some modifications to the recorded code. Without realizing it, you have just been introduced to the way that many VBA developers work. Many developers record as much as possible and then make needed changes to the recorded code. This makes VBA development fast and easy.

Q&A

Q Do I have to record a macro to produce the code for chart creation or can I write it from scratch?

A If you prefer to write code from scratch, you are more than welcome to do so. The techniques presented in this hour are simply the way to do it with minimum effort on your part.

Q I've noticed a drawback to recording macros: I often get more code than I need. For example, when I changed font settings, the macro recorder included everything on that tab in the dialog box. Doesn't this result in inefficient code?

A You can argue that the macro recorder doesn't always give you the most efficient code. But realize that you can always edit the code and delete any lines that you feel are unnecessary. You might want to comment the lines you think you don't want in the recorded code, and run the procedure to see the impact of not having those lines before you actually delete them.

Workshop

The quiz questions and exercise are provided for your further understanding. See Appendix A, "Answers," for the answers.

Quiz

1. What VBA statement would you use to create a chart?
2. What property of the `Application` object returns the current active chart?
3. What property of the `Chart` object controls the type of chart that is displayed?
4. What method of the `Chart` object controls what is being charted?
5. Which is not a property of the `Chart` object: `ChartArea`, `ChartType`, `ChartLocation` or `ChartTitle`?
6. True or False. Creating a chart is recordable by the macro recorder.
7. The `Workbook` object's _____ property returns the active chart.

Exercise

Create a UserForm with five option buttons on it. The option buttons should have the following captions and be named appropriately:

- Pie
- 3D Pie

- Clustered Column
- Stacked Column
- 3D Stacked Column

Create a procedure named `PickAChartType` that, based on the number of columns selected in the range to be charted, enables either the pie option buttons or the column buttons. When the procedure runs, the UserForm should display and the user can selected the type of chart he or she wants. Based on the selection made, a chart should be created.

Hint: Make the variable that is to store the selected range a public variable.

Hour 19

Pivot Tables

Some of the worksheets you work with have hundreds of rows and dozens of columns. One way to deal with this issue is to freeze your titles. But this doesn't help you much in analyzing the large amount of data. Excel provides a great tool, called a pivot table, that will solve both the problem of viewing and analyzing large amounts of data.

The highlights of this hour include

- Why you want to use pivot tables
- Overview of pivot tables concepts
- Recording a macro to create a pivot table
- Modifying the recorded pivot table code

Working with Pivot Tables

Probably the most underused data-analysis feature of Excel is pivot tables. Pivot tables are used to summarize large amounts of data by presenting the data in a three-dimensional format. The presented format allows you to filter the information to various levels of detail. Figure 19.1 shows an example of a pivot table.

FIGURE 19.1

This pivot table is used to view and analyze sales information.

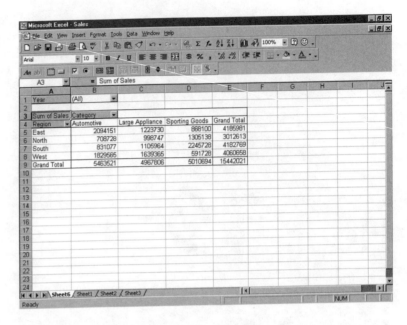

Pivot tables have several features that make them very attractive to work with:

- Built-in filtering

  Pivot tables automatically have filters built into them, allowing you to view only the detail you want.

- Dynamic layout

  Pivot tables have a dynamic layout that can be easily changed by just dragging the fields shown in the pivot table to other areas in the pivot table.

- Automatic totaling of report data

  Whatever field you decide to use as your summary data is automatically totaled. You can also change the type of calculation being performed on the summarized data.

- Supports a wide range of data sources

  You can create a pivot table based on a wide variety of data sources, including Excel lists, any worksheet range that has labeled columns, and external database files.

Pivot Table Overview

When you create a pivot table, you are asked to select fields for the following four areas:

- Page Fields

  Page fields are the main level of filter in a pivot table. When selecting a page field, ask yourself how you primarily want to organize your data.

- Row Fields

  Row fields are a lower or secondary level of detail.

- Column Fields

  Column fields are another lower or secondary level of detail.

- Data Items

  Data items are the fields that you want to summarize. Examples of good candidates for data items include sales, costs, units on hand, and so on.

Take a look at the worksheet shown in Figure 19.2. In this worksheet, you have three candidates that can either be page, row, or column fields. Year, Region, and Category can be used for any of the fields. You just need to decide what your focus is. The best candidate for a data item is the Sales field.

FIGURE 19.2

This range of data is a candidate for pivot table usage.

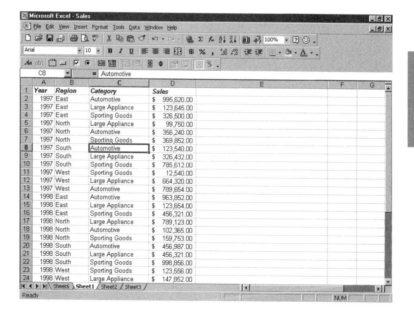

If you decided that Region was to be the page field, Year was to be the row field, and Category was to be the column field, your resulting pivot table would look like the one shown in Figure 19.3.

FIGURE 19.3

The resulting pivot table.

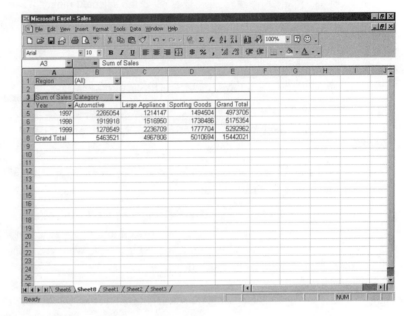

You can have multiple page, row, column, and data fields if you want to do so. This can be quite useful when working with data that has numerous rows and columns to give you several filtering options.

Creating a Pivot Table Using Code

In Hour 18, "Charts," you used the macro recorder to generate the code to create a chart. You are going to do the same thing in this hour. You are going to record a macro to generate the basic code for creating a pivot table.

Open the Sales.xls file located at the book's companion Web site. You'll notice that the worksheet in this workbook has four columns: Year, Region, Category, and Sales.

Because you want Excel to treat the data on this worksheet as a list, the heading rows have a font different from the rest of the rows on the worksheet.

You are going to create a pivot table based on a list, so the Microsoft Excel List or Database option button should be selected. You are creating a pivot table, so the Pivot Table option button should also be selected. Click Next to move to the next step in pivot table creation. Verify that range A1:D37 is the selected range and click Next. You want to place this pivot table on a new sheet, so select the New Worksheet option button and click Finish. A new sheet is added to your workbook and an empty pivot table is displayed (see Figure 19.4).

FIGURE 19.4

When the wizard is finished, you are presented with an empty pivot table. You are now ready to create its layout.

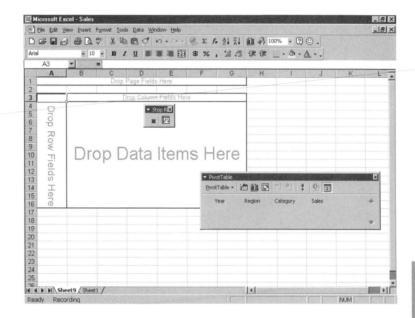

Drag the Year field from the PivotTable toolbar to the section of the pivot table labeled Drop Page Fields Here. Next, drag the Region field from the PivotTable toolbar to the section of the pivot table labeled Drop Row Fields Here. Drag the Category field from the PivotTable toolbar to the section of the pivot table labeled Drop Column Fields Here. The final thing you need to do to create the layout of your pivot table is to drag the Sales field from the PivotTable toolbar to the section of the pivot table labeled Drop Data Items Here. The completed pivot table is shown in Figure 19.5. Stop recording your macro.

Before examining the recorded code, take a moment to experiment with the functionality of the pivot table. Beside the Year field, which currently says (All), is a down-arrow button. Click this button and select 1997. Click OK. Now just the sales information for 1997 is displayed in the pivot table. Click the down-arrow button beside the Category field heading in the pivot table. Remove the checks from Automotive and Large

19

Appliances. Click OK. Now just the Sporting Goods figures for 1997 are displayed for the pivot table. Click the down-arrow button beside the Category field heading in the pivot table again. Check Automotive and Large Appliances. Click OK. Select (All) for the Year field. Now all the information is displayed again.

FIGURE 19.5

After you place the Sales field in the pivot table, data is displayed.

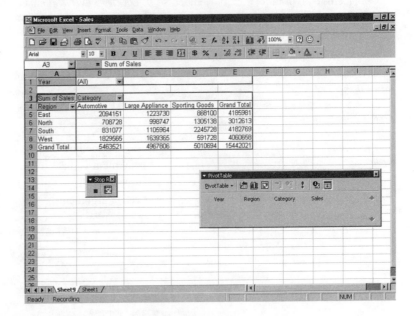

Reviewing the Recorded Code

Go to the Visual Basic Editor by pressing Alt+F11. From the Project Explorer, open the Modules folder and open Module1. You'll see your recorded macro listed. Listing 19.1 shows the complete procedure.

LISTING 19.1   The MyPivotTable Procedure

```
 1: Sub MyPivotTable()
 2:     ActiveWorkbook.PivotCaches.Add(SourceType:=xlDatabase, SourceData:= _
 3:         "Sheet1!R1C1:R37C4").CreatePivotTable _
        TableDestination:="", TableName:= _
 4:         "PivotTable6"
 5:     ActiveSheet.PivotTableWizard TableDestination:=ActiveSheet.Cells(3, 1)
 6:     ActiveSheet.Cells(3, 1).Select
 7:     ActiveSheet.PivotTables("PivotTable6").SmallGrid = False
 8:     With ActiveSheet.PivotTables("PivotTable6").PivotFields("Year")
 9:         .Orientation = xlPageField
10:         .Position = 1
```

```
11:      End With
12:      With ActiveSheet.PivotTables("PivotTable6").PivotFields("Region")
13:          .Orientation = xlRowField
14:          .Position = 1
15:      End With
16:      With ActiveSheet.PivotTables("PivotTable6").PivotFields("Category")
17:          .Orientation = xlColumnField
18:          .Position = 1
19:      End With
20:      With ActiveSheet.PivotTables("PivotTable6").PivotFields("Sales")
21:          .Orientation = xlDataField
22:          .Position = 1
23:      End With
24: End Sub
```

The first statement in this macro performs the Add method on the PivotCaches collection. The interesting thing about this statement is that two methods are actually being executed. In conjunction with the Add method, the CreatePivotTable method is being executed. Note that the TableDestination argument is set to an empty string. This instructs Excel to create the pivot table on a new sheet:

```
ActiveWorkbook.PivotCaches.Add(SourceType:=xlDatabase, SourceData:= _
    "Sheet1!R1C1:R37C4").CreatePivotTable TableDestination:="", TableName:= _
    "PivotTable1"
```

After the new sheet and pivot table are created, a series of properties are set:

```
ActiveSheet.PivotTableWizard TableDestination:=ActiveSheet.Cells(3, 1)
ActiveSheet.Cells(3, 1).Select
ActiveSheet.PivotTables("PivotTable6").SmallGrid = False
```

The rest of the procedure has to do with setting the fields for the pivot table:

```
With ActiveSheet.PivotTables("PivotTable6").PivotFields("Year")
    .Orientation = xlPageField
    .Position = 1
End With
With ActiveSheet.PivotTables("PivotTable6").PivotFields("Region")
    .Orientation = xlRowField
    .Position = 1
End With
With ActiveSheet.PivotTables("PivotTable6").PivotFields("Category")
    .Orientation = xlColumnField
    .Position = 1
End With
With ActiveSheet.PivotTables("PivotTable6").PivotFields("Sales")
    .Orientation = xlDataField
    .Position = 1
End With
```

19

If you were to run this macro again, you would get an error because the recorded macro passed a value to the `TableName` argument when the pivot table was created. To make this procedure more generic, make the changes (changes are in bold) shown in Listing 19.2.

LISTING 19.2 The Generic Version of the `MyPivotTable` Procedure

```
 1: Sub MyPivotTable()
 2:     Dim ptSales As PivotTable
 3:
 4:     Set ptSales = ActiveWorkbook.PivotCaches.Add(SourceType:=xlDatabase, _
           SourceData:= _
 5:         "Sheet1!R1C1:R37C4").CreatePivotTable(TableDestination:="")
 6:     ActiveSheet.PivotTableWizard TableDestination:=ActiveSheet.Cells(3, 1)
 7:     ActiveSheet.Cells(3, 1).Select
 8:     ptSales.SmallGrid = False
 9:     With ptSales.PivotFields("Year")
10:         .Orientation = xlPageField
11:         .Position = 1
12:     End With
13:     With ptSales.PivotFields("Region")
14:         .Orientation = xlRowField
15:         .Position = 1
16:     End With
17:     With ptSales.PivotFields("Category")
18:         .Orientation = xlColumnField
19:         .Position = 1
20:     End With
21:     With ptSales.PivotFields("Sales")
22:         .Orientation = xlDataField
23:         .Position = 1
24:     End With
25: End Sub
```

Now you don't have to worry about the name issue when creating a new pivot table. If you return to your workbook, you can now run this procedure as many times as you like.

Summary

You now know how to use a pivot table to make working with large amounts of data easier. To further your goal of learning VBA, you recorded a macro that created a pivot table and then modified the macro so that you can use the procedure multiple times.

Q&A

Q **Do pivot tables automatically refresh when I change the data they are based on?**

A No, you can refresh a pivot table either by clicking the Refresh button on the Pivot Table toolbar or by executing the RefreshTable method.

Q **If I know I want to use the same name every time I create a certain pivot table, what do I need to do?**

A The easiest way to handle this is to delete the sheet where the pivot table resided when the user exited the workbook. Then, place the code to create the pivot table in the workbook's Auto_Open procedure so that it is generated when the user opens the workbook.

Q **Can I use the Add method on the PivotTables collection to create a pivot table object instead of using the CreatePivotTable method in conjunction with the Add method of the PivotCaches collection?**

A Yes. First, execute the Add method on the PivotCaches collection. Use the resulting object as the value of the PivotCache argument of the PivotTables collection's Add method.

Workshop

The quiz questions and exercise are provided for your further understanding. See Appendix A, "Answers," for the answers.

Quiz

1. True or False. You can only create a pivot table based on an Excel list or range.
2. Name the two collections you worked with when creating a pivot table.
3. Which property of the PivotField object assigns the location of the field (that is, page, row, column, or data)?
4. True or False. You can have only one row field.
5. Name the four areas of a pivot table.
6. Which method creates the actual pivot table report?
7. True or False. Creating a pivot table is recordable by the macro recorder.

19

Exercise

Open the Instock workbook located on the companion Web Site. Begin recording a
macro named InStockPivot. Create a pivot table, using Figure 19.6 as your guide. Select
Housewares as the Dept. and Atlanta as the Location. Stop recording the macro. Modify
the recorded code to name the pivot table Instock and to delete all sheets except the
Stock Info sheet in the workbook.

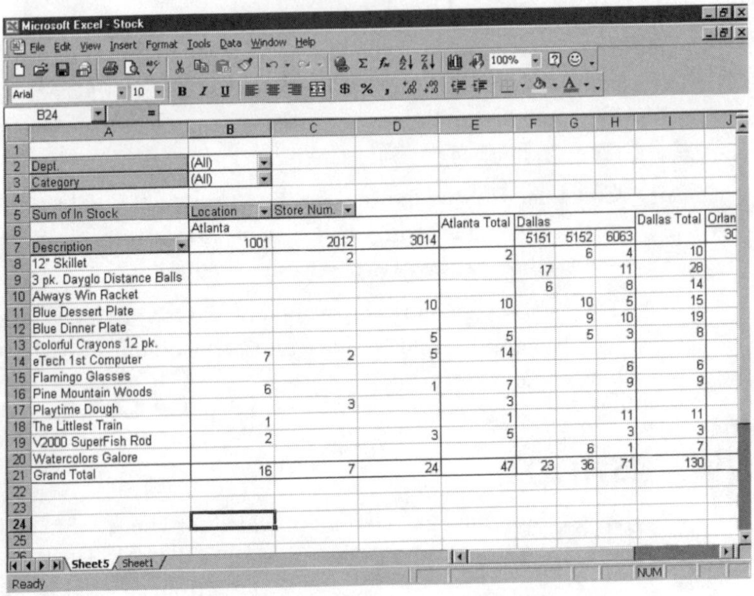

FIGURE 19.6

*InStockPivot Example
Screen.*

HOUR **20**

Introduction to Data Access

In this hour, you are working with an add-in called MS Query. Using MS Query, you can create a query to import data from an external data source. The best part about this tool is that you can record the process using Excel's macro recorder!

The highlights of this hour include

- A discussion of database formats that you can retrieve data from
- An overview of the ways you can retrieve external data
- How to use MS Query to retrieve data
- Making modification to your recorded MS Query macro

Available Databases

You might be surprised to find out that just about any database that you can access via your computer is available to Excel. Some of the available database formats are

- Microsoft Access
- Microsoft SQL Server
- Microsoft FoxPro
- Oracle
- Paradox
- dBASE
- ASCII text files
- SYLK

You might be wondering why you would want to import database data into Excel. Excel does certain things better than databases. These things include calculations, analysis, and charting. By importing data into Excel, you can use these features on your data.

Access Methods

You've actually already worked with one of the database access methods available in Excel. Pivot tables can be used to bring external data into Excel. Other ways to bring external data into Excel include

- MS Query
- ADO (ActiveX Data Objects)
- DAO (Data Access Objects)
- ODBC (Open Database Connectivity)

ADO is the preferred method for accessing data from Microsoft Access and other databases quickly and efficiently. DAO is supported primarily for backward compatibility to older versions of Access. ODBC can be used to connect to a variety of databases, including Microsoft SQL Server and Oracle. This hour focuses on the use of Microsoft Query to bring external data into Excel.

Accessing Data Using MS Query

The easiest way to access data from Excel is using an add-in called MS Query. MS Query is a tool that helps you connect to a data source and retrieve data. The retrieved data is placed in a worksheet. MS Query has a major benefit for the Excel developer—it is recordable by the macro recorder! This can be a great timesaver, but it does have a price. As you probably guessed, MS Query is the slowest method as far as performance for data access. You'll need to decide which is most important to you: speedy, easy development or better application performance.

If you decide to use MS Query as part of your application solution, MS Query needs to be installed on your users' machines. It doesn't install as part of a typical install, but it does install as part of a full install. It can also be installed any time after Excel has been installed.

The database you are going to use in this hour is the Northwind database. The Northwind database is a sample database that installs with Microsoft Access. To create a macro that retrieves data from the Northwind database, complete the following steps:

1. Close all open workbooks. Open a new workbook.

2. Start recording a macro named MSQueryExample that is stored in this workbook.

3. Select Data, Get External Data, New Database Query. The Choose Data Source Dialog box displays (see Figure 20.1). You can either select from a data source that has already been defined or create a new data source.

FIGURE 20.1

The Choose Data Source dialog lists data sources that have already been defined on your system.

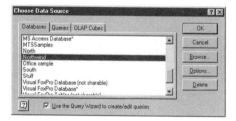

4. Select Northwind and click OK. The Query Wizard - Choose Columns dialog displays (see Figure 20.2).

20

FIGURE 20.2

After you are connected to your data source, the next step is to select the columns for your query.

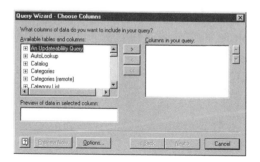

5. A list of queries and tables displays. To see the available columns, click the plus sign next to the item in the Available Tables and Columns list box. Locate and select Products. Click the plus sign next to products to see a list of columns. Select Product ID and click the Add button (>) to add the column to the Columns in Your Query list box. Add Product Name, Unit Price, and Units in Stock. Click Next. The Filter Data dialog displays (see Figure 20.3).

FIGURE 20.3

A filter lets you retrieve just the records you want.

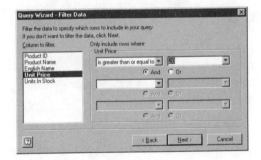

6. Select Unit Price from the Columns to Filter list box. From the first drop-down list box, select Is Greater Than or Equal To. Enter 15 in the next box. This creates a filter that shows only items that have a price of more than $15. Click Next. The Sort Order dialog displays (see Figure 20.4).

FIGURE 20.4

After selecting your filter, you can choose a sort order.

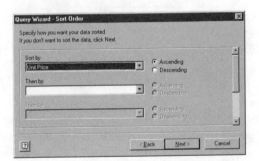

7. Select Unit Price from the Sort by drop-down list. Click Next. The Finish dialog displays (see Figure 20.5).

8. Click Finish to return the data to Excel. The Returning External Data to Microsoft Excel dialog displays (see Figure 20.6).

FIGURE 20.5

MS Query gives you several options as to what to do with the retrieved data.

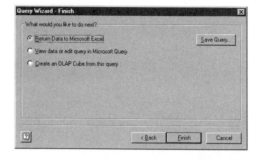

FIGURE 20.6

The last step before actually bringing the data into Excel is to tell Excel where to place the data.

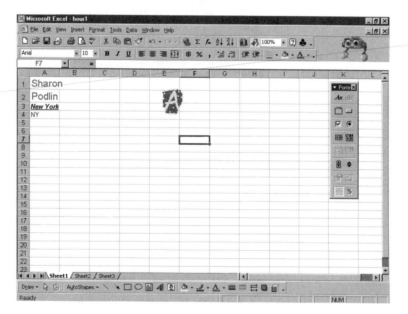

9. You are going to place the data on the current worksheet in cell A1. If A1 is not listed in this dialog box, select it. Click OK. After a few moments, the data displays in your worksheet and is ready for you to work with (see Figure 20.7).

10. Stop recording your macro.

Now you are ready to look at the code that was generated by your work. View the `MSQueryExample` procedure in the Visual Basic Editor. What might surprise you is that the resulting code is a large `With` statement. Listing 20.1 shows the complete procedure.

20

FIGURE 20.7

The data is returned to your workbook.

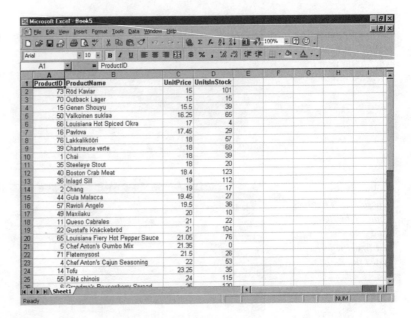

LISTING 20.1 The `MSQueryExample` Procedure

```
1: Sub MSQueryExample()
2:
3:     With ActiveSheet.QueryTables.Add(Connection:=Array(Array( _
4:         "ODBC; _
               DBQ=C:\Program Files\Microsoft Office\Office\Samples\
               ➥Northwind.mdb; DefaultDir=C:\Program Files\
               ➥Microsoft Office\Office\Samples;"),
               ➥Array("Driver={Microsoft Access Driver
               ➥(*.mdb)};DriverId=281; FIL=MS Access;
               ➥ImplicitCommitSync=Yes;MaxBufferSize=512;
               ➥MaxScanRows=8;Page"), Array("Timeout=5;
               ➥SafeTransactions=0;Threads=3; UID=admin;
               ➥UserCommitSync=Yes;")), Destination:=Range
               ➥("A1")).CommandText = Array("SELECT
               ➥Products.ProductID, Products.ProductName,
               ➥ Products.UnitPrice, Products.UnitsInStock"
               ➥& Chr(13) &"" & Chr(10) & "FROM `C:\Program
               ➥Files\Microsoft Office\Office\Samples\
               ➥Northwind`.Products Products" & Chr(13)
               ➥& "" & Chr(10) & "WHERE (Products.UnitPri"
5:         "ce>=15)" & Chr(13) & "" & Chr(10) &
               ➥"ORDER BY Products.UnitPrice")
6:     .Name = "Query from Northwind"
7:     .FieldNames = True
8:     .RowNumbers = False
```

```
 9:          .FillAdjacentFormulas = False
10:          .PreserveFormatting = True
11:          .RefreshOnFileOpen = False
12:          .BackgroundQuery = True
13:          .RefreshStyle = xlInsertDeleteCells
14:          .SavePassword = True
15:          .SaveData = True
16:          .AdjustColumnWidth = True
17:          .RefreshPeriod = 0
18:          .PreserveColumnInfo = True
19:          .Refresh BackgroundQuery:=False
20:      End With
21: End Sub
```

The first major statement executed is the Add method. This statement contains the connection information about the data source you connected to include file location and dri-
ver information:

```
ActiveSheet.QueryTables.Add(Connection:=Array(Array( _
        "ODBC;DBQ=C:\Program Files\Microsoft Office\Office\Samples\
              ➥Northwind.mdb;DefaultDir=C:\Program Files\
              ➥Microsoft Office\Office\Samples;" ), Array( _
              ➥"Driver={Microsoft Access Driver (*.mdb)};
              ➥DriverId=281; FIL=MS Access;
              ➥ImplicitCommitSync=Yes;MaxBufferSize=512;
              ➥MaxScanRows=8;Page"), Array("Timeout=5;
              ➥SafeTransactions=0; Threads=3;UID=admin;
              ➥UserCommitSync=Yes;")), Destination:=Range("A1"))
```

After the connection is made, the QueryTable's CommandText property is set. This is actually a Select statement that selects the appropriate data based on the selections you
made through the Query Wizard:

```
.CommandText = Array( _
"SELECT Products.ProductID, Products.ProductName, Products.UnitPrice,
➥Products.UnitsInStock" & Chr(13) & "" & Chr(10) &
➥"FROM `C:\Program Files\Microsoft Office\Office\Samples\Northwind`
➥.Products Products" & Chr(13) & "" & Chr(10) &
➥"WHERE (Products.UnitPrice>=15)" & Chr(13) & "" &
➥Chr(10) & "ORDER BY Products.UnitPrice")
```

The rest of the procedure sets miscellaneous properties. You can already see the major
benefit of MS Query that I talked about. By being recordable, development is a breeze!

You are probably asking yourself how to modify this type of macro. A perfect example
of how you might want to modify something like this is to set it up to prompt the user
for what price he is looking for. To do this, modify the procedure as shown in Listing
20.2. Changes are in bold.

20

LISTING 20.2   The Modified `MSQueryExample` Procedure

```
 1: Sub MSQueryExample()
 2:     Dim sngPrice As Single
 3:     Dim sMessage As String
 4:
 5:     Worksheets.Add
 6:     sMessage = "You wish to see prices greater than: "
 7:     sngPrice = Application.InputBox(sMessage, "Enter Price", Type:=1)
 8:
 9:     With ActiveSheet.QueryTables.Add(Connection:=Array(Array( _
10:         "ODBC; DBQ=C:\Program Files\Microsoft Office\Office\Samples\
          ➥Northwind.mdb; DefaultDir=C:\Program Files\Microsoft
          ➥Office\Office\Samples;" ), Array("Driver=
          ➥{Microsoft Access Driver (*.mdb)};DriverId=281;
          ➥FIL=MS Access;ImplicitCommitSync=Yes;
          ➥MaxBufferSize=512; MaxScanRows=8;Page"),Array
          ➥("Timeout=5;SafeTransactions=0; Threads=3;UID=admin;
          ➥UserCommitSync=Yes;")), Destination:=Range("A1"))
11:         .CommandText = Array("SELECT Products.ProductID,
          ➥Products.ProductName, Products.UnitPrice,
          ➥Products.UnitsInStock" & Chr(13) & "" & Chr(10) &
          ➥"FROM `C:\Program Files\Microsoft Office\Office\
          ➥Samples\Northwind`.Products Products" & Chr(13) &
          ➥"" & Chr(10) & "WHERE (Products.UnitPrice>="
          ➥& sngPrice & ")" & Chr(13) & "" & Chr(10)
          ➥& "ORDER BY Products.UnitPrice")
12:         .Name = "Query from Northwind"
13:         .FieldNames = True
14:         .RowNumbers = False
15:         .FillAdjacentFormulas = False
16:         .PreserveFormatting = True
17:         .RefreshOnFileOpen = False
18:         .BackgroundQuery = True
19:         .RefreshStyle = xlInsertDeleteCells
20:         .SavePassword = True
21:         .SaveData = True
22:         .AdjustColumnWidth = True
23:         .RefreshPeriod = 0
24:         .PreserveColumnInfo = True
25:         .Refresh BackgroundQuery:=False
26:     End With
27: End Sub
```

In the modified example, you start by creating a couple of variables. The first variable will store the value that the user enters. The second variable, sMessage, is simply used to hold the text for the input box.

The actual procedure begins by adding a blank worksheet. This allows you to ensure that the data isn't accidentally overwriting anything. Next, you prompt your user for input. You use that input in the Select statement in the place of the 15 that was there.

Run the modified procedure. When prompted, enter 20 for the price. You'll see that a worksheet is added to the workbook, and that the rows that are returned all have prices of twenty or more dollars. This was a simple and useful modification of recorded code.

MS Query isn't limited to working with a single table. You can create a query based on multiple linked tables as well.

Another way to work with MS Query as a development tool is to create all the queries you need using MS Query and then save them to a query file. Then, you'll use a saved query in your procedure. To see an example of working with a saved query, select cell A1 in your returned data. If it isn't already displayed, show the External Data toolbar. Click the button. Click Next until the Finish dialog of the Query Wizard displays. Click Save Query. Enter Prices as the name of the query and click Save. Then, click Finish to dismiss the Query Wizard dialog box.

Now you are ready to use the saved query. Add a new sheet to your workbook. Record a macro named PricesExample. Select Data, Get External Data, Run Saved Query. From the Run Query dialog, select Prices and click Get Data. Click OK when prompted about where to return the data. After the data is retrieved, stop recording the macro. Go to the Visual Basic Editor and take a look at what was recorded. Listing 20.3 shows the resulting recorded code.

LISTING 20.3 The PricesExample Procedure

```
 1: Sub PricesExample()
 2:
 3:     With ActiveSheet.QueryTables.Add(Connection:= _
 4:         "FINDER;C:\WINNT\Profiles\Administrator\Application
              ➥Data\Microsoft\Queries\Prices.dqy"_
 5:         , Destination:=Range("A1"))
 6:         .Name = "Prices"
 7:         .FieldNames = True
 8:         .RowNumbers = False
 9:         .FillAdjacentFormulas = False
10:         .PreserveFormatting = True
11:         .RefreshOnFileOpen = False
12:         .BackgroundQuery = True
13:         .RefreshStyle = xlInsertDeleteCells
14:         .SavePassword = True
15:         .SaveData = True
```

20

LISTING **20.3**   continued

```
16:          .AdjustColumnWidth = True
17:          .RefreshPeriod = 0
18:          .PreserveColumnInfo = True
19:          .Refresh BackgroundQuery:=False
20:      End With
21: End Sub
```

The main differences between this procedure and the MSQueryExample are the Add method and that PricesExample does not set the CommandText property. The drawback to this approach is that you can't prompt the user for information to plug into the query. But if you have a standard query that doesn't require user input, this is a good way to go.

Summary

You now know two ways to retrieve external data. As discussed in Hour 19, "Pivot Tables," you can retrieve external data using pivot tables. In this hour, you learned to retrieve data using MS Query. Both of these techniques are recordable by the macro recorder making them great for the Excel developer who is pressed for time.

In the next hour, you are going to learn to access data using ADO (ActiveX Data Objects). This technique gives the most control and best performance of the methods discussed in this book.

Q&A

Q Can I use the queries I created with Access with MS Query?

A Yes and no: You can create a new query using MS Query based on a query that exists in Access, but you can't run an Access query from the Data, Get External Data, Run Saved Query menu.

Q What if I want to modify the query I created using MS Query?

A On the Finish dialog box of the Query Wizard is an option to View Data or Edit Query in Microsoft Query. This option takes you to Query's interface, which is similar to the one found in Access for working with queries.

Q Do I have to have Access on my system to be able to read Access data to my Excel workbook?

A No, you just need to have the MS Query add-in installed.

Workshop

The quiz questions and exercise are provided for your further understanding. See Appendix A, "Answers," for the answers.

Quiz

1. What is the name of the collection to which a query is added when using MS Query?

2. What is the name of the property that stores the `Select` statement for the query you create?

3. True or False: If you use MS Query while recording a macro, you will have to make several modifications to the generated code.

4. True or False: MS Query only works with Access databases.

5. True or False: MS Query can retrieve data from multiple tables.

6. What is the major benefit you gain from using MS Query to retrieve data?

7. Name four different ways to retrieve external data into Excel.

Exercise

Create a copy the `MSQueryExample` procedure and name the copy `PriceAndMore`. Create a simple UserForm with four option buttons on it. The option buttons should have the following captions:

- Product ID
- Product Name
- Unit Price
- Units In Stock

Modify the `PriceAndMore` procedure so that based on the user's selection from the UserForm the data is sorted appropriately.

20

Hour 21

Accessing Data Using ADO

You've accessed external data before this hour, but you've relied on things that you recorded. What if requiring users to have the MS Query add-in is not an option? What if you want more control and better performance than you can get through MS Query? Then you need to use ADO.

The highlights of this hour include

- A discussion of what ADO is
- An overview of the ADO objects
- How to add a reference to the ADO library
- Using ADO to bring data into a worksheet

What Is ADO?

ActiveX Data Objects (ADO) lets you develop applications that access and manipulate data in a database through an OLE DB provider. Instead of using pivot tables and MS Query, you can interact directly with your data using ADO. This means you have more control over your data with less system overhead.

NEW TERM *OLE DB* is a set of Component Object Model (COM) interfaces that provide uniform access to data stored in diverse information sources.

The goal of ADO is to gain access to, edit, and update data sources. This means you can use ADO to bring data into a worksheet, update it, and then return the updated data to the table.

The Access Database Objects

As its name implies, ActiveX Data Objects provides an object model for you to use when accessing and manipulating data. You'll be using several key objects when working with this model:

- The Connection object—This object represents a connection to the data source you are using. After you have a connection to a data source, you can execute commands on that data source.
- The Command object—The Command object represents a command. Commands are queries or statements that can be processed by the data source.
- The Parameter object—The Parameter object works hand in hand with the Command object. The Parameter object represents a parameter of a Command.
- The Recordset object—The Recordset object is the real heart of the ADO object model. You use Recordset objects to manipulate data through your connection. A Recordset object represents the entire set of records from a table or the results of a query.
- The Field object—The Field object represents a column in a Recordset.
- The Error object—The Error object represents an error returned from a data source. Any operation involving ADO objects can generate one or more provider errors. As each error occurs, one or more Error objects are placed in the Errors collection of the Connection object.

Overview of Using ADO

Most Excel developers have one goal when working with ADO: to get data from a database into a workbook. The basic steps for accomplishing this goal are as follows:

1. Making a connection to a data source.
2. Gaining access to a recordset.
3. Getting records from the recordset.
4. Closing the connection to the data source.

Adding a Reference to the ADO Library

Before you begin to write code, you need to create a reference to the ADO library. Use the following steps to do this:

1. Select Tools, References. The References dialog displays.
2. Locate Microsoft ActiveX Data Objects 2.0 Library and place a check in its box.
3. Click OK. The reference is added to your application.

Writing Data from a Database to a Worksheet

Because it is one of the key things that most Excel developers want to do, you will begin your exploration of ADO by writing data from a database to a worksheet. In a new workbook, create the procedure found in Listing 21.1.

LISTING 21.1 The GoGetProducts Procedure

```
 1:    Sub GoGetProducts()
 2:       Dim rsProducts As ADODB.Recordset
 3:       Set rsProducts = New ADODB.Recordset
 4:       rsProducts.Open Source:="Products", _
 5:          activeconnection:="Provider=Microsoft.Jet.OLEDB.4.0;Data Source= _
 6: C:\Program Files\Microsoft Office\Office\Samples\Northwind.mdb", _
 7:          CursorType:=adOpenStatic, _
 8:          LockType:=adLockOptimistic, _
 9:          Options:=adCmdTable
10:       With Worksheets("Sheet1")
11:          .Range("A1").CurrentRegion.Clear
```

continues

21

> The breaks in this code are done due to limitation to line length in this book. I recommend you enter broken lines as one long line in your procedure.

```
12:          Application.Intersect(.Range(.Rows(1),
             ➥ .Rows(rsProducts.RecordCount)),
             ➥ .Range(.Columns(1),.Columns(rsProducts.Fields.Count))).
             ➥ Value = TransposeArray(rsProducts.GetRows
             ➥ (rsProducts.RecordCount))
13:      End With
14:
15:      rsProducts.Close
16: End Sub
```

Right from the start, this procedure works with the `Recordset` object. Take a look at the `Recordset`'s `Open` method. Its `Source` argument is set to the name of the table, in this case Products. The `activeconnection` argument's value provides necessary connection information. You are connecting to an Access database named Northwind:

```
Dim rsProducts As ADODB.Recordset
Set rsProducts = New ADODB.Recordset
rsProducts.Open Source:="Products", _
    activeconnection:="Provider=Microsoft.Jet.OLEDB.4.0;Data Source= _
C:\Program Files\Microsoft Office\Office\Samples\Northwind.mdb", _
    CursorType:=adOpenStatic, _
    LockType:=adLockOptimistic, _
    Options:=adCmdTable
```

After you have access to the recordset, you are ready to bring it into the worksheet. This is where things start looking a little strange. Data within an ADO recordset is organized as a 2-dimensional table, with each column representing a record within the recordset and each row representing a field. Yes, it is the opposite of what you would think it would be.

Because of this, you need to transpose the recordset before you copy it to the worksheet. That way, records go down the rows and fields go across the columns. If you are a seasoned Excel user, you might think to use Excel's `Transpose` function. The problem is that for large arrays, the `Transpose` method might fail. To get around this, you are going to create your own version of the `Transpose` function, as shown in Listing 21.2. In the `GoGetProducts` procedure, you'll first clear cell A1's current region and then use the `Intersect` method in conjunction with your version of the `Transpose` function (`MyTranspose`). The `Intersect` method returns a `Range` object that represents the rectangular intersection of two or more ranges. It's used because you want to create an intersection between the array represented by your recordset and the range on your worksheet:

```
With Worksheets("Sheet1")
    .Range("A1").CurrentRegion.Clear
    Application.Intersect(.Range(.Rows(1), .Rows(rsProducts.RecordCount)), _
                          .Range(.Columns(1), .Columns
                        ➥ (rsProducts.Fields.Count))).Value = _
                          MyTranspose(rsProducts.GetRows
                        ➥ (rsProducts.RecordCount))
End With
```

The final thing the procedure does is close the connection to the recordset:

```
rsProducts.Close
```

Earlier, I mentioned that you need to create a function that is in essence your own version of the Transpose function. Go ahead and enter that procedure now.

LISTING 21.2   The MyTranspose Function

```
 1: Function MyTranspose(ByRef ArrayOriginal As Variant) As Variant
 2:     Dim x As Integer
 3:     Dim y As Integer
 4:     Dim i As Integer
 5:     Dim j As Integer
 6:     Dim ArrayTranspose() As Variant
 7:
 8:     x = UBound(ArrayOriginal, 1)
 9:     y = UBound(ArrayOriginal, 2)
10:
11:     ReDim ArrayTranspose(y, x)
12:
13:     For i = 0 To x
14:         For j = 0 To y
15:             ArrayTranspose(j, i) = ArrayOriginal(i, j)
16:         Next
17:     Next
18:
19:     MyTranspose = ArrayTranspose
20:
21: End Function
```

21

All this function does is moves the elements in one dimension of an array to the other dimension of an array.

You are now ready to run the GoGetProducts procedure. Go to your workbook and run the procedure. In a few moments, you'll have data in your workbook as shown in Figure 21.1!

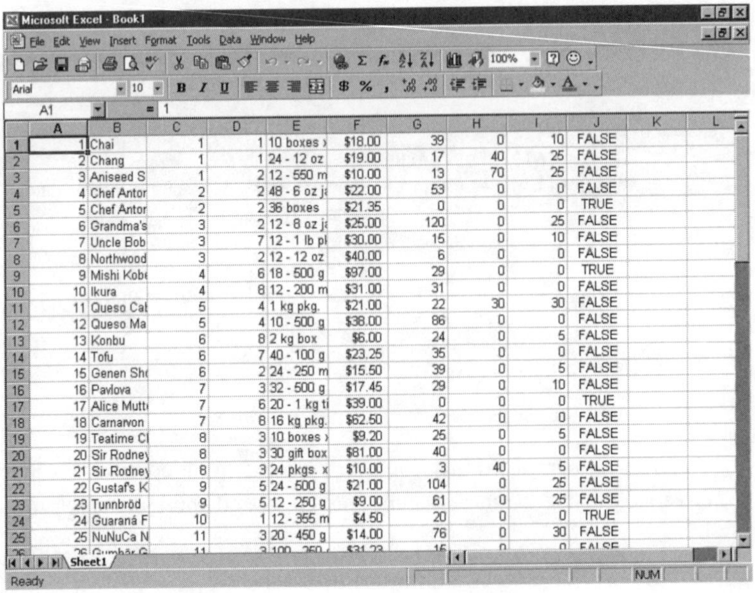

	A	B	C	D	E	F	G	H	I	J
1	1	Chai	1	1	10 boxes x	$18.00	39	0	10	FALSE
2	2	Chang	1	1	24 - 12 oz	$19.00	17	40	25	FALSE
3	3	Aniseed S	1	2	12 - 550 m	$10.00	13	70	25	FALSE
4	4	Chef Antor	2	2	48 - 6 oz ja	$22.00	53	0	0	FALSE
5	5	Chef Antor	2	2	36 boxes	$21.35	0	0	0	TRUE
6	6	Grandma's	3	2	12 - 8 oz ja	$25.00	120	0	25	FALSE
7	7	Uncle Bob	3	7	12 - 1 lb pl	$30.00	15	0	10	FALSE
8	8	Northwood	3	2	12 - 12 oz	$40.00	6	0	0	FALSE
9	9	Mishi Kobe	4	6	18 - 500 g	$97.00	29	0	0	TRUE
10	10	Ikura	4	8	12 - 200 m	$31.00	31	0	0	FALSE
11	11	Queso Cat	5	4	1 kg pkg.	$21.00	22	30	30	FALSE
12	12	Queso Ma	5	4	10 - 500 g	$38.00	86	0	0	FALSE
13	13	Konbu	6	8	2 kg box	$6.00	24	0	5	FALSE
14	14	Tofu	6	7	40 - 100 g	$23.25	35	0	0	FALSE
15	15	Genen Sho	6	2	24 - 250 m	$15.50	39	0	5	FALSE
16	16	Pavlova	7	3	32 - 500 g	$17.45	29	0	10	FALSE
17	17	Alice Mutt	7	6	20 - 1 kg ti	$39.00	0	0	0	TRUE
18	18	Carnarvon	7	8	16 kg pkg.	$62.50	42	0	0	FALSE
19	19	Teatime Cl	8	3	10 boxes x	$9.20	25	0	5	FALSE
20	20	Sir Rodney	8	3	30 gift box	$81.00	40	0	0	FALSE
21	21	Sir Rodney	8	3	24 pkgs. x	$10.00	3	40	5	FALSE
22	22	Gustaf's K	9	5	24 - 500 g	$21.00	104	0	25	FALSE
23	23	Tunnbröd	9	5	12 - 250 g	$9.00	61	0	25	FALSE
24	24	Guaraná F	10	1	12 - 355 m	$4.50	20	0	0	TRUE
25	25	NuNuCa N	11	3	20 - 450 g	$14.00	76	0	30	FALSE

FIGURE 21.1
Data is retrieved to the worksheet using ADO.

Summary

In this hour, you were provided with a quick overview of ADO concepts. Then, you saw how to bring data from a table to your worksheet using ADO.

In the next hour, you are going to build on your ADO knowledge. You'll be creating a UserForm that allows your user to navigate and update records.

Q&A

Q Is Access the only database format that I can use with ADO?

A Actually, you can use several other formats, including SQL Server and FoxPro.

Q Is a recordset always a table?

A No, a recordset can also be based on a command—that is, a query.

Workshop

The quiz questions and exercise are provided for your further understanding. See Appendix A, "Answers," for the answers.

Quiz

1. Which argument of the Open method is used to pass the name of the object to be used as the recordset?

2. True or False: To access data through ADO, you just write the appropriate code.

3. Which object stores information about problems you had while using ADO?

4. True or False: You can access data only from Microsoft Access using ADO.

5. Which object represents the records you are working with via ADO?

6. How do you terminate a connection to an ADO source?

7. Name the four steps for working with ADO.

Exercise

Create a UserForm with 3 option button on it. The option buttons' captions should be Suppliers, Products, and Orders. Write the necessary code to enable a user to select the table from which to bring data into the user's workbook.

21

HOUR **22**

More on ADO

In this hour, you are going to expand on your knowledge of ADO. You are going to focus on the Recordset object and its properties and methods. By using those properties and methods, you are going to create a UserForm that displays data from a database using ADO.

The highlights of this hour include

- How to retrieve fields from a recordset to a form
- Adding record navigation to your form
- How to update members of your recordset

Retrieving Fields to a UserForm

Rather than bringing data directly into a worksheet, you might want to present it in a UserForm. This gives your user a nice, friendly interface to work with. You'll also find the approach of working with UserForms somewhat different than that of working with worksheets. Start by creating the UserForm:

1. Add a UserForm to your workbook.
2. Using Figure 22.1 as a guide, add controls to the form.

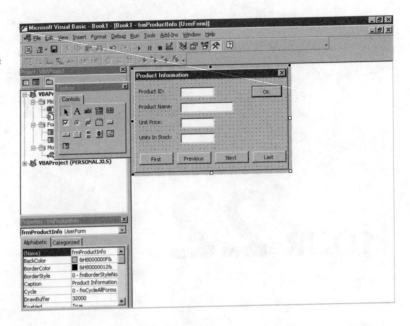

FIGURE 22.1
*This form will be used
to display data from an
Access database.*

3. Set the following properties:

Name	Property
txtProductID	
txtProductName	
txtUnitPrice	
txtUnitsInStock	
cmdOK	Default=True

4. Set the form's Caption to Product Information and name the form
   frmProductInfo.

The next step is to add a reference to the Microsoft ActiveX Data Objects 2.0 library by
using the Tools menu. Now you are ready to enter the first procedure. You want the data
to display as soon as you display the form, so enter the code in Listing 22.1 in the
UserForm's Activate event procedure.

LISTING 22.1 The UserForm_Activate Procedure

```
 1: Private Sub UserForm_Activate()
 2:     cnnProduct.Open "Provider=Microsoft.Jet.OLEDB.4.0;Data _
 3: Source=C:\Program Files\Microsoft Office\Office\Samples\Northwind.mdb"
 4:
 5: rstProduct.Open _
"Select ProductID, ProductName, UnitPrice, UnitsInStock from Products", _
 6: cnnProduct, adOpenKeyset, _
 7:        adLockOptimistic, adCmdText    _
txtProductID.Text = rstProduct.Fields(0).Value
 8:     txtProductName.Text = rstProduct.Fields(1).Value
 9:     txtUnitPrice.Text = rstProduct.Fields(2).Value
10:     txtUnitsInStock.Text = rstProduct.Fields(3).Value
11:
12: End Sub
```

This procedure begins by opening a connection to the database. Then it uses a Select statement to create the recordset. The values of the fields are then used to set the Text properties of the text boxes. Notice that field indexing begins with 0. You also need to place the following lines in the form's General Declarations area:

```
Dim cnnProduct As New ADODB.Connection
Dim rstProduct As New ADODB.Recordset
```

Add the following lines for the cmdOK_click procedure:

```
frmProductInfo.Hide
cnnProduct.Close
```

Go ahead and run the form. You'll see the values of the first record of the recordset displayed in the form. The next step is to move from record to record.

Adding Record Navigation

A recordset has five move methods to allow you to navigate through it: Move, MoveFirst, MoveNext, MovePrevious, and MoveLast. Move moves a certain number of rows, and the other methods move to a specific record. Add four command buttons to the bottom of your UserForm as shown in Figure 22.2.

Caption	Name
First	cmdFirst
Previous	cmdPrevious
Next	cmdNext
Last	cmdLast

FIGURE 22.2

The form is being enhanced to include navigation.

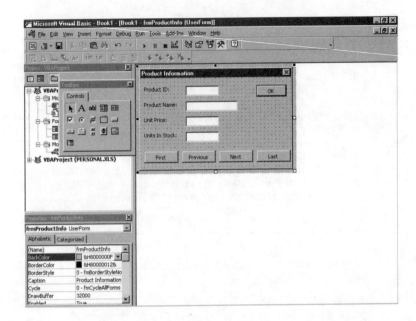

You are going to use four of the Move methods for these buttons. But before you add the code to these command buttons, you are going to write a procedure to set the fields' Value properties to the text boxes' Text properties because you need this code for each of these procedures. The procedure you need to create is shown in Listing 22.2.

LISTING 22.2 The FillFields Procedure

```
1: Sub FillFields()
2:     txtProductID.Text = rstProduct.Fields(0).Value
3:     txtProductName.Text = rstProduct.Fields(1).Value
4:     txtUnitPrice.Text = rstProduct.Fields(2).Value
5:     txtUnitsInStock.Text = rstProduct.Fields(3).Value
6: End Sub
```

Now enter the code for the navigation command buttons. Listing 22.3 has the code you need.

LISTING 22.3 The Move Procedures

```
1: Private Sub cmdFirst_Click()
2:     rstProduct.MoveFirst
3:     FillFields
4:
```

```
 5: End Sub
 6:
 7: Private Sub cmdLast_Click()
 8:     rstProduct.MoveLast
 9:     FillFields
10: End Sub
11:
12: Private Sub cmdNext_Click()
13:
14:     rstProduct.MoveNext
15:     If rstProduct.EOF Then
16:         rstProduct.MoveLast
17:     End If
18:     FillFields
19: End Sub
20:
21: Private Sub cmdPrevious_Click()
22:     rstProduct.MovePrevious
23:     If rstProduct.BOF Then
24:         rstProduct.MoveFirst
25:     End If
26:     FillFields
27: End Sub
```

The final code needs to go in the OK button. Listing 22.4 has the complete procedure for the OK button's Click event procedure.

LISTING 22.4   The cmdOK_Click Procedure

```
Private Sub cmdOK_Click()
    Dim iNumRows As Integer

    Worksheets("Product Requests").Activate
    Range("A1").Select
    Selection.CurrentRegion.Select
    iNumRows = Selection.Rows.Count
    Range("A1").Select
    Selection.Offset(iNumRows, 0).Value = txtProductID.Text
    Selection.Offset(iNumRows, 1).Value = txtProductName.Text
    Selection.Offset(iNumRows, 2).Value = txtUnitPrice.Text

    frmProductInfo.Hide
    cnnProduct.Close

End Sub
```

Run your form. You can now use the buttons to move forward and backward through your records. Looking at the procedures that are pretty simple, cmdFirst and cmdLast are the easiest procedures. cmdNext and cmdPrevious are a little more complex. As you use these Move methods, you do not know when you hit the beginning or end of the recordset. This requires some checking. The Recordset object has BOF and EOF properties that can be tested to see whether you're beyond one of the boundaries of the recordset. You test this with an If structure. If you are beyond a boundary, your code can issue the appropriate MoveFirst or MoveLast method to correct the situation.

Updating Data

You might want your user to be able to make changes to the data displayed in the form and have those changes be reflected in the database. This is done using the Update method. Add a command button under the OK button named cmdUpdate with a caption of Update (see Figure 22.3). Enter the code for the button's Click event, as shown in Listing 22.5.

FIGURE 22.3

The next enhancement to the form is the ability to update information.

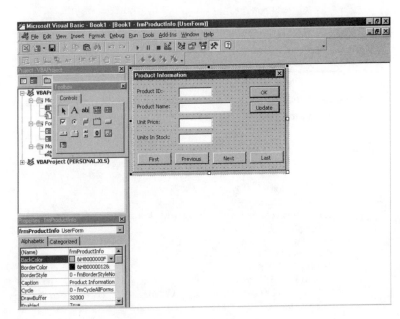

LISTING 22.5   The cmdUpdate_Click Procedure

```
1: Private Sub cmdUpdate_Click()
2:     rstProduct.Fields("ProductName").Value = txtProductName.Text
3:     rstProduct.Fields("UnitPrice").Value = txtUnitPrice.Text
4:     rstProduct.Fields("UnitsInStock").Value = txtUnitsInStock.Text
5: End Sub
```

22

Notice that this procedure does not set the Value property of the ProductID field. This is because the ProductID field is a primary key and should not be modified. To test your procedure, run the form. Change the Unit Price of the first field to 19. Click Update. Click Next, and then click Previous to return to the record. The updated price is still there.

Adding Search Capabilities

The last feature you are going to add to your form is the ability to search for a particular Product ID. To do this, you are going to use the recordset's Find method. The Find method always begins from the current record. Because of this, you are going store the current record location to a variable via the recordset's Bookmark property, and then exe-cute the MoveFirst method to go to the beginning of the recordset. If there isn't a match to the item being located, you can return to the record that was previously displayed by setting the Bookmark property back to its previous value. Add a command button under the Update button. Name the button cmdFind and set its caption to Find. Enter the code shown in Listing 22.6 for the Find button.

LISTING 22.6   The cmdFind_Click Procedure

```
 1: Private Sub cmdFind_Click()
 2:     Dim varBookmark
 3:     varBookmark = rstProduct.Bookmark
 4:     Dim strLookup As String, strFind As String
 5:     strLookup = InputBox("Enter product ID", "Locate Product ID")
 6:     If strLookup = "" Then Exit Sub
 7:     rstProduct.MoveFirst
 8:     strFind = "[ProductID] = '" & strLookup & "'"
 9:     rstProduct.Find strFind, 0, adSearchForward, rstProduct.Bookmark
10:     If rstProduct.EOF Then
11:         MsgBox "Product not found.", vbInformation, "Find Failure"
12:         rstProduct.Bookmark = varBookmark
13:         Exit Sub
14:     End If
15:     FillFields
16:
17: End Sub
```

Run the form. Click the Find button and enter 17. When you click OK, you'll see the field you were looking for.

Summary

In this hour, you covered several methods of the Recordset object. If you need to bring data into Excel from another data source you'll definitely need the skills that you learned in this hour. Now you know how to navigate through, update, and search a recordset. You also know how to display data from a database in a UserForm. These types of operations are critical to your application if you are supporting database integration.

Q&A

Q Why don't I work with Database or Table objects instead of Recordset objects?

A If you look at the ADODB library in the Object Browser, you'll find that as far as ADO is concerned there aren't Database and Table objects available for your direct manipulation. All data manipulation takes place via the Recordset object.

Q Is ADO the best way to work with external data?

A That depends on your needs. If you need to gain access to data with minimum coding you might want to use MS Query or pivot tables. Another alternative is to use Automation or ODBC. You are the best judge of what is best for your situation.

Workshop

The quiz questions and exercise are provided for your further understanding. See Appendix A, "Answers," for the answers.

Quiz

1. What method do you execute to move to the last record in a recordset?
2. How do you test to see whether you are at the beginning of a recordset?
3. What method is used to write changes to a recordset?
4. What property of the Recordset object stores the current record location?
5. What method is used to search a recordset?
6. What property of the Field object is used to retrieve the contents of a field?
7. True or False. Recordset information can be retrieved either to a worksheet or to a UserForm.

Exercise

Add a sheet to your workbook. Name the sheet Product Requests. In cell A1, enter Product ID. In cell B1, enter Product Name. In cell C1, enter Unit Price.

Modify the cmdOK procedure to write the information in the form to the Product Requests sheet.

22

HOUR 23

Using Automation

Although Excel can do many things and do them well, it cannot do everything. For example, Excel is not a good choice for creating a letter (although I have heard of people using it for that purpose, I don't recommend it!). Fortunately, you have a whole world of functionality available through Microsoft Office. In this hour, you will learn to control other applications using VBA code in Excel.

The highlights of this hour include

- A discussion of what Automation is
- An overview of Automation basics
- How to add a reference to an Automation server
- Using the Object Browser to view an object library's information
- How to create an instance to an Automation server
- Using Automation to control Microsoft Word

What Is Automation?

NEW TERM
Automation, previously known as OLE Automation, is a technology that allows you to incorporate the functionality of Windows applications into your VBA code. *Automation* is the process of controlling one application through another. Anything you can do with Word, PowerPoint, Outlook, Access, Project, and numerous other applications can also be done in your Excel VBA applications by using Automation. By using these applications as tools, you can give your application new capabilities that would otherwise require you to do extreme amounts of coding or simply be impossible to do using only Excel. What if you wanted to track hours in Project and graph them in Excel? How about generating slide shows based on the values found in a worksheet? Sounds like a job for PowerPoint!

NEW TERM
To use Automation, you must own a copy of the application whose functionality you want to incorporate into your application and that application must support Automation. Windows-based applications that fully support Automation are said to *expose*, or make available, their collection of objects, properties, methods, and events. By using these exposed objects, you can use the application's features. If you and your users already have Microsoft Office and other OLE-compliant applications, why not use them? They're already paid for and they offer familiar interfaces to your user.

Automation Basics

NEW TERM
When working with Automation, you need to understand the roles that each application performs. When working with Automation, you are going to have a controller application and a server application. A *controller application* controls an Automation server application. Visual Basic is an excellent example of a controller application. A *server application* exposes objects that can be manipulated by other applications. In your applications, Excel will be the controller application.

Dynamic Data Exchange (DDE) and the SendKeys method are available for use with applications that do not support Automation.

Referencing an Automation Server

NEW TERM
Most applications that support Automation provide an object library. An *object library* provides information to the controller application about available objects in the server application. To use the object library information, you need to reference the object library from your controller application, that is, Excel. In this hour, you are going

to control Microsoft Word via Automation. This means Word is the server application and that you need to add a reference to it. Select the Tools, References menu while in the VBA Editor. The References dialog shown in Figure 23.1 displays. Place a check by Microsoft Word 9.0 Object Library and click OK. The reference is added to your project.

If you don't have Word 2000, you won't have this object library listed. Therefore, you can't perform Automation using Word. The information in this hour should still work if you have the previous version of Word (Word 8.0). Just select Microsoft Word 8.0 Object Library instead. If the most recent version of Word you have installed on your system is Word 95, the examples in this hour will not work because Word 95 does not support VBA. Word 97 (Word 8.0) was the first version of Word that used Visual Basic for Applications. Prior to that release, Word used WordBasic as its Automation language.

FIGURE 23.1

The References dialog is used to make object libraries available for use with Automation.

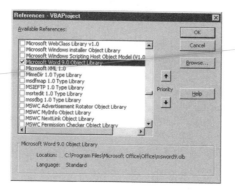

Viewing an Object Library's Contents

The Object Browser allows you to view an object library's exposed objects. The Object Browser lists all properties, events, and methods for the exposed objects. To view Microsoft Word's object library information, select View, Object Browser to display the Object Browser window (see Figure 23.2). Select Word from the project/library list (the first drop-down list) to display the contents of the Word object library. You can select an object and view its properties and methods. When you are done, close the Object Browser.

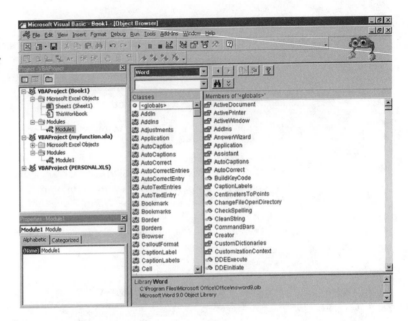

FIGURE 23.2
The Object Browser is a useful tool for listing objects in a specific library.

Creating an Instance of an Automation Server

Adding a reference to an Automation server just makes it available for your use. It doesn't mean that you can actually use it. To use the object library, you have to create an instance of the server. This is done with code. You are going to do this by using the `CreateObject` statement. `CreateObject` is used to create a new instance of a server, meaning that you can use the server application's objects, methods, and properties in your procedure. Listing 23.1 shows the code needed to create a reference to Word.

LISTING 23.1 Creating an Instance to Word

```
1: Dim y As Word.Application
2: Set y = CreateObject("Word.Application")
```

After you create an instance to the server application, you use its objects, methods, and properties just as you would use Excel's objects, methods, and properties.

Okay, now it's time to point out a little detail to you. Word uses VBA as its Automation language. Excel uses VBA as its Automation language. Word has a macro recorder. Excel has a macro recorder. Does this give you any ideas? This means that you can record a macro in Word and copy the resulting code into your Excel procedure! You do have to make a minor change to the code, but you'll see that in a few moments.

Using Automation to Control Microsoft Word

You are going to create a simple application that inserts the values from a range of cells into a letter. Before you begin your macro, you need to set up a couple of things. First, you need to create the letter in Word (in reality you could create the letter using code from Excel, but we aren't going to do this). Start Word and create the following letter:

23

To Sales Manager:

Below you'll find the latest sales figures. If you have any questions please do not hesitate to contact me.

Sincerely,

The Boss

NEW TERM Save this letter as Sales. Now you are going to make a couple of changes to this letter by adding bookmarks. *Bookmarks* are named locations within a Word document. To add the needed bookmarks, complete the following steps:

1. Position the insertion point at the beginning of *Sales Manager*.
2. Select Insert, Bookmark. The Bookmark dialog displays.
3. Enter Region for the bookmark name and click Add. You've created the first bookmark.
4. Add a blank line before *Sincerely*. Position the insertion point on that blank line. Add a bookmark named SalesInfo to this location.
5. Save the document and close it. Minimize Word.

The next step of this process will be done in Excel. Create the worksheet that you see in Figure 23.3. This worksheet's information is going to eventually be copied and pasted into the Sales document.

Return to Word and start recording a macro named SaleStuff (you'll need a blank document open).

To record a macro in Word, use the same steps that you would use in Excel. Select Tools, Macro, Record New Macro.

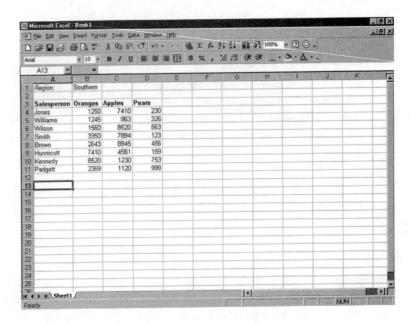

FIGURE 23.3
This is the sales infor-
mation needed by the
Sales document.

To complete the macro, use the following steps:

1. Select File, Open and open the Sales document.
2. Select Edit, Go To. Select Bookmark from the Go To What list box. Select Region as the first bookmark to go to. Click Go To.
3. Select SalesInfo as the next bookmark to go to and click Go To.
4. Click Close to dismiss the dialog box.
5. Stop recording the macro.

Select Tools, Macro, Macros to access the Macro dialog. Select SaleStuff and click Edit to view the recorded code. There's a lot of extra code in this procedure. Edit the proce-dure so that it matches the one in Listing 23.2.

LISTING 23.2   The Edited `SaleStuff` Procedure

```
1: Sub SaleStuff()
2:
3:     Documents.Open FileName:="sales.doc"
4:     Selection.GoTo What:=wdGoToBookmark, Name:="Region"
5:     Selection.GoTo What:=wdGoToBookmark, Name:="SalesInfo"
6:
7: End Sub
```

This code will act as the foundation for the procedure you are going to create in Excel. Cut this procedure. Close Word. Return to Excel and open the Visual Basic Editor. Add a module to this workbook and paste the code into the module. The next step is to edit the code. First, you need to create an instance to Word. Then you need to make a little change to the code you pasted. Each line of the code needs to begin with the variable that you set when you created an instance to Word. The easiest way to do this is with a `With` statement. Modify your procedure to match the one found in Listing 23.4.

LISTING 23.4   Adding an Instance to Word

```
1: Sub SaleStuff()
2:     Dim y As Word.Application
3:     Set y = CreateObject("Word.Application")
4:
5:     With y
6:         .Documents.Open Filename:="sales.doc"
7:         .Selection.GoTo What:=wdGoToBookmark, Name:="Region"
8:         .Selection.GoTo What:=wdGoToBookmark, Name:="SalesInfo"
9:     End With
10:
11: End Sub
```

You are almost done now. You just need to add the code to copy the information from Excel and paste it into Word. Listing 23.5 shows the completed procedure. Changes are in bold.

LISTING 23.5   The Final Version of the `SaleStuff` Procedure

```
1: Sub SaleStuff()
2:     Dim y As Word.Application
3:     Set y = CreateObject("Word.Application")
4:
5:     With y
6:         .Visible = True
7:     'The path listed in the next step may be different
8:     'on your own machine. Change as needed.
9:         .Documents.Open Filename:="d:\excel vba\sales.doc"
10:         Worksheets("Sheet1").Range("B1").Copy
11:         .Selection.GoTo What:=wdGoToBookmark, Name:="Region"
12:         .Selection.Paste
13:         Application.CutCopyMode = False
14:         Worksheets("Sheet1").Range("A3:D11").Select
15:         Selection.Copy
16:         .Selection.GoTo What:=wdGoToBookmark, Name:="SalesInfo"
17:         .Selection.Paste
18:         Application.CutCopyMode = False
19:     End With
20:
21: End Sub
```

The first change you made was to set Word's `Visible` property to `True`. This displays Word in the foreground so that you can see what is going on:

```
.Visible = True
```

Next, you opened the Sales document. After opening the Sales document, you copied range B1, which contained the region's name. You went to the bookmark that was named Region and pasted the range B1 contents there. You also set Excel's `CutCopyMode` property to `False` to get rid of the marquee that displays around a range that has been cut or copied:

```
.Documents.Open Filename:="d:\excel vba\sales.doc"
 Worksheets("Sheet1").Range("B1").Copy
.Selection.GoTo What:=wdGoToBookmark, Name:="Region"
.Selection.Paste
Application.CutCopyMode = False
```

You repeated the same basic thing for the next range of cells:

```
Worksheets("Sheet1").Range("A3:D11").Select
Selection.Copy
.Selection.GoTo What:=wdGoToBookmark, Name:="SalesInfo"
.Selection.Paste
Application.CutCopyMode = False
```

To summarize, when working with Automation, you want to

- Set up the file in the server application
- Set up your workbook in Excel
- Record as much as you can in the server application
- Record as much as you can in Excel
- Cut the recorded code from the server application and combine it with the recorded code in Excel
- Add the necessary statements to create an instance of the server application in your Excel procedure (`CreateObject`)
- Make necessary changes to the pasted code that came from the server application

Save your workbook as Hour23. If you have Word open, close it. Run the SaleStuff macro. You'll see Word start and the Sales document open. In a few moments, the copied information from Excel is pasted into the document, as shown in Figure 23.4. This was a simple example, and in real life you would probably want to format the final letter more, but you get the idea.

To best run the macro again, close Word and do not save the changes made to the Sales document.

FIGURE 23.4

The completed Sales letter.

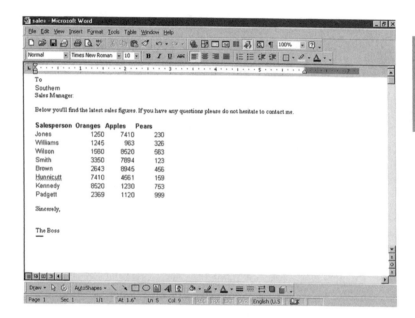

23

Summary

As much as you can do with Excel, you are bound by what it does best: number crunching, charting, reporting, and so on. Looking beyond those boundaries, you see that other applications do things really well, such as document creation or presentation generation. You now know how to exploit the strengths of applications via your Excel VBA application by incorporating Automation. By using Automation, you are in fact adding whatever Excel lacks. This truly extends what you can accomplish as a programmer.

Q&A

Q Do all Windows applications support Automation?

A No, only those applications that are designed to implement Automation support automation. Not all vendors elect to do this.

Q Do DOS-based applications support Automation?

A No, DOS-based applications cannot support Automation. To control a DOS-based application try using the SendKey method, which is documented in VBA online Help.

Workshop

The quiz questions and exercise are provided for your further understanding. See Appendix A, "Answers," for the answers.

Quiz

1. What statement do you use to add an instance to an Automation server application?
2. True or False. Other than Excel and VBA native objects, you can only view referenced library objects in the Object Browser.
3. In the application created in this hour, Excel was the _____ application.
4. True or False. Excel can only act as a controller application.
5. How do you add a reference to an object library?
6. True or False. You have to be able to access Word from your system to be able to use it in Automation.
7. True or False. Most Microsoft Office applications support some level of Automation.

Exercise

Create a new workbook named Orders. Create the worksheet shown in Figure 23.5. Create a document in Word named Invoice Letter, as shown in Figure 23.6. Add needed bookmarks. Create a procedure that uses the information in the selected row to add the appropriate information in the Invoice Letter document.

FIGURE 23.5

Data from this work-sheet is used to populate a letter via Automation.

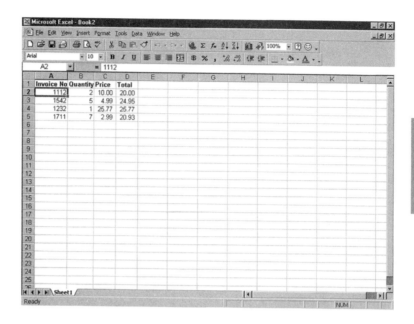

FIGURE 23.6

This letter is used in Hour 23's Automation exercise.

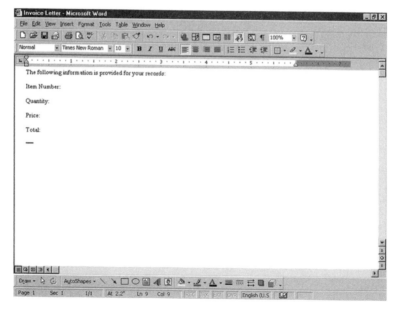

HOUR 24

Running Procedures

What if you want a certain procedure to run whenever you open or close a particular workbook? What if you want a procedure to run when a user activates a sheet in your workbook? Excel provides ways to accomplish these and other tasks and they are the focus of this hour.

The highlights of this hour include

- Using Excel `Auto_Open` and `Auto_Close` procedures
- Implementing event procedures
- Creating add-ins

Running Procedures Automatically

You might have procedures that you want to run automatically when a user opens or closes a workbook. Excel has made this task very easy to do. If you want a procedure to run when a workbook opens, name the procedure `Auto_Open`.

`Auto_Open` procedures are useful for a variety of tasks:

- Initializing variable values
- Adding menus and toolbar buttons
- Initializing values on a worksheet
- Displaying a welcome screen for your application
- Changing options such as gridline display and zero display
- Inserting worksheets
- Performing formatting tasks
- Deleting unwanted data from workbooks

If you want a procedure to run when you close a workbook, name it `Auto_Close`. Types of actions you might want to perform in an `Auto_Close` procedure include:

- Deleting unnecessary worksheets
- Saving the workbook to another name as a backup
- Returning display settings you might have turned off, such as the status bar, gridlines, toolbars, and so on

You can have only one `Auto_Open` and one `Auto_Close` procedure per workbook.

The names of these procedures are not case sensitive.

If you open a workbook from VBA, its `Auto` procedures do not run. If you want the `Auto` procedures to run, use the `RunAutoMacros` method.

To see an example of using an automatic procedure, create a new workbook. Create a procedure named `Auto_Open in a new module`. Enter the code found in Listing 24.1 in this procedure.

LISTING 24.1 Auto_Open Procedure Example

```
 1: Sub Auto_Open()
 2:     Range("A1").Value = "Date:"
 3:
 4:     Range("B1").FormulaR1C1 = "=NOW()"
 5:     Columns("B:B").EntireColumn.AutoFit
 6:
 7:     With ActiveWindow
 8:         .DisplayHorizontalScrollBar = False
 9:         .DisplayVerticalScrollBar = False
10:     End With
11:     With Application
12:         .DisplayFormulaBar = False
13:         .DisplayStatusBar = False
14:     End With
15: End Sub
```

24

This procedure will enter a date and turn off scrollbars, the formula bar, and the status bar. You'll want to undo this when you exit the workbook, so create the Auto_Close procedure shown in Listing 24.2.

LISTING 24.2 Auto_Close Procedure Example

```
 1: Sub Auto_Close()
 2:
 3: With ActiveWindow
 4:         .DisplayHorizontalScrollBar = True
 5:         .DisplayVerticalScrollBar = True
 6:     End With
 7:     With Application
 8:         .DisplayFormulaBar = True
 9:         .DisplayStatusBar = True
10:     End With
11: End Sub
```

To test your procedures, save the workbook as Hour24. Close the workbook and then open it again. You'll see that the date has been added to cell B1, and the scrollbars, the formula bar, and the status bar are not displayed (see Figure 24.1). Close the workbook and those items return.

FIGURE 24.1

*Automatic procedures
are useful for cus-
tomizing the Excel
environment.*

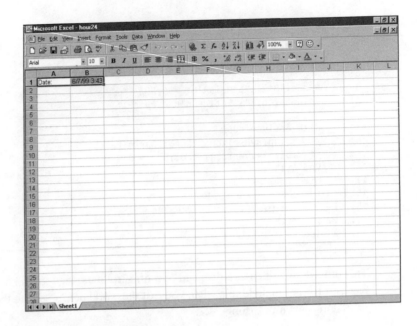

Running Event Procedures

The procedures you write can be made to respond to certain events. Examples of the
events are double-clicking, activating a sheet, going to a window, and entering a value in
a cell. If you want to assign a macro to an action, you need to use an On procedure. Excel
supports a dozen On procedures:

- **OnAction**

  Runs when a specified object is clicked.

- **OnCalculate**

  Runs after a worksheet is recalculated.

- **OnData**

  Runs when data arrives from an application other than Excel.

- **OnDoubleClick**

  Runs when the specified object is double-clicked.

- **OnEntry**

  Runs when the user enters data in a worksheet. Doesn't run until the user presses
  Enter or moves to another cell.

- **OnKey**

  Runs when the user presses a specified combination of keys.

- **OnRepeat**

  Runs when the user executes a `Repeat` command.

- **OnSheetActivate**

  Runs when the specified sheet is switched to from another sheet.

- **OnSheetDeactivate**

  Runs when the focus is switched from the specified sheet to another sheet.

- **OnTime**

  Runs at a specified date and time if Excel is running and the workbook with the `OnTime` procedure is loaded.

- **OnUndo**

  Runs when the user undoes a command.

- **OnWindow**

  Runs when the user switches to a specified window, or when the Excel application window is activated or opened.

24

> Many of these events are referred to as *hidden* in online help, meaning that they do not appear in the Object Browser. This does not mean that they are unavailable.

Typically, these `On` properties are set in the `Auto_Open` procedure of a workbook. There are lots of ways you can use these properties. For example, you might want to execute a save whenever the `OnData` event occurs. Or you might want to validate data when an `OnEntry` event occurs. To see a simple demonstration of how events work, complete the following steps:

1. Open a new workbook. This workbook needs to have at least two worksheets in it.

2. Create an `Auto_Open` procedure with the following code:
   ```
   Worksheets("Sheet1").OnSheetActivate = "TryIt"
   ```

3. Create a new procedure named `TryIt`. Enter the following code for the procedure:
   ```
   MsgBox "You're back!"
   ```

4. Save the workbook as Event.

5. Open the workbook and go to Sheet2.

6. Now go to Sheet1. The message box displays.

7. Click OK to dismiss the message box.

To further experiment with these properties, add the following line to your `Auto_Open` procedure:

```
Worksheets("Sheet1").OnEntry = "ValidateA1"
```

Next, create the procedure shown in Listing 24.3.

LISTING 24.3   The `ValidateA1` Procedure

```
1: Sub ValidateA1()
2:     If Range("A1").Value < 5 Then
3:         MsgBox "Invalid value"
4:         Range("A1").Clear
5:         Range("A1").Activate
6:     End If
7:
8: End Sub
```

Now go to Sheet1 and select cell A1. Type 4 and press Enter. You'll get a message box telling you that you've entered an invalid value. Press OK to dismiss the message box.

Creating Add-ins

You've seen a couple of ways to have procedures run automatically, but what if you want your application to load automatically when Excel starts? If this is the case, you can save and distribute your workbook as an add-in. Add-ins are workbooks that can't be read or modified, but can contain custom information such as custom sheet layouts and procedures. Add-ins can manipulate themselves and save their changes. Examples of the type information that you might want to store in an add-in include

- User-defined functions
- Custom dialog boxes
- Custom menus
- Custom toolbars

In the following steps, you create a workbook with a function that calculates commission. Then you save that workbook as an add-in and use it. Complete the following steps:

1. Create a new workbook. Create a function in the workbook named `CalcComm`.

2. Enter the following code for the `CalcComm` procedure:
   ```
   Function CalcComm(x As Variant)
       CalcComm = x * 0.3
   End Function
   ```

3. Save the workbook as MyFunctions.

4. Select File, Save As. Select Microsoft Excel Add-in for the file type. Your save directory automatically becomes the AddIns folder. Click Save to create the add-in.

5. Close all workbooks.

6. Create a new workbook.

7. Select Tools, Add-ins. The Add-ins dialog displays.

8. Click Browse. Select MyFunctions and click OK. Click OK to close the Add-ins dialog box.

9. If you look at your Window menu, you'll see the only workbook open is the new one you created.

10. In cell A1, enter `100`. In cell B1, type `=calccomm(A1)` and press Enter. The commission is calculated.

Hopefully, this small demonstration has given you some ideas on how to use add-ins.

Summary

In this hour, you learned the skills you need to automate the execution of your procedures. You learned that by naming a procedure `Auto_Open`, it runs when the workbook opens; by naming a procedure `Auto_Close`, it runs when you close the workbook. You learned about the `On` properties and how to use them to execute your macros. Finally, you learned how to make your Automation solution into an add-in so that it is automatically loaded with Excel.

Q&A

Q Do I have to do anything other than name a procedure Auto_Open to get it to run automatically?

A No, the name itself acts as a trigger to run.

Q If I want an add-in to always be available, where do I store it?

A Store it in your PERSONAL workbook.

Workshop

The quiz questions and exercise are provided for your further understanding. See Appendix A, "Answers," for the answers.

24

Quiz

1. If you wanted a procedure to run when you retrieved data using MS Query, which event property would you use?

2. True or False. You can have multiple Auto_Open procedures in the same workbook.

3. Name at least two event properties that perform data validation to which you could assign a procedure.

4. True or False. You have to manually load custom add-ins every time you want to use them.

5. You need to save an external Word file when you close a certain workbook. How would you do this?

6. Name at least two things you may want to do via a custom add-in.

Exercise

Create a new workbook. Create a procedure named Auto_Open. This procedure needs to

- Enter Date:, Name:, and Company Name: in cells A1 through C1.
- Use the Now function in cell B1 to enter the system date.
- Use the UserName property of the Application object to insert your name in cell B2.
- Use the OrganizationName property of the Application object to insert your company name in cell B3.
- Resize to best fit columns A and B.

Test your work.

APPENDIX A

Answers for Hour 1

1. Is VBA found only in Excel?

   No, it can be found in other Microsoft Office applications, including Word and Access.

2. What language is VBA based on?

   Visual Basic.

3. True or False. You can use Excel's built-in functions in your VBA applications.

   True.

4. When you edit your macro code, you work in the _____ (three words).

   Visual Basic Editor

5. Name two limitations of the macro recorder.

   Using a macro, you can't prompt a user for information while the macro is running, or perform different actions based on user input or cell values.

Answers for Hour 2

1. True or False. A shortcut key can be assigned only when you first record a macro.

   False.

2. Where are the three locations that you can save a macro?

   This workbook, a new workbook, and the personal macro workbook.

3. Where is the personal macro workbook located?

   \XLSTART

4. True or False. The personal macro workbook is automatically opened when you start Excel.

   True.

5. True or False. Excel will not allow you to assign your macro to one of its already defined shortcut keys.

   False.

6. What are the basic steps for assigning a macro to a graphic?

   Add the graphic to your sheet.

   Right-click the graphic and select Assign Macro.

Answers for Hour 3

Quiz

1. Name two controls that allow a user to select from one possible option among multiple options.

   Option buttons and list boxes.

2. True or False. A UserForm can be added only when the Visual Basic Editor is active.

   True.

3. How do you link a control to a cell?

   Right-click the control, select Format Control. Go to the Control tab and enter the appropriate cell in the Cell Link box.

4. True or False. The grid that displays on the UserForm when you are looking at it in the Visual Basic Editor also displays when you run the form.

   False.

5. _____ are controls that display static text.

   Labels

Exercises

No answers.

Answers for Hour 4

1. What are the three levels of scope?

   Procedural-level (also called a local variable), module-level, and public.

2. You need a variable that will store numbers greater than 0 and less than 100. What data type should you use?

   Integer is the best choice.

3. What is the maximum number of characters in a procedure, variable, or constant name?

   255.

4. True or False. A procedure name can begin with a number.

   False.

5. Where are public variables declared?

   In the General Declarations section of a module.

6. True or False. Constants can only be defined within a procedure.

   False. They can be defined in the General Declarations area of a module as well.

7. Which function key do you press to execute a procedure?

   F5.

The complete procedure for Hour 4's exercise is as follows:

```
Public Sub VarAndConst()
    Dim sTest As String
    Const iNumber As Integer = 2

    sTest = "This is a test."

    MsgBox "sTest's value is: " & sTest
    MsgBox "iNumber's value is: " & iNumber
End Sub
```

Answers for Hour 5

Quiz

1. What is the string concatenation character?

   &

2. What is the data type of the value returned from a message box?

   Integer.

3. What is the data type of the value returned from the InputBox method?

   It depends on the value provided for the type argument.

4. What are some of the things that you set for a message box via the *buttons* argument?

   Types of buttons, icon displayed, and which button is the default button.

5. True or False. In VBA, arguments can only be passed positionally.

   False. You can use named arguments.

Exercise

The following is the completed procedure for the exercise:

```
Public Sub YourInfo()
    Dim sName As String
    Dim sCity As String
    Dim sAge As String

    sName = Application.InputBox("Enter your name: ", Type:=2)
    sCity = Application.InputBox("Enter your home city: ", Type:=2)
    sAge = Application.InputBox("Enter your age: ", Type:=1 + 2)

    MsgBox sName & " lives in " & sCity & " and is " & sAge & "."

End Sub
```

Answers for Hour 6

Quiz

1. What are the two primary control-of-flow statements?

   The If statement and the Select Case statement.

2. True or False. The If and Select Case statements are case sensitive.

   True.

3. What method do you use to display a built-in Excel dialog box?

Show.

4. How do you convert a string to all uppercase?

By using the UCase function.

Exercise

The following are the completed procedures for this exercise:

```
Sub ClickTest()
    Dim iResponse As Integer

    iResponse = MsgBox("Do you wish to continue?", vbOKCancel)

    If iResponse = vbOK Then
        MsgBox "OK was clicked."
    Else
        MsgBox "Cancel was clicked."
    End If
End Sub

Sub Discount()
    Dim iDiscountCategory As Integer

    iDiscountCategory = InputBox("Enter discount code: ")
    Select Case iDiscountCategory
        Case 1
            MsgBox "Discount is 5%."
        Case 2
            MsgBox "Discount is 10%."
        Case 3
            MsgBox "Discount is 15%."
        Case 4
            MsgBox "Discount is 20%."
        Case Else
            MsgBox "Invalid discount code."
    End Select

End Sub
```

A

Answers for Hour 7

Quiz

1. What are the two main types of loops in VBA?

For statement and Do statement.

2. What statements allow you to beak out of a loop?

   `Exit For` and `Exit Do`.

3. What are the two types of `Do` loops?

   `Do While` and `Do Until`.

4. True or False. The condition of a `Do` loop must be placed at the top of the loop.

   False.

Exercises

First, create a procedure named `EnterHours`. Using a `For` statement, allow your user to enter an employee's hours for five days and then calculate the total number of hours. Display the total in a message box.

Next, create another procedure named `Salary`. Prompt the user for the hourly wage of the employee. The minimum hourly wage at the company is six dollars. Using a `Do` loop, continue to display the input box until the minimum amount is entered. Use this rate to calculate the amount of salary based on the number of hours calculated by `EnterHours`. Display the total in a message box.

Hint: Declare the variable that is to hold the number of hours as a public variable.

Run `EnterHours` first and then run `Salary`.

The following is the code needed to complete this exercise:

```
Public sngNumberOfHours As Single

Public Sub EnterHours()
    Dim iCounter As Integer

    For iCounter = 1 To 5

        sngNumberOfHours = sngNumberOfHours + InputBox
        ("Please number of hours for day " & iCounter)
    Next

    MsgBox "Total of hours: " & sngNumberOfHours

End Sub

Public Sub Salary()
    Dim sngRate As Single
    Dim sngSalary As Single

    Do While sngRate < 6
        sngRate = InputBox("Enter the employee's hourly rate: ")
```

```
        If sngRate < 6 Then
            MsgBox "Minimum rate is 6.00"
        End If
    Loop

    MsgBox "Salary is: " & sngRate * sngNumberOfHours
End Sub
```

Answers for Hour 8

Quiz

1. How do you set a property?

   `Object.propertyname = value`

2. How do you call a method?

   `Object.Method`

3. What statement do you use to assign an object to an object variable?

   The `Set` statement.

4. True or False. Only objects have properties and methods, not collections.

   False. Collections have properties and methods. For example, collections have the `Add` method and the `Count` property.

5. How do you create a new element in a collection?

   Using the `Add` method.

Exercise

For the `Application` object:

- The directory path where Excel is installed: `Path`
- The operating system being used: `OperatingSystem`
- The name of the registered user of this copy of Excel: `UserName`

For the `Workbook` object:

- Whether the workbook has been saved: `Saved`

The procedure created for this exercise should be similar to the following:

```
Sub TellMeMore()
    MsgBox "Excel is installed at " & Application.Path
    MsgBox "Excel is installed on the " & Application.OperatingSystem
    MsgBox Application.UserName & "is the registered user."
    MsgBox "This workbook has " & Worksheets.Count
    MsgBox "Workbook saved? " & ThisWorkbook.Saved
End Sub
```

A

Answers for Hour 9

Quiz

1. How would you use the MAX function in VBA to determine the largest number in the range A1:C5?

   ```
   SngResult = Application.Max(Range("A1:C5"))
   ```

2. Which object is the outer-most level in the object hierarchy?

   The Application object.

3. What method do you use to create either a new Workbook object or a new Worksheet object?

   The Add method.

4. Using VBA code, how do you remove a worksheet from a workbook?

   Using the Worksheet object's Delete method.

5. Which property returns the workbook in which the current procedure is located? Which object has this property?

   The ThisWorkbook property of the Application object returns the workbook in which the executing procedure is located.

6. True or False. You cannot run an Excel 4.0 macro in VBA.

   False. You can run Excel 4.0 macros in VBA using the Application object's Run method.

Exercise

The following are the completed procedures for the exercise:

```
Sub Hour9Lab()
    Dim wbH9Workbook As Workbook
    Dim wsH9Worksheet As Worksheet

    Set wbH9Workbook = Workbooks.Add
    Set wsH9Worksheet = wbH9Workbook.Worksheets.Add

    wsH9Worksheet.Name = "Sharon"

    wbH9Workbook.SaveAs ("Hour9Lab")

End Sub

Sub SaveHour9()

    If Workbooks("Hour9Lab").Saved = True Then
```

```
        MsgBox "This workbook has already been saved."
    Else
        Workbooks("Hour9Lab").Save
        MsgBox "The workbook has been saved."
    End If
End Sub
```

Answers for Hour 10

Quiz

1. True or False. In VBA, a range always refers to multiple cells.

   False. A single cell is considered a range as well.

2. Which Range object property is useful for accessing one range based on the address of another range?

   The Offset property.

3. If you want to increase the value of each cell in a range, which statement would you use to do this with the least code?

   The For Each statement.

4. Which property enables you to select an unknown range based on the location of another range?

   The CurrentRegion property.

5. How would you find out how many cells there were in a range?

   By using the Count property.

6. What property is used to remove the contents of a range?

   The Clear method.

7. You must set several properties for the same object. What is the most efficient way to do this?

   Using the With statement.

Exercise

The following is the answer to the exercise:

```
Sub ReducePrices()
    Dim x As Range
    Dim bProblems As Boolean

    'The For Each statement lets you work with
    'the cells in the range.
```

```
For Each x In Range("B2:B6")
    x.Value = x.Value - 5
    'Test to see if the prices are now
    'zero of less.
    If x.Value <= 0 Then
        'Because you want to make the price and
        'the item name bold and red you need to
        'start by selecting the item name.
        x.Offset(0, -1).Select
        'Resize is used to select both the price
        'and the item name.
        Selection.Resize(1, 2).Select
        With Selection
            .Font.Bold = True
            .Font.Color = vbRed
        End With
        'This variable is used to determine
        'if there was a problem
        bProblems = True
    End If

Next

    If bProblems = True Then
        MsgBox "Some of the prices are zero or less!"
    End If

End Sub
```

Answers for Hour 11

Quiz

1. Name three ways to get to online help.

   Via the Object Browser, by pressing F1 from the Code window, or by using the Help menu.

2. The Object Browser is a great source for listing objects, events, properties, and

   _____.

   methods

3. What keys do you press to go to the beginning of a module?

   Ctrl+Home.

4. _____ is a small pop-up box that displays information about functions and their parameters as you type.

   QuickInfo

5. Where do you go to control the use of features such as Auto Quick Info and Auto Syntax Check?

The Options dialog.

6. True or False. The examples provided through online help are viewable only—meaning that they cannot be copied and placed in your own code.

False. You can easily copy and paste code examples from the Help system. That's what they are there for!

Exercise

Using whatever tool you prefer (Help or the Object Browser), locate the following information:

The method used to perform a spell check (Hint: Check the Application object): CheckSpelling_____

Property that contains the location where Excel is installed: Path_____

Property that tells you whether a workbook has been saved: Saved_____

Method used to force manual calculation: Calculate_____

Property used to hide (make invisible) a worksheet: Visible_____

Method used to empty the contents of a range: Clear_____

Hour 12

Quiz

1. What mode occurs when you reach a breakpoint?

Break mode, meaning that the procedure's execution is paused.

2. How do you determine the order in which the procedure code is executed?

By stepping through the code.

3. How do you display the value of properties and variables in the Immediate window?

Using Print or ?.

4. Name a way other than a breakpoint to pause the application.

By using a watch expression.

5. True or False. When a procedure is placed in Break mode, its variable's values aren't available for your viewing.

False. One the main reasons for placing a procedure in Break mode is to check the current status of variables.

6. Name the two forms of stepping through code execution.

Step Over and Step Into.

7. True or False. Watches never affect program execution.

False. Watches can be used to place a procedure in Break mode.

Exercise

The problem with this procedure is that the Select Case statement is case sensitive. The corrected procedure is listed below (correction is in bold):

```
Sub Hour12Exercise()
    Dim sWhichState As String

    sWhichState = InputBox("Enter the state for shipping: ")

    Select Case UCase(sWhichState)
        Case "FL"
            MsgBox "Shipping is 3.50."
        Case "NY"
            MsgBox "Shipping is 5.00."
        Case "OH"
            MsgBox "Shipping is 2.00."
        Case "CA"
            MsgBox "Shipping is 6.00."
        Case Else
            MsgBox "We don't ship there."
    End Select

End Sub
```

Answers for Hour 13

Quiz

1. What are three main steps to creating an error handler?

(1) Set an error trap. (2) Write an error-handling routine. (3) Provide an exit from the error-handling routine.

2. Name the object and its property that are used to return the error number.

The Err object's Number property. (You actually only need to refer to the Err object because the Number property is its default property.)

3. Which statement returns you to the line that caused the error?

   `On Error Resume.`

4. What character do you place at the end of a line to make it a line label?

   A colon (:).

5. What statement would you execute to skip a line that caused an error?

   `On Error Resume Next.`

6. True or False. Each procedure must have its own error handling routine.

   False. You can implement a centralized error handler.

7. Which logically construct is best to use when creating an error handler?

   A `Select Case` statement.

Exercise

Create the following procedure:

```
Sub ProcWithError()
    Workbooks.Open "C:\nosuchfile.wkb"
End Sub
```

Add code to implement an error handler that displays a message and resumes on the next line of the procedure.

The following is the completed procedure for the exercise:

```
Sub ProcWithError()
    On Error GoTo MyErrorHandler

    Workbooks.Open "C:\nosuchfile.wkb"
    Exit Sub
MyErrorHandler:
    MsgBox "This file does not exist."
    Resume Next
End Sub(c)Answers for Hour 14
```

Quiz

1. True or False. The grid displays on a UserForm when you run it.

   False. The grid displays only when the form is in Design mode.

2. Which property is used to set an accelerator key for a control?

   The `Accelerator` property.

3. How do you identify a command button as the one to execute when you press Enter?

   By setting its `Default` property to `True`.

4. Which property do you set to select an option button?

   The Value property.

5. True or False. Aligning controls requires setting properties.

   False. You can align controls by using either the Format menu or the Align button on the UserForm toolbar.

6. What happens when you set a command button's Cancel property to True?

   The button executes if the user presses the Esc key.

7. What sets the initial tab order for controls on a form?

   The creation order of the controls on the form.

Exercise

In this exercise, you are going to be creating the form shown in Figure 14.6. Name the form frmSplash and set its Caption to Welcome to Guest Expenses! Table 14.3 shows needed property settings.

After creating the form, you may want to run it. Even for a simple form, like the one you created in this exercise, it's a good idea to run it to see how it will look once it's integrated into your completed application.

Answers for Hour 15

Quiz

1. How do you disable a control?

   By setting its Enabled property to False.

2. How do you display a form?

   By using the form's Show method.

3. In which procedure do you place form initialization code?

   In the UserForm_Activate procedure.

4. How do you remove a form from memory?

   By executing Unload.

5. If you need to return to a control via code, what method do you use?

   Using the control's SetFocus method.

6. Where do I store the values used by controls like list boxes?

   The easiest place is in a named range on a worksheet.

7. Which list box property controls which list item is displayed?

The ListIndex property determines which item in the list box's list of values is displayed.

8. Name a place to put validation code.

In the Click event procedure of a Save or OK button.

Exercise

Create a procedure named ShowSplash. The ShowSplash procedure needs to display frmSplash.

Enter the necessary code for the cmdOK button on frmSplash to display the frmGuestExpenses form.

Go to Sheet1 of the Guest Expenses workbook. Assign ShowSplash to the command button on that form. Run and test your application.

The following are the answers to the exercise:

To display frmSplash, you would use the following code. (This is the code that executes when you click the command button on Sheet1. Place this code in a module.)

```
Sub ShowSplash()
    frmSplash.Show
End Sub
```

To display frmGuestExpenses, you would use the following code. (This is the code that executes when you click the OK button on frmSplash.)

```
Private Sub cmdOK_Click()
    frmGuestExpenses.Show
    Unload Me
End Sub
```

Answers for Hour 16

Quiz

1. What collection do toolbars belong to?

The CommandBars collection.

2. Which property is used to assign a macro to a toolbar button?

The OnAction property.

3. Name the collection that toolbar buttons belong to.

The Controls collection.

4. What method do you use to remove a toolbar?

   The `Delete` method.

5. How do you display a toolbar using VBA code?

   By setting the toolbar's `Visible` property to `True`.

6. Which property is used to control the image displayed on a toolbar button?

   The `FaceID` sets the image on the button.

7. True or False. A toolbar automatically displays when it is created.

   False. You must set the toolbar's `Visible` property to `True` to display it.

Exercise

Create a procedure named `Hour16Toolbar`. This procedure needs to create and display a new toolbar named Hour16 that has 3 buttons on it: New (ID is 2520), Open (ID is 23), and Save (ID is 3).

Create another procedure named `DeleteTB` that deletes the Hour16 toolbar. Run and test your procedures.

The following is the answer for this hour's exercise:

```
Sub Hour16Toolbar()
    Dim cbHour16 As CommandBar

    Set cbHour16 = CommandBars.Add(Name:="Hour16")

    With cbHour16
        .Visible = True
        .Controls.Add Type:=msoControlButton, ID:=2520, Before:=1
        .Controls.Add Type:=msoControlButton, ID:=23, Before:=2
        .Controls.Add Type:=msoControlButton, ID:=3, Before:=3
    End With
End Sub

Sub DeleteTB()
    CommandBars("Hour16").Delete
End Sub
```

Answers for Hour 17

Quiz

1. What method do you use to create a menu?

   The `Add` method.

2. What property of a custom control (menu item) do you assign a procedure to?

   The `OnAction` property.

3. What type of control is a menu?

   `msoControlPopup`

4. How do you get rid of a menu using VBA code?

   With the `Delete` method.

5. What dialog box must be open for you to modify menus?

   The Customize dialog box, which can be accessed by right-clicking a menu bar or toolbar and selecting Customize.

6. When creating a command bar using the `Add` method, what property is used to automatically delete the command bar when the container application is closed?

   Set the optional `Temporary` argument to `True` to make the new command bar temporary. Temporary command bars are deleted when the container application is closed. The default value is `False`.

7. How to you display a menu bar?

   By setting the menu bar's Visible property to `True`.

Exercises

The following are the completed exercises for this hour:

```
Sub Exercise17()

    Dim Ex17menubar As CommandBar
    Dim mymenu As Object
    Dim mymenuitem As Object

    Set Ex17menubar = CommandBars.Add _
        (Name:="Exercise17", Position:=msoBarTop, MenuBar:=True, _
Temporary:=True)

    With Ex17menubar
        .Controls.Add Type:=msoControlPopup, ID:=30002, Before:=1
        .Controls.Add Type:=msoControlPopup, ID:=30003, Before:=2
        .Controls.Add Type:=msoControlPopup, ID:=30010, Before:=3
        .Visible = True
    End With

    CommandBars("Worksheet Menu Bar").Visible = False
End Sub

Sub DeleteExercise17()
    CommandBars("Exercise17").Delete
```

Answers for Hour 18

Quiz

1. What VBA statement would you use to create a chart?

   `Charts.Add.`

2. What property of the `Application` object returns the current active chart?

   The `ActiveChart` property.

3. What property of the `Chart` object controls the type of chart that is displayed?

   The `ChartType` property.

4. What method of the `Chart` object controls what is being charted?

   The `SourceData` method.

5. Which is not a property of the `Chart` object: `ChartArea`, `ChartType`, `ChartLocation`, or `ChartTitle`?

   `ChartLocation` is not a property of the `Chart` object.

6. True or False. Creating a chart is recordable by the macro recorder.

   True. You can easily record chart creation.

7. The `Workbook` object's _____ property returns the active chart.

   `ActiveChart.`

Exercises

The UserForm you create should be similar to the one in Figure 18.5.

FIGURE 18.5

The completed UserForm for the exercise.

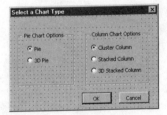

In the General Declarations section of a module, you'll need to enter the following line of code:

`Dim rCurrRange As Range`

The following procedure sets the `rCurrRange` variable and displays the UserForm:

```
Sub PickAChartType()
    Set rCurrRange = Selection
    frmChartType.Show
End Sub
```

The following procedures are associated with the UserForm:

```
 1: Private Sub cmdCancel_Click()
 2:     frmChartType.Hide
 3:
 4: End Sub
 5:
 6: Private Sub cmdOK_Click()
 7:
 8:     If optPie.Value = True Then
 9:         Charts.Add
10:         ActiveChart.ChartType = xlPie
11:         ActiveChart.SetSourceData Source:=rCurrRange, PlotBy:= _
12:             xlColumns
13:         ActiveChart.Location Where:=xlLocationAsObject, Name:="Sheet1"
14:         ActiveChart.ApplyDataLabels _
            Type:=xlDataLabelsShowPercent, LegendKey:=False _
15:             , HasLeaderLines:=True
16:     ElseIf opt3DPie.Value = True Then
17:         Charts.Add
18:         ActiveChart.ChartType = xl3DPie
19:         ActiveChart.SetSourceData Source:=rCurrRange, PlotBy:= _
20:             xlColumns
21:         ActiveChart.Location Where:=xlLocationAsObject, Name:="Sheet1"
22:         ActiveChart.ApplyDataLabels _
            Type:=xlDataLabelsShowPercent, LegendKey:=False _
23:             , HasLeaderLines:=True
24:     ElseIf optStackedColumn.Value = True Then
25:         Charts.Add
26:         ActiveChart.ChartType = xlColumnStacked
27:         ActiveChart.SetSourceData Source:=rCurrRange
28:         ActiveChart.Location Where:=xlLocationAsObject, Name:="Sheet1"
29:     ElseIf optClusterColumn.Value = True Then
30:         Charts.Add
31:         ActiveChart.ChartType = xlColumnClustered
32:         ActiveChart.SetSourceData Source:=rCurrRange
33:         ActiveChart.Location Where:=xlLocationAsObject, Name:="Sheet1"
34:     ElseIf opt3DStackedColumn.Value = True Then
35:         Charts.Add
36:         ActiveChart.ChartType = xl3DColumnStacked
37:         ActiveChart.SetSourceData Source:=rCurrRange
38:         ActiveChart.Location Where:=xlLocationAsObject, Name:="Sheet1"
39:     End If
40:
41:     With ActiveChart
42:         .HasTitle = True
```

```
43:            .ChartTitle.Characters.Text = "Sales"
44:            .ChartTitle.Select
45:      End With
46:
47:      Selection.AutoScaleFont = True
48:      With Selection.Font
49:            .Name = "Arial"
50:            .FontStyle = "Bold Italic"
51:            .Size = 14
52:            .Strikethrough = False
53:            .Superscript = False
54:            .Subscript = False
55:            .OutlineFont = False
56:            .Shadow = False
57:            .Underline = xlUnderlineStyleNone
58:            .ColorIndex = xlAutomatic
59:            .Background = xlAutomatic
60:      End With
61:
62:      frmChartType.Hide
63:
64: End Sub
65:
66: Private Sub UserForm_Click()
67:
68: End Sub
69:
70: Private Sub UserForm_Initialize()
71:    If rCurrRange.Columns.Count = 2 Then
72:          optPie.Enabled = True
73:          optPie.Value = True
74:          opt3DPie.Enabled = True
75:          opt3DPie.Value = False
76:          optClusterColumn.Enabled = False
77:          optClusterColumn.Value = False
78:          optStackedColumn.Enabled = False
79:          optStackedColumn.Value = False
80:          opt3DStackedColumn.Enabled = False
81:          opt3DStackedColumn.Value = False
82:          lblInfo.Caption = "The recommended type for your data is a pie."
83:    ElseIf rCurrRange.Columns.Count > 2 Then
84:          optClusterColumn.Enabled = True
85:          optClusterColumn.Value = True
86:          optStackedColumn.Enabled = True
87:          optStackedColumn.Value = False
88:          opt3DStackedColumn.Enabled = True
89:          opt3DStackedColumn.Value = False
90:          optPie.Enabled = False
91:          optPie.Value = False
92:          opt3DPie.Enabled = False
93:          opt3DPie.Value = False
```

```
94:          lblInfo.Caption = "The recommended type for your data is a column."
95:      Else
96:          MsgBox "Selection is not suitable for a chart."
97:          frmChartType.Hide
98:          End
99:      End If
100:
101: End Sub
```

Answers for Hour 19

Quiz

1. True or False. You can only create a pivot table based on an Excel list or range.

   False. You can create a pivot table from a variety of other sources, including external databases and other pivot tables.

2. Name the two collections you worked with when creating a pivot table.

   The `PivotCaches` collection and the `PivotTables` collection.

3. Which property of the `PivotField` object assigns the location of the field (that is, page, row, column or data)?

   The `Orientation` property.

4. True or False. You can have only one row field.

   False. You can have multiple row fields, as well as column, page, and data fields.

5. Name the four areas of a pivot table.

   Page Fields, Row Fields, Column Fields, Data Items

6. Which method creates the actual pivot table report?

   The `CreatePivotTable` method.

7. True or False. Creating a pivot table is recordable by the macro recorder.

   True. Recording pivot table creation is the easiest way to generated the needed VBA code.

A

Exercise

The following is the completed macro for this hour's exercise:

```
1: Sub InStockPivot()
2:     Dim x As Worksheet
3:
4:     'The following line has been added so that the
5:     'message box with the delete sheets alert
```

```
6:        'won't display.
7:        Application.DisplayAlerts = False
8:
9:        For Each x In Worksheets
10:           If x.Name <> "Stock Info" Then
11:               x.Delete
12:           End If
13:       Next x
14:
15:       Application.DisplayAlerts = True
16:
17:       ActiveWorkbook.PivotCaches.Add(SourceType:=xlDatabase, SourceData:= _
18:           "Stock Info!R1C1:R45C6").CreatePivotTable
              TableDestination:="", TableName:= _
19:           "InStock"
20:       ActiveSheet.PivotTableWizard TableDestination:=ActiveSheet.Cells(3, 1)
21:       ActiveSheet.Cells(3, 1).Select
22:       ActiveSheet.PivotTables("InStock").SmallGrid = False
23:           With ActiveSheet.PivotTables("InStock").PivotFields("Category")
24:           .Orientation = xlPageField
25:           .Position = 1
26:       End With
27:       With ActiveSheet.PivotTables("InStock").PivotFields("Dept.")
28:           .Orientation = xlPageField
29:           .Position = 2
30:       End With
31:       With ActiveSheet.PivotTables("InStock").PivotFields("Store Num.")
32:           .Orientation = xlColumnField
33:           .Position = 1
34:       End With
35:       With ActiveSheet.PivotTables("InStock").PivotFields("Location")
36:           .Orientation = xlColumnField
37:           .Position = 1
38:       End With
39:       With ActiveSheet.PivotTables("InStock").PivotFields("Description")
40:           .Orientation = xlRowField
41:           .Position = 1
42:       End With
43:       With ActiveSheet.PivotTables("InStock").PivotFields("In Stock")
44:           .Orientation = xlDataField
45:           .Position = 1
46:       End With
47:       ActiveSheet.PivotTables("InStock").PivotFields("Dept.").CurrentPage = _
48:           "Housewares"
49:       With ActiveSheet.PivotTables("InStock").PivotFields("Location")
50:           .PivotItems("Dallas").Visible = False
51:           .PivotItems("Orlando").Visible = False
52:       End With
53: End Sub
```

Answers for Hour 20

Quiz

1. What is the name of the collection to which a query is added when using MS Query?

   The `QueryTables` collection.

2. What is the name of the property that stores the `Select` statement for the query you create?

   The `CommandText` property.

3. True or False. If you use MS Query while recording a macro, you will have to make several modifications to the generated code.

   False. Unless you want to add customizations, such as user prompts, you don't have to change the code at all.

4. True or False. MS Query only works with Access databases.

   False. MS Query works with a variety of database formats.

5. True or False. MS Query can retrieve data from multiple tables.

   True. MS Query isn't limited to working with a single table. You can create a query based on multiple linked tables.

6. What is the major benefit you gain from using MS Query to retrieve data?

   It is recordable.

7. Name four different ways to retrieve external data to Excel.

   MS Query, ADO (ActiveX Data Objects), DAO (Data Access Objects), ODBC (Open Database Connectivity)

A

Exercise

Create a copy the `MSQueryExample` procedure and name the copy `PriceAndMore`. Create a simple UserForm with four option buttons on it. The option buttons should have the following captions:

- Product ID
- Product Name
- Unit Price
- Units In Stock

Modify the `PriceAndMore` procedure so that based on the user's selection from the UserForm the data is sorted appropriately.

The following is the completed code for the exercise:

```
1: Public sSortChoice As String
2:
3: 'Changes are in bold.
4: Sub PriceAndMore()
5:     Dim sngPrice As Single
6:     Dim sMessage As String
7:
8:
9:     Worksheets.Add
10:     sMessage = "You wish to see prices greater than: "
11:     sngPrice = Application.InputBox(sMessage, "Enter Price", Type:=1)
12:     frmSort.Show
13:     With ActiveSheet.QueryTables.Add(Connection:=Array(Array( _
14:         "ODBC;DBQ=C:\Program Files\Microsoft Office\Office\Samples\
             ➥Northwind.mdb; DefaultDir=C:\Program Files\Microsoft
             ➥Office\Office\Samples;"), Array("Driver=
             ➥{Microsoft Access Driver (*.mdb)};DriverId=281;
             ➥FIL=MS Access;ImplicitCommitSync=Yes;MaxBufferSize=512;
             ➥MaxScanRows=8;Page), Array("Timeout=5;SafeTransactions=0;
             ➥Threads=3; UID=admin;UserCommitSync=Yes;")),
             ➥Destination:=Range("A1"))
15:         .CommandText = Array( _
16:         "SELECT Products.ProductID, Products.ProductName,
             ➥ Products.UnitPrice,
             ➥ Products.UnitsInStock" & Chr(13) & "" & Chr(10) &
             ➥ "FROM `C:\Program Files\Microsoft Office\Office\Samples\Northwind`
             ➥.Products Products" & Chr(13) & "" & Chr(10) &
             ➥ "WHERE (Products.UnitPrice>=" & sngPrice & ")" & Chr(13) &
             ➥ "" & Chr(10) & "ORDER BY Products." & sSortChoice)
17:         .Name = "Query from Northwind"
18:         .FieldNames = True
19:         .RowNumbers = False
20:         .FillAdjacentFormulas = False
21:         .PreserveFormatting = True
22:         .RefreshOnFileOpen = False
23:         .BackgroundQuery = True
24:         .RefreshStyle = xlInsertDeleteCells
25:         .SavePassword = True
26:         .SaveData = True
27:         .AdjustColumnWidth = True
28:         .RefreshPeriod = 0
29:         .PreserveColumnInfo = True
30:         .Refresh BackgroundQuery:=False
31:     End With
32: End Sub
```

The following is the code associated with the UserForm:

```
Private Sub cmdCancel_Click()
```

```
        frmSort.Hide
        End
End Sub

Private Sub cmdOK_Click()
    If optProductID = True Then
        sSortChoice = "ProductID"
    ElseIf optProductName = True Then
        sSortChoice = "ProductName"
    ElseIf optUnitPrice = True Then
        sSortChoice = "UnitPrice"
    Else
        sSortChoice = "UnitsInStock"
    End If
    frmSort.Hide

End Sub
```

Answers for Hour 21

Quiz

1. Which argument of the Open method is used to pass the name of the object to be used as the recordset?

   The Source argument.

2. True or False. To access data through ADO, you just write the appropriate code.

   False. You must also add a reference through the Tools menu of the Visual Basic Editor.

3. Which object stores information about problems you had while using ADO?

   The Error object.

4. True or False. You can access data only from Microsoft Access using ADO.

   False. You can use a variety of other sources including Microsoft FoxPro and Microsoft SQL Server.

5. Which object represents the records you are working with via ADO?

   You use Recordset objects to manipulate data through your connection. A Recordset object represents the entire set of records from a table or the results of a query.

6. How do you terminate a connection to an ADO source?

   By using the Close statement.

7. Name the four steps for working with ADO.

A

Make a connection to a data source. Gain access to a recordset. Get records from the recordset. Close the connection to the data source.

Exercise

Create a UserForm with 3 option button on it. The option buttons' captions should be Suppliers, Products, and Orders. Write the necessary code to allow a user to select the table from which to bring data into the user's workbook.

The following are the answers for the exercise.

The code for the UserForm is as follows:

```
Private Sub cmdCancel_Click()
    frmPickADatabase.Hide

End Sub

Private Sub cmdOK_Click()
    If optSuppliers.Value = True Then
        sUserChoice = "Suppliers"
    ElseIf optProducts.Value = True Then
        sUserChoice = "Products"
    Else
        sUserChoice = "Orders"
    End If
    frmPickADatabase.Hide
    GoGetData


End Sub
```

The code for the other necessary procedures, which need to reside in a module, is as follows. (If you used the same module you used for the rest of the hour, you don't have to reenter the MyTranspose function.)

```
1: Public sUserChoice As String
2:
3: Function MyTranspose(ByRef ArrayOriginal As Variant) As Variant
4:     Dim x As Integer
5:     Dim y As Integer
6:     Dim i As Integer
7:     Dim j As Integer
8:     Dim ArrayTranspose() As Variant
9:
10:    x = UBound(ArrayOriginal, 1)
11:    y = UBound(ArrayOriginal, 2)
12:
13:    ReDim ArrayTranspose(y, x)
14:
```

```
15:      For i = 0 To x
16:          For j = 0 To y
17:              ArrayTranspose(j, i) = ArrayOriginal(i, j)
18:          Next
19:      Next
20:
21:      MyTranspose = ArrayTranspose
22:
23: End Function
24:
25:
26:   Sub GoGetData()
27:      Dim rsData As ADODB.Recordset
28:      Set rsData = New ADODB.Recordset
29:      rsData.Open Source:=sUserChoice, _
30:          activeconnection:="Provider=Microsoft.Jet.OLEDB.4.0;
              ➥Data Source=C:\Program Files\Microsoft Office\Office\
              ➥Samples\Northwind.mdb", _
31:          CursorType:=adOpenStatic, _
32:          LockType:=adLockOptimistic, _
33:          Options:=adCmdTable
34:      With Worksheets("Sheet1")
35:          .Range("A1").CurrentRegion.Clear
36:
37:          Application.Intersect(.Range(.Rows(1),
              ➥.Rows(rsData.RecordCount)),_
38:              .Range(.Columns(1),
              ➥.Columns(rsData.Fields.Count))).Value =
39:              MyTranspose(rsData.GetRows(rsData.RecordCount))
40:
41:      End With
42:
43:
44:      rsData.Close
45:
46: End Sub
```

Answers for Hour 22

Quiz

1. What method do you execute to move to the last record in a recordset?

   The MoveLast method.

2. How do you test to see whether you are at the beginning of a recordset?

   By testing whether the BOF property is True.

3. What method is used to write changes to a recordset?

The Update method.

4. What property of the Recordset object stores the current record location?

The Bookmark property.

5. What method is used to search a recordset?

The Find method.

6. What property of the Field object is used to retrieve the contents of a field?

The Value property.

7. True or False. Recordset information can be retrieved either to a worksheet or to a UserForm.

True. You can bring data from a recordset to a worksheet or to a UserForm.

Exercise

The following is the code for this hour's exercise. Changes are in bold:

```
 1: Private Sub cmdOK_Click()
 2:     Dim iNumRows As Integer
 3:
 4:     Worksheets("Product Requests").Activate
 5:     Range("A1").Select
 6:     Selection.CurrentRegion.Select
 7:     iNumRows = Selection.Rows.Count
 8:     Range("A1").Select
 9:     Selection.Offset(iNumRows, 0).Value = txtProductID.Text
10:     Selection.Offset(iNumRows, 1).Value = txtProductName.Text
11:     Selection.Offset(iNumRows, 2).Value = txtUnitPrice.Text
12:
13:     frmProductInfo.Hide
14:     cnnProduct.Close
15:
16: End Sub
```

Answers for Hour 23

Quiz

1. What statement do you use to add an instance to an Automation server application?

The CreateObject statement.

2. True or False. Other than Excel and VBA native objects, you can only view referenced library objects in the Object Viewer.

True. Only native and referenced object information can be viewed in the Object Viewer.

3. In the application created in this hour, Excel was the _____ application.
controller

4. True or False. Excel can only act as a controller application.

False. Excel is both controller and server application.

5. How do you add a reference to an object library?

Using the Tools, References menu available in the Visual Basic Editor.

6. True or False. You have to be able to access Word from your system to be able to use it in Automation.

True. You must have access to the server application to be able to automate it.

7. True or False. Most Microsoft Office applications support some level of Automation.

True. Most of the Office applications support Automation, either as a controller or a server or both.

Exercise

The following is the complete procedure for this exercise:

```
1: Sub Hour23exercise()
2:      'This code assumes the active cell
3:      'is in column A.
4:
5:      Dim y As Word.Application
6:      Set y = CreateObject("Word.Application")
7:
8:      With y
9:          .Visible = True
10:         'Your document location may be different from the
11:         'one shown below. Make necessary changes.
12:         .Documents.Open Filename:="d:\excel vba\Invoice Letter.doc"
13:          ActiveCell.Copy
14:         .Selection.GoTo What:=wdGoToBookmark, Name:="InvoiceNumber"
15:         .Selection.Paste
16:         Application.CutCopyMode = False
17:         ActiveCell.Offset(0, 1).Select
18:         Selection.Copy
19:         .Selection.GoTo What:=wdGoToBookmark, Name:="Quantity"
20:         .Selection.Paste
21:         Application.CutCopyMode = False
22:         Selection.Offset(0, 1).Select
23:         Selection.Copy
24:         .Selection.GoTo What:=wdGoToBookmark, Name:="Price"
25:         .Selection.Paste
26:         Application.CutCopyMode = False
27:         Selection.Offset(0, 1).Select
28:         Selection.Copy
```

A

```
29:            .Selection.GoTo What:=wdGoToBookmark, Name:="Total"
30:            .Selection.Paste
31:            Application.CutCopyMode = False
32:        End With
33:
34: End Sub
```

Answers for Hour 24

Quiz

1. If you wanted a procedure to run when you retrieved data using MS Query, which event property would you use?

   The OnData property.

2. True or False. You can have multiple Auto_Open procedures in the same workbook.

   False. You can have one Auto_Open and one Auto_Close procedure per workbook.

3. Name at least two event properties that perform data validation to which you could assign a procedure.

   You could use OnCalculate, OnEntry, OnSheetDeactivate, and OnKey.

4. True or False. You have to manually load custom add-ins every time you want to use them.

   False. After you select an add-in via the Tools menu, it is loaded with Excel from that point forward.

5. You need to save an external Word file when you close a certain workbook. How would you do this?

   Write a procedure that uses Automation to save the external Word file and assign it the name Auto_Close.

6. Name at least two things you may want to do via a custom add-in.

   Store user-defined functions, custom dialog boxes, custom menus and custom toolbars.

Exercise

The following is the code for the completed exercise:

```
Sub Auto_Open()
    With ActiveSheet
        .Range("A1").Value = "Date:"
        .Range("B1").FormulaR1C1 = "=NOW()"
        .Range("A2").Value = "Name:"
```

```
        .Range("B2").Value = Application.UserName
        .Range("A3").Value = "Company Name:"
        .Range("B3").Value = Application.OrganizationName
        .Columns("A:A").EntireColumn.AutoFit
        .Columns("B:B").EntireColumn.AutoFit
    End With
End Sub
```

A

INDEX

mcp.com
The Authoritative Encyclopedia of Computing

Resource Centers
Books & Software
Personal Bookshelf
WWW Yellow Pages
Online Learning
Special Offers
Site Search
Industry News

▶ Choose the online ebooks
that you can view from your
personal workspace on our site.

About MCP   Site Map   Product Support

Turn to the *Authoritative* Encyclopedia of Computing

You'll find over 150 full text books online, hundreds of
shareware/freeware applications, online computing classes
and 10 computing resource centers full of expert advice
from the editors and publishers of:

- Adobe Press
- BradyGAMES
- Cisco Press
- Hayden Books
- Lycos Press
- New Riders

- Que
- Que Education & Training
- Sams Publishing
- Waite Group Press
- Ziff-Davis Press

mcp.com
The Authoritative Encyclopedia of Computing

Get the best
information and
learn about latest
developments in:

- Design

- Graphics and
Multimedia

- Enterprise Computing
and DBMS

- General Internet
Information

- Operating Systems

- Networking and
Hardware

- PC and Video Gaming

- Productivity
Applications

- Programming

- Web Programming
and Administration

- Web Publishing

When you're looking for computing information, consult the authority.
The Authoritative Encyclopedia of Computing at mcp.com.

Get **FREE** books and more...when you register this book online for our Personal Bookshelf Program

http://register.samspublishing.com/

SAMS

 Register online and you can sign up for our *FREE Personal Bookshelf Program...*unlimited access to the electronic version of more than 200 complete computer books—immediately! That means you'll have 100,000 pages of valuable information onscreen, at your fingertips!

 Plus, you can access product support, including complimentary downloads, technical support files, book-focused links, companion Web sites, author sites, and more!

 And you'll be automatically registered to receive a *FREE subscription to a weekly email newsletter* to help you stay current with news, announcements, sample book chapters, and special events, including sweepstakes, contests, and various product giveaways!

We value your comments! Best of all, the entire registration process takes only a few minutes to complete, so go online and get the greatest value going—absolutely FREE!

Don't Miss Out On This Great Opportunity!

Sams is a brand of Macmillan Computer Publishing USA.

For more information, please visit *www.mcp.com*

Copyright ©1999 Macmillan Computer Publishing USA

Other Related Titles

Sams Teach Yourself Word 2000 Automation in 24 Hours
0-672-31652-8
Pam Palmer
$19.99 USA / $28.95 CAN

Sams Teach Yourself Microsoft Excel 2000 Programming in 21 Days
0-672-31543-2
Matthew Harris
$29.99 USA / $42.95 CAN

Sams Teach Yourself Visual Basic 6 in 21 Days
0-672-31310-3
Greg M. Perry
$29.99 USA / $42.95 CAN

Sams Teach Yourself Beginning Programming in 24 Hours
0-672-31355-3
Greg M. Perry
$19.99 USA / $28.95 CAN

Sams Teach Yourself Microsoft FrontPage 2000 in 24 Hours
0-672-31500-9
Dick Oliver and Rogers Cadenhead
$19.99 USA / $28.95 CAN

Sams Teach Yourself Access 2000 in 24 Hours
0-672-31289-1
Timothy Buchannan and Craig Eddy
$19.99 USA / $28.95 CAN

Sams Teach Yourself Microsoft Powerpoint 2000 in 24 Hours
0-672-31432-0
Alexandria Haddad
$19.99 USA / $28.95 CAN

Sams Teach Yourself Visual Basic 6 in 24 Hours
0-672-31533-5
Greg M. Perry and Sanjaya Hettihewa
$19.99 USA / $28.95 CAN

Sams Teach Yourself Visual C++ 6 in 24 Hours
0-672-31303-0
Mickey Williams
$24.99 USA / $35.95 CAN

Sams Teach Yourself Microsoft Outlook 2000 Programming in 24 Hours
0-672-31651-X
Sue Mosher
$19.99 USA / $28.95 CAN

VBA for Microsoft Office 2000 Unleashed
0-672-31567-X
Paul McFedries
$39.99 USA / $59.95 CAN

SAMS

www.samspublishing.com

All prices are subject to change.